Citroën Diesel Engine
Service and Repair Manual

A K Legg LAE MIMI and Finn Deacon

Models covered
This manual covers the Citroën 1769 cc and 1905 cc (1.7 and 1.9 litre) diesel engines used in the Visa, C15/Champ Van and BX models (including the 1.7 litre turbocharged engine used in the BX)

Does not cover specific application to ZX or Xantia models

(1379 -168 - 6Y4)

© Haynes Publishing 1996

A book in the **Haynes Service and Repair Manual Series**

ABCDE
FGHIJ
KLMNO
PQ

2

Printed by **J H Haynes & Co Ltd, Sparkford, Nr Yeovil, Somerset BA22 7JJ, England**

Haynes Publishing
Sparkford, Nr Yeovil, Somerset BA22 7JJ, England

Haynes North America, Inc
861 Lawrence Drive, Newbury Park, California 91320, USA

Editions Haynes S.A.
147/149, rue Saint Honoré, 75001 PARIS, France

Haynes Publishing Nordiska AB
Box 1504, 751 45 UPPSALA, Sweden

ISBN 1 85960 223 1

British Library Cataloguing in Publication Data
A catalogue record for this book is available from the British Library

Contents

LIVING WITH YOUR CITROËN DIESEL

Introduction

MAINTENANCE

Routine maintenance and servicing

Contents

About this manual

The aim of this manual is to help you get the best value from your vehicle. It can do so in several ways. It can help you decide what work must be done (even should you choose to get it done by a garage), provide information on routine maintenance and servicing, and give a logical course of action and diagnosis when random faults occur. However, it is hoped that you will use the manual by tackling the work yourself. On simpler jobs it may even be quicker than booking the car into a garage and going there twice, to leave and collect it. Perhaps most important, a lot of money can be saved by avoiding the costs a garage must charge to cover its labour and overheads.

The manual has drawings and descriptions to show the function of the various components so that their layout can be understood. Then the tasks are described and photographed in a step-by-step sequence so that even a novice can do the work.

Unlike most Haynes manuals, which cover a particular vehicle in different trim levels and engine sizes, this book covers one engine and its associated equipment as fitted to a range of vehicles. Items which are common to diesel and petrol models - e.g. bodywork, transmission and running gear - are not covered in this book.

The vehicles used in the preparation of this manual and which appear in many of the photographs, were a BX diesel, a Visa diesel and a BX Turbo diesel.

Acknowledgements

Thanks are due to Champion, who supplied replacement component information. Certain illustrations are the copyright of Citroën Cars Limited, and are used with their permission. Illustrations denoted by the line '© Robert Bosch Limited' are used by kind permission of that company. Thanks are also due to Sykes-Pickavant Limited, who provided some of the workshop tools, and to all those people at Sparkford who helped in the production of this manual.

We take great pride in the accuracy of information given in this manual, but vehicle manufacturers make alterations and design changes during the production run of a particular vehicle of which they do not inform us. No liability can be accepted by the authors or publishers for loss, damage or injury caused by any errors in, or omissions from, the information given.

Working on your car can be dangerous. This page shows just some of the potential risks and hazards, with the aim of creating a safety-conscious attitude.

General hazards

Scalding

• Don't remove the radiator or expansion tank cap while the engine is hot.
• Engine oil, automatic transmission fluid or power steering fluid may also be dangerously hot if the engine has recently been running.

Burning

• Beware of burns from the exhaust system and from any part of the engine. Brake discs and drums can also be extremely hot immediately after use.

Crushing

• When working under or near a raised vehicle, always supplement the jack with axle stands, or use drive-on ramps. *Never venture under a car which is only supported by a jack.*
• Take care if loosening or tightening high-torque nuts when the vehicle is on stands. Initial loosening and final tightening should be done with the wheels on the ground.

Fire

• Fuel is highly flammable; fuel vapour is explosive.
• Don't let fuel spill onto a hot engine.
• Do not smoke or allow naked lights (including pilot lights) anywhere near a vehicle being worked on. Also beware of creating sparks (electrically or by use of tools).
• Fuel vapour is heavier than air, so don't work on the fuel system with the vehicle over an inspection pit.
• Another cause of fire is an electrical overload or short-circuit. Take care when repairing or modifying the vehicle wiring.
• Keep a fire extinguisher handy, of a type suitable for use on fuel and electrical fires.

Electric shock

• Ignition HT voltage can be dangerous, especially to people with heart problems or a pacemaker. Don't work on or near the ignition system with the engine running or the ignition switched on.

• Mains voltage is also dangerous. Make sure that any mains-operated equipment is correctly earthed. Mains power points should be protected by a residual current device (RCD) circuit breaker.

Fume or gas intoxication

• Exhaust fumes are poisonous; they often contain carbon monoxide, which is rapidly fatal if inhaled. Never run the engine in a confined space such as a garage with the doors shut.
• Fuel vapour is also poisonous, as are the vapours from some cleaning solvents and paint thinners.

Poisonous or irritant substances

• Avoid skin contact with battery acid and with any fuel, fluid or lubricant, especially antifreeze, brake hydraulic fluid and Diesel fuel. Don't syphon them by mouth. If such a substance is swallowed or gets into the eyes, seek medical advice.
• Prolonged contact with used engine oil can cause skin cancer. Wear gloves or use a barrier cream if necessary. Change out of oil-soaked clothes and do not keep oily rags in your pocket.
• Air conditioning refrigerant forms a poisonous gas if exposed to a naked flame (including a cigarette). It can also cause skin burns on contact.

Asbestos

• Asbestos dust can cause cancer if inhaled or swallowed. Asbestos may be found in gaskets and in brake and clutch linings. When dealing with such components it is safest to assume that they contain asbestos.

Special hazards

Hydrofluoric acid

• This extremely corrosive acid is formed when certain types of synthetic rubber, found in some O-rings, oil seals, fuel hoses etc, are exposed to temperatures above 400°C. The rubber changes into a charred or sticky substance containing the acid. *Once formed, the acid remains dangerous for years. If it gets onto the skin, it may be necessary to amputate the limb concerned.*
• When dealing with a vehicle which has suffered a fire, or with components salvaged from such a vehicle, wear protective gloves and discard them after use.

The battery

• Batteries contain sulphuric acid, which attacks clothing, eyes and skin. Take care when topping-up or carrying the battery.
• The hydrogen gas given off by the battery is highly explosive. Never cause a spark or allow a naked light nearby. Be careful when connecting and disconnecting battery chargers or jump leads.

Air bags

• Air bags can cause injury if they go off accidentally. Take care when removing the steering wheel and/or facia. Special storage instructions may apply.

Diesel injection equipment

• Diesel injection pumps supply fuel at very high pressure. Take care when working on the fuel injectors and fuel pipes.

⚠️ *Warning: Never expose the hands, face or any other part of the body to injector spray; the fuel can penetrate the skin with potentially fatal results.*

Remember...

DO

• Do use eye protection when using power tools, and when working under the vehicle.

• Do wear gloves or use barrier cream to protect your hands when necessary.

• Do get someone to check periodically that all is well when working alone on the vehicle.

• Do keep loose clothing and long hair well out of the way of moving mechanical parts.

• Do remove rings, wristwatch etc, before working on the vehicle – especially the electrical system.

• Do ensure that any lifting or jacking equipment has a safe working load rating adequate for the job.

DON'T

• Don't attempt to lift a heavy component which may be beyond your capability – get assistance.

• Don't rush to finish a job, or take unverified short cuts.

• Don't use ill-fitting tools which may slip and cause injury.

• Don't leave tools or parts lying around where someone can trip over them. Mop up oil and fuel spills at once.

• Don't allow children or pets to play in or near a vehicle being worked on.

History of the diesel engine

Rudolf Diesel invented the first commercially successful compression ignition engine at the end of the 19th century. Compared with the spark ignition engine, the diesel had the advantages of lower fuel consumption, the ability to use cheaper fuel, and the potential for much higher power outputs. Over the following two or three decades such engines were widely adopted for stationary and marine applications, but the fuel injection systems used were not capable of high-speed operation. This speed limitation, and the considerable weight of the air compressor needed to operate the injection equipment, made the first diesel engines unsuitable for use in road-going vehicles.

In the 1920s the German engineer Robert Bosch developed the in-line injection pump, a device which is still in extensive use today. The use of hydraulic systems to pressurise and inject the fuel did away with the need for a separate air compressor and made possible much higher operating speeds. The so-called high-speed diesel engine became increasingly popular as a power source for goods and public transport vehicles, but for a number of reasons (including specific power output, flexibility and cheapness of manufacture) the spark ignition engine continued to dominate the passenger car and light commercial market.

In the 1950s and 60s, diesel engines became increasingly popular for use in taxis and vans, but it was not until the sharp rises in oil prices in the 1970s that serious attention was paid to the small passenger car market.

Subsequent years have seen the growing popularity of the small diesel engine in cars and light commercial vehicles, not only for reasons of fuel economy and longevity but also for environmental reasons. Every major European car manufacturer now offers at least one diesel-engined model. The diesel's penetration of the UK market has been relatively slow, due in part to the lack of the considerable fuel price differential in favour of diesel which exists in other parts of Europe, but it has now gained widespread acceptance and this trend looks set to continue.

Principles of operation

All the diesel engines covered in this book operate on the familiar four-stroke cycle of induction, compression, power and exhaust. Two-stroke diesels do exist, and may in future become important, but they are not used in light vehicles at present. Most have four cylinders, some larger engines have six, and five- and three-cylinder engines also exist.

Induction and ignition

The main difference between diesel and petrol engines is in the means by which the fuel/air mixture is introduced into the cylinder and then ignited. In the petrol engine the fuel is mixed with the incoming air before it enters the cylinder, and the mixture is then ignited at the appropriate moment by a spark plug. At all conditions except full throttle, the throttle butterfly restricts the airflow and cylinder filling is incomplete.

In the diesel engine, air alone is drawn into the cylinder and then compressed. Because of the diesel's high compression ratio (typically 20 : 1) the air gets very hot when compressed - up to 750°C. As the piston approaches the end of the compression stroke, fuel is injected into the combustion chamber under very high pressure in the form of a finely atomised spray. The temperature of the air is high enough to ignite the injected fuel as it mixes with the air. The mixture then burns and provides the energy which drives the piston downwards on the power stroke.

When starting the engine from cold, the temperature of the compressed air in the cylinders may not be high enough to ignite the fuel. The preheating system overcomes this problem. The engines in this book have automatically-controlled preheating systems, using electric heater plugs (glow plugs) which heat the air in the combustion chamber just

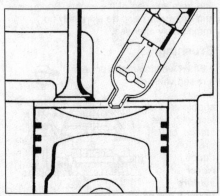

Injection into pre-chamber

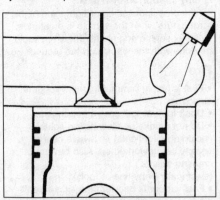

Injection into turbulence chamber

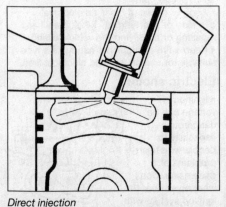

Direct injection

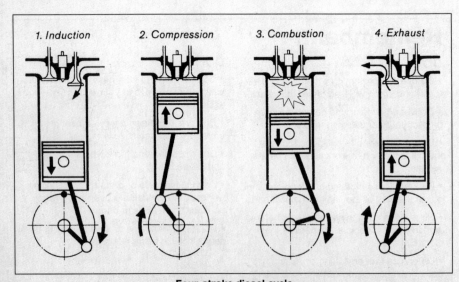

1. Induction   *2. Compression*   *3. Combustion*   *4. Exhaust*

Four-stroke diesel cycle
© Robert Bosch Limited

Direct and indirect injection
© Robert Bosch Limited

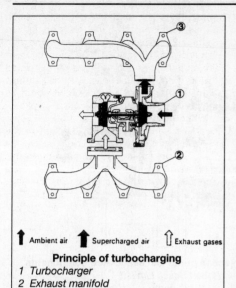

Principle of turbocharging
1 Turbocharger
2 Exhaust manifold
3 Inlet manifold

↑ Ambient air   ↑ Supercharged air   ↑ Exhaust gases

before and during start-up.

On most diesel engines there is no throttle valve in the inlet tract. Exceptions to this are those few engines which use a pneumatic governor, which depends on a manifold depression being created. Even more rarely a throttle valve may be used to create manifold depression for the operation of a brake servo, though it is more usual for a separate vacuum pump to be fitted for this purpose.

Direct and indirect injection

In practice, it is difficult to achieve smooth combustion in a small-displacement engine by injecting the fuel directly into the combustion chamber. To get around this problem the technique of indirect injection is widely used. With indirect injection, the fuel is injected into a pre-combustion or swirl chamber in the cylinder head, alongside the main combustion chamber.

Indirect injection engines are less efficient than direct injection ones and also require more preheating when starting from cold, but these disadvantages are offset by smoother and quieter operation.

Mechanical construction

The pistons, crankshaft and bearings of a diesel engine are generally of more robust construction than in a petrol engine of comparable size, because of the greater loads imposed by the higher compression ratio and the nature of the combustion process. This is one reason for the diesel engine's longer life. Other reasons include the lubricating qualities of diesel fuel on the cylinder bores, and the fact that the diesel engine is generally lower-revving than its petrol counterpart, having much better low-speed torque characteristics and a lower maximum speed.

Turbocharging

Turbochargers have long been used on large diesel engines and are becoming common on small ones. The turbocharger uses the energy of the escaping exhaust gas to drive a turbine which pressurises the air in the inlet manifold. The air is forced into the cylinders instead of being simply sucked in. If more air is present, more fuel can be burnt and more power developed from the same size engine.

Greater benefit can be gained from turbocharging if the pressurised air is cooled before it enters the engine. This is done using an air-to-air heat exchanger called an intercooler. The cooled air is denser and contains more oxygen in a given volume than warm air straight from the turbocharger.

Exhaust emissions

Because combustion in the correctly functioning diesel engine nearly always occurs in conditions of excess oxygen, there is little or no carbon monoxide (CO) in the exhaust gas. A further environmental benefit is that there is no added lead in diesel fuel.

At the time of writing there is no need for complicated emission control systems on the diesel engine, though simple catalytic converters are beginning to appear on production vehicles. Increasingly stringent emission regulations may result in the adoption of exhaust gas recirculation (EGR) systems and carbon particle traps.

Knock and smoke

The image of the diesel engine for many years was of a noisy, smoky machine, and to some extent this was justified. It is worth examining the causes of knock and smoke, both to see how they have been reduced in modern engines and to understand what causes them to get worse.

There is inevitably a small delay (typically 0.001 to 0.002 sec) between the start of fuel injection and the beginning of proper combustion. This delay, known as ignition lag, is greatest when the engine is cold and idling. The characteristic diesel knock is caused by the sudden increase in cylinder pressure which occurs when the injected fuel has mixed with the hot air and starts burning. It is therefore an unavoidable part of the combustion process, though it has been greatly reduced by improvements in combustion chamber and injection system design. A defective injector (which is not atomising the fuel as it should for optimum combustion) will also cause the engine to knock.

Smoke is caused by incorrect combustion, but unlike knock it is more or less preventable. During start-up and warm-up a certain amount of white or blue smoke may be seen, but under normal running conditions the exhaust should be clean. The thick black smoke which is all too familiar from old or badly-maintained vehicles is caused by a lack of air for combustion, either because the air inlet is restricted (clogged air cleaner) or because too much fuel is being injected (defective injectors or pump). Causes of smoke are examined in more detail in the Reference Chapter.

Fuel supply and injection systems

Fuel supply

The fuel supply system is concerned with delivering clean fuel, free of air, water or other contaminants, to the injection pump. It always includes a fuel tank, a water trap and a fuel filter (which may be combined in one unit),

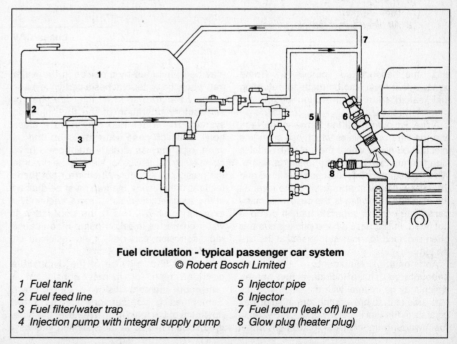

Fuel circulation - typical passenger car system
© Robert Bosch Limited

1 Fuel tank
2 Fuel feed line
3 Fuel filter/water trap
4 Injection pump with integral supply pump
5 Injector pipe
6 Injector
7 Fuel return (leak off) line
8 Glow plug (heater plug)

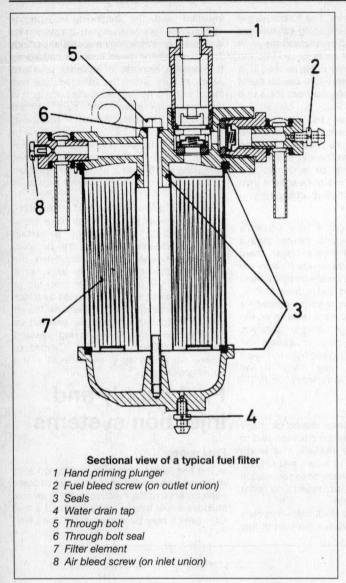

Sectional view of a typical fuel filter

1 Hand priming plunger
2 Fuel bleed screw (on outlet union)
3 Seals
4 Water drain tap
5 Through bolt
6 Through bolt seal
7 Filter element
8 Air bleed screw (on inlet union)

Bosch PE in-line injection pump and associated components
© Robert Bosch Limited

1 Pump   3 Lift pump
2 Governor housing   4 Drivegear and advance mechanism

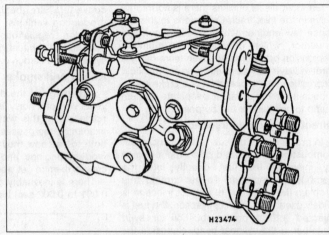

Lucas/CAV distributor injection pump, type DPC

and the associated pipework. Some arrangement must also be made for returning fuel leaked from the injection pump and injectors to the tank.

A fuel lift pump is fitted between the tank and the filter on vehicles which use an in-line injection pump, or where the fuel tank outlet is significantly lower than the injection pump. When a distributor injection pump is fitted and the tank outlet is at about the same level as the injection pump (as is the case with many passenger cars), a separate fuel lift pump is not fitted. In this case a hand priming pump is often provided for use when bleeding the fuel system.

Additional refinements may be encountered. These include a fuel heater, which may be integral with the filter or on the tank side of it, to prevent the formation of wax crystals in the fuel in cold weather. A "water in fuel" warning light on the instrument panel

may be illuminated by a device in the water trap when the water reaches a certain level.

The water trap and fuel filter are vital for satisfactory operation of the fuel injection system. The water trap may have a glass bowl, in which case water build-up can be seen, or it may as already mentioned have some electrical device for alerting the driver to the presence of water. Whether or not these features are present, the trap must be drained at the specified intervals, or more frequently if experience shows this to be necessary. If water enters the injection pump it can cause rapid corrosion, especially if the vehicle is left standing for any length of time.

The fuel filter may be of the disposable cartridge type, or it may consist of a renewable element inside a metal bowl. Sometimes a coarser pre-filter is fitted upstream of the main filter. Whatever the type, it must be renewed at the specified intervals.

Considering the damage which can be caused to the injection equipment by the entry of even small particles of dirt, it is not worth using cheap replacement filters, which may not be of the same quality as those of reputable manufacture.

Fuel injection pump

The pump is a mechanical device attached to the engine. Its function is to supply fuel to the injectors at the correct pressure, at the correct moment in the combustion cycle and for the length of time necessary to ensure efficient combustion. The pump responds to depression of the accelerator pedal by increasing fuel delivery, within the limits allowed by the governor. It is also provided with some means of cutting off fuel delivery when it is wished to stop the engine.

Some kind of governor is associated with the injection pump, either integral with it or attached to it. All vehicle engine governors regulate fuel delivery to control idle speed and maximum speed; the variable-speed governor also regulates intermediate speeds. Operation of the governor may be mechanical or hydraulic, or it may be controlled by manifold depression.

Other devices in or attached to the pump include cold start injection advance or fast idle units, turbo boost pressure sensors and anti-stall mechanisms.

Fuel injection pumps are normally very reliable. If they are not damaged by dirt, water or unskilled adjustment they may well outlast the engine to which they are fitted.

Fuel injectors

One fuel injector is fitted to each cylinder. The function of the injector is to spray an evenly atomised quantity of fuel into the combustion or pre-combustion chamber when the fuel pressure exceeds a certain value, and to stop the flow of fuel cleanly when the pressure drops. Atomisation is achieved by a spring-loaded needle which vibrates rapidly against its seat when fuel under pressure passes it. The needle and seat assembly together are known as the injector nozzle.

Injectors in direct injection engines are usually of the multi-hole type, while those in indirect engines are of the pintle type. The "throttled pintle" injector gives a progressive build-up of injection, which is valuable in achieving smooth combustion.

The injector tips are exposed to the temperatures and pressures of combustion, so not surprisingly they will in time suffer from carbon deposits and ultimately from erosion and burning. Service life will vary according to factors such as fuel quality and operating conditions, but typically one could expect to clean and recalibrate a set of injectors after about 80 000 km (50 000 miles), and perhaps to renew them or have them reconditioned after 160 000 km (100 000 miles).

Injector pipes

The injector pipes are an important part of the system and must not be overlooked. The dimensions of the pipes are important and it should not be assumed that just because the end fittings are the same, a pipe from a different engine can be used as a replacement. Securing clips must be kept tight and the engine should not be run without them, as damage from vibration or fuel cavitation may result.

Introduction to the Citroën diesel engine

The Citroën diesel engines covered in this manual were first fitted to BX models in early 1984, Visa models in early 1985 and C15 Vans, that were renamed Champ Vans in 1993.

They are built at the highly automated Citroën factory at Tremery in France and are given the code names of XUD 7 for the 1.7, XUD 9 for the 1.9 and XUD 7TE for the turbo engine.

Compared with petrol engines of similar capacity the diesel version is extremely quiet, whilst being driven. Only a certain amount of engine clatter is heard at idle and when first started. Routine maintenance tasks are few, but essential, and are easily carried out. Work on the fuel injection pump will require the use of one or two dial test indicators.

Outside the engine bay the vehicles, to which these engines are fitted, are much the same as petrol-engined versions. For complete coverage of a particular vehicle, the appropriate main manual will be needed as well.

Front three-quarter view of Citroën XUD engine. Timing belt cover has been removed

1 Timing belt
2 Oil filler cap and ventilation hose
3 Injectors
4 Diagnostic socket
5 Temperature sensors
6 Fast idle thermo unit
7 Thermostat cover
8 Injection pump (Roto-diesel)
9 Coolant hose to oil cooler
10 Drivebelt tension adjusting bolt
11 Flywheel
12 Alternator
13 Oil filter
14 Sump
15 Alternator drivebelt
16 Crankshaft pulley
17 Water pump
18 Timing belt intermediate roller
19 Injection pump sprocket
20 Timing belt tensioner
21 Right-hand engine mounting
   bracket
22 Camshaft sprocket

Lubricants and fluids

1 Engine .... Multigrade engine oil, viscosity SAE 15W/40
2 Manual transmission .... Gear oil, viscosity SAE 75W/80W
3 Automatic transmission .... Dexron II type ATF
4 Hydraulic system (BX models) .... Green LHM fluid
5 Brake hydraulic system (Visa models) .... Hydraulic fluid to SAE J1703 C
Vacuum pump (Visa models) .... SAE 10W 30

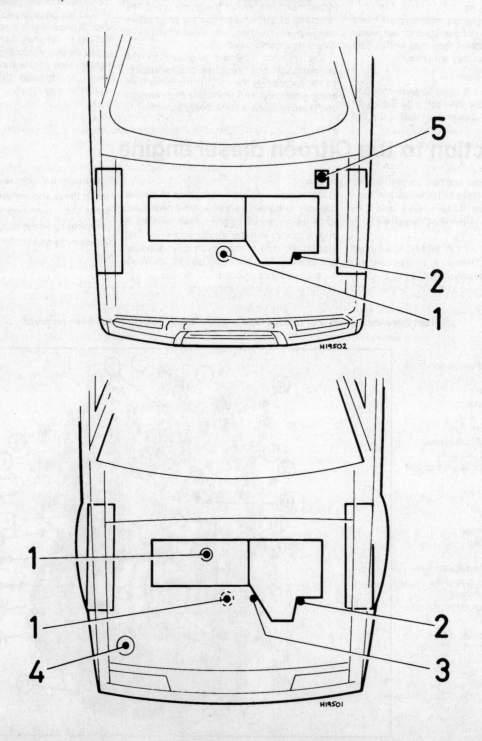

Chapter 1
Routine maintenance and servicing

Contents

Degrees of difficulty

Easy, suitable for novice with little experience 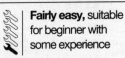	**Fairly easy,** suitable for beginner with some experience 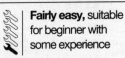	**Fairly difficult,** suitable for competent DIY mechanic 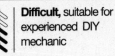	**Difficult,** suitable for experienced DIY mechanic	**Very difficult,** suitable for expert DIY or professional

Specifications

Capacities

Automatic transmission fluid, drain and refill	2.5 litres
Cooling system:	
Visa Saloon/Van	7.5 litres
BX (non-Turbo)	7.0 litres
BX (Turbo)	6.5 litres
Engine oil, drain and refill (including filter)	5.0 litres
Fuel tank:	
Visa Saloon	43 litres
C15/Champ Van	47 litres
BX up to early 1993 (except Turbo and TZD non-Turbo models)	52 litres
BX (TZD non-Turbo)	60 litres
BX (from early 1993, and all Turbo models)	66 litres
Manual transmission oil (refer to owners handbook)	2.0± 0.2 litres
Vacuum pump (Visa models)	40 cc

Cooling

Antifreeze content:	
for protection down to -15°C (5°F)	28%
for protection down to -30°C (-22°F)	50%

Brakes

Minimum rear brake shoe lining thickness	1.0 mm

Vacuum pump (Visa models)

Drivebelt tension	Approx 5.0 mm deflection midway between pulleys

Engine

Idle speed:

  Roto-diesel injection pump:

C15	800 ± 50 rpm
BX	775 ± 25 rpm
Visa	750 rpm

  Bosch injection pump:

Automatic transmission	825 ± 25 rpm
Manual transmission	775 ± 25 rpm
Oil filter type	Champion F104

Air filter:

BX models up to mid-1987 (round type)	Champion W117
BX models from mid-1987 (square type)	Champion U543
Visa Saloon/C15 Van	Champion W117

Fuel filter type:

  BX models and C15 Van:

Roto-diesel	Champion L132
Bosch	Champion L135

  Visa Saloon:

Roto-diesel	Champion L131 or L137
Bosch	Champion L136

Tyres

Pressures - bar (lbf/in²):	Front	Rear
Visa:		
145 SR 13 tyres	2.2 (32)	2.0 (29)
155 SR 13 tyres	2.3 (33)	2.6 (38)
BX:		
Saloon	2.1 (30)	2.1 (30)
Estate	2.3 (33)	2.5 (36)

Torque wrench settings

	Nm	lbf ft
Fuel filter through-bolt	10	7
Rear hub nut (Visa)	190	140

Maintenance schedule

The maintenance schedules below are basically those recommended by us for vehicles driven daily. Servicing intervals are determined by mileage or time elapsed - this is because fluids and systems deteriorate with age as well as with use. Follow the time intervals if the appropriate mileage is not covered within the specified period.

Vehicles operating under adverse conditions may need more frequent maintenance. "Adverse conditions" include climatic extremes, full-time towing or taxi work, driving on unmade roads, and a high proportion of short journeys. The use of inferior fuel (such as may be found in some foreign countries) can cause early degradation of the engine oil. Consult a dealer for full guidance.

Some of the procedures, where indicated, are described in detail in the relevant main manual for the vehicle. Refer to Haynes Manual No. 908 for BX models and No. 620 for Visa models. Note that Manual No. 620, also covers the C15 Van.

At weekly intervals, or before a long journey

- ☐ Check battery (Section 3)
- ☐ Check brake fluid level, investigate any sudden loss of fluid (Section 4)
- ☐ Check coolant level (Section 5)
- ☐ Check engine oil level (Section 6)
- ☐ Check the operation of lights, wipers and horn (Section 7)
- ☐ Check tyre pressures and condition (including spare) (Section 8)
- ☐ Check washer fluid level(s) (Section 9)

Every 6 000 miles (10 000 km) or 6 months, whichever comes first

Note: *On pre 1989 models, the mileage intervals were at 5000 miles (7500 km). The time intervals however, are the same.*

- ☐ Check handbrake adjustment (Section 10)
- ☐ Check hydraulic circuit (Section 11)
- ☐ Check hydraulic system fluid level (BX models), (Section 12)
- ☐ Check the steering gear and driveshaft components (Section 13)
- ☐ Clean oil filler cap (where applicable), (Section 14)
- ☐ Drain water from fuel filter (Section 15)
- ☐ Examine exhaust system for corrosion and leakage (Section 16)
- ☐ Renew the engine oil and filter (Section 17)
- ☐ Check brake disc pads for wear (refer to the relevant main manual)
- ☐ Check brake discs for wear (refer to the relevant main manual)
- ☐ Check front wheel alignment (refer to the relevant main manual)
- ☐ Check the automatic transmission fluid level (refer to the relevant main manual)
- ☐ Lubricate all controls, linkages, door locks and hinges (refer to the relevant main manual)

Every 12 000 miles (20 000 km) or 12 months, whichever comes first

Note: *On pre 1989 models, the mileage intervals were at 10 000 miles (15 000 km). The time intervals however, are the same.*
Along with the work specified in the previous schedule, where applicable ...

- ☐ Check drivebelt tension (Section 18)
- ☐ Check idling speed (Section 19)
- ☐ Check vacuum pump (Visa models) (Section 20)

- ☐ Inspect rear brake shoes (Visa models) (Section 21)
- ☐ Lubricate clutch pedal and cable (Section 22)
- ☐ Renew fuel filter (before winter, regardless of mileage) (Section 23)
- ☐ Check clutch adjustment (refer to the relevant main manual)
- ☐ Check wheel bearings (refer to the relevant main manual)
- ☐ Check seat belts and anchorages (refer to the relevant main manual)

Every 18 000 miles (30 000 km) or 18 months, whichever comes first

Note: *On pre 1989 models, the mileage intervals were at 15 000 miles (22 500 km). The time intervals however, are the same.*
Along with the work specified in previous schedules, where applicable ...

- ☐ Clean the hydraulic system filter (BX models) (refer to the main manual)

Every 24 000 miles (40 000 km) or 2 years, whichever comes first

Note: *On pre 1989 models, the mileage intervals were at 20 000 miles (30 000 km). The time intervals however, are the same.*
Along with the work specified in previous schedules, where applicable...

- ☐ Renew air cleaner element (refer to Chapter 4)
- ☐ Renew automatic transmission fluid (if applicable) (refer to the relevant main manual)

Every 30 000 miles (45 000 km) or 2 years, whichever comes first

Along with the work specified in previous schedules, where applicable ...

- ☐ Renew coolant (Section 24)
- ☐ Renew brake fluid (Visa models) (refer to the relevant main manual)

Every 36 000 miles (60 000 km)

- ☐ Renew hydraulic system fluid (BX models) (refer to the main manual)
- ☐ Check transmission fluid level (manual transmission models) (Section 25)

Every 48 000 miles (80 000 km)

- ☐ Renew timing belt (refer to Chapter 2)

1

Underbonnet view of a Visa diesel (air cleaner removed)

1 Coolant filler cap and expansion tank
2 Injectors
3 Accelerator cable
4 Brake vacuum pump
5 Fusebox
6 Servo unit
7 Speedometer cable
8 Brake fluid reservoir
9 Washer pump
10 Washer reservoir
11 Front suspension upper mounting
12 Brake master cylinder
13 Battery
14 Heater plug relay
15 Clutch cable
16 Reversing light switch
17 Top hose
18 Radiator
19 Fast idle thermo unit
20 Engine oil dipstick and filler cap
21 Starter motor
22 Oil filler
23 Injection pump (Bosch)
24 Alternator
25 Fuel filter
26 Right hand engine mounting

Front underbody view of a Visa diesel

1 Subframe
2 Exhaust pipe
3 Right hand driveshaft support bracket
4 Lower engine mounting
5 Exhaust resonator
6 Engine oil drain plug
7 Transmission
8 Track control arm
9 Anti-roll bar
10 Track rod
11 Final drive oil drain plug

Underbonnet view of a BX diesel (air cleaner removed)

1   Injectors
2   Oil filler cap and ventilation hose
3   Valve cover
4   HP pump drivebelt
5   HP pump
6   Washer reservoir
7   Battery
8   Front suspension hydraulic unit
9   Heater plug relay
10 Clutch cable
11 Thermostat cover
12 Reversing lamp switch
13 Radiator
14 Top hose
15 Fast idle thermo unit
16 Bonnet lock
17 Starter motor
18 Accelerator cable
19 Engine oil dipstick
20 Diagnostic socket
21 Injection pump (Roto-diesel)
22 Coolant filler cap
23 Hydraulic system reservoir
24 Fuel filter
25 Right hand engine mounting
26 Washer reservoir

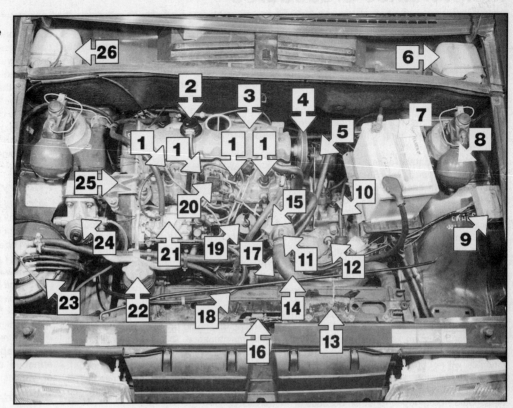

Underbonnet view of a BX Turbo model - intercooler removed for clarity

1   LHM fluid reservoir
2   Fuel filter
3   Suspension units
4   Air cleaner to turbo trunking
5   Turbo to intercooler trunking
6   Inlet manifold
7   Brake pipe unions
8   Battery
9   ABS control block
10 Air cleaner
11 Air intake
12 Intercooler air inlet duct
13 Engine oil filler/dipstick
14 Cold start accelerator
15 Richness limiter
16 Fuel injectors
17 Crankcase ventilation oil trap
18 Thermostat housing
19 Expansion tank cap
20 Hydraulic pump drive pulley

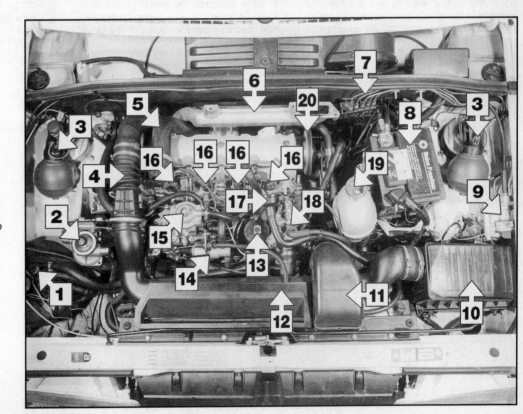

1

Maintenance procedures

1 Introduction

1   This Chapter is designed to help the home mechanic maintain his/her vehicle for safety, economy, long life and peak performance.

2 The Chapter contains a master maintenance schedule, followed by Sections dealing specifically with each task in the schedule. Visual checks, adjustments, component renewal and other helpful items are included. Refer to the accompanying illustrations of the engine compartment and the underside of the vehicle for the locations of the various components.

3 Servicing your vehicle according to the mileage/time maintenance schedule and the following Sections will provide a planned maintenance programme, which should result in a long and reliable service life. This is a comprehensive plan, so maintaining some items but not others at the specified service intervals, will not produce the same results.

4 As you service your vehicle, you will discover that many of the procedures can - and should - be grouped together, because of the particular procedure being performed, or because of the proximity of two otherwise-unrelated components to one another. For example, if the vehicle is raised for any reason, the exhaust can be inspected at the same time as the suspension and steering components.

5 The first step in this maintenance programme is to prepare yourself before the actual work begins. Read through all the Sections relevant to the work to be carried out, then make a list and gather all the parts and tools required. If a problem is encountered, seek advice from a parts specialist, or a dealers service department.

2 Intensive maintenance

1 If, from the time the vehicle is new, routine maintenance schedule is followed closely, frequent checks made of fluid levels and high-wear items, as recommended, the engine will be kept in relatively good running condition. The need for additional work will be minimised.

2 It is possible that there will be times when the engine is running poorly due to the lack of regular maintenance. This is even more likely if a used vehicle, which has not received regular and frequent maintenance checks, is bought. In such cases, additional work may need to be carried out, outside of the regular maintenance intervals.

3 If engine wear is suspected, a compression test (refer to Chapter 2) will provide valuable information regarding the overall performance of the main internal components. Such a test can be used as a basis to decide on the extent of the work to be carried out. If, for example, a compression test indicates serious internal engine wear, conventional maintenance as described in this Chapter will not greatly improve the performance of the engine. It may also prove a waste of time and money, unless extensive overhaul work is carried out first.

4 The following series of operations are those most often required to improve the performance of a generally poor-running engine:

Primary operations

a) Clean, inspect and test the battery
b) Check all the engine related fluids
c) Check the condition and tension of the drivebelts
d) Check the condition of the air filter, and renew if necessary
e) Check the fuel filter
f) Check the condition of all hoses, and check for fluid leaks
g) Check the idle speed, anti-stall and mixture settings, as applicable

5 If the above operations do not prove fully effective, carry out the following secondary operations:

Secondary operations

All items listed under "Primary operations", plus the following:
a) Check the charging system
b) Check the preheating system
c) Check the fuel system

Weekly or before a long journey

3 Battery fluid - check

> ⚠ **Warning: Read the 'Safety First!' section in the front of this manual, before checking the battery.**

1 Make sure that the battery tray is in good condition and that the clamps are tight **(see illustration)**.

2 Corrosion on the tray, retaining clamp and the battery terminals, can be removed with a solution of water mixed with baking soda. Thoroughly rinse all cleaned areas with clean water. Any metal parts of the tray damaged by corrosion should be covered with a zinc-based primer, then painted **(see Haynes hint)**.

3 Approximately every three months and definitely before the winter months, check the charge condition of the battery (and if applicable, the electrolyte levels).

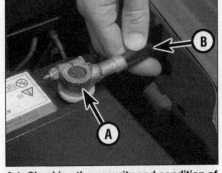

3.1 Checking the security and condition of the battery clamps

Applying petroleum jelly to the battery clamps

4 Brake fluid - check

> ⚠ **Warning: Brake hydraulic fluid can harm your eyes and damage painted surfaces, so use extreme caution when handling and pouring it. Do not use fluid that has been standing open for some time, as it absorbs moisture from the air that can cause a dangerous loss of braking effectiveness.**

1 On Visa models the braking system is similar to that for petrol engine models, but there is insufficient vacuum for a vacuum servo unit. A vacuum pump, belt-driven from the camshaft, is therefore employed. The vacuum servo unit and master cylinder are located on the left-hand side of the bulkhead **(see illustration)**. A cross-tube mounted inside the passenger compartment links the brake pedal to the vacuum servo unit.

2 On BX models the braking system is virtually identical to that on petrol-engined models.

3 If the reservoir requires repeated topping-up this indicates a fluid leak somewhere in the system, that should be investigated immediately.

> **HAYNES HiNT** *The fluid level in the master cylinder will drop slightly as the brake linings wear down, but the fluid level must never be allowed to drop below the "MIN" mark.*

4 If a leak is suspected, the car should not be driven until the braking system has been checked. Never take any risks where brakes are concerned.

4.1 Brake master cylinder on Visa models

5 Coolant level - check

> ⚠ **Warning: Wait until the engine is cold before starting this procedure**

1 With the engine cold, depress the filler cap and turn it anti-clockwise to remove it **(see illustration)**.

2 Check that on Visa models the coolant is up to the level plate visible through the filler neck. On BX models withdraw the black plastic tube from the radiator filler neck and check that the coolant level is on the upper limit of the "threaded" section.

3 If necessary top-up the system with the recommended coolant then refit the filler cap.

6 Engine oil level - check

1 The vehicle must be parked on level ground and the engine must have been stopped for approximately 10 minutes to allow oil in circulation to return to the sump.

2 Withdraw the dipstick from its tube, wipe the end with a piece of clean rag, re-insert it fully and then withdraw it again. Read the oil level on the end of the dipstick; it should be between the two cut-outs that represent the maximum and minimum oil levels **(see illustrations)**.

3 It is not strictly necessary to top-up the engine oil until it reaches the minimum cut-out, but on no account allow the level to fall any lower. The amount of oil needed to top-up from minimum to maximum is 1 litre for 1.7 models and approximately 1.5 litres for 1.9 models.

4 When topping-up is necessary, use clean engine oil of the specified type, preferably of the same make and grade as that already in the engine. Top up by removing the filler cap from the valve cover or the filler tube as

5.1 Filling the radiator on BX models

1

6.2A Withdrawing the engine oil dipstick (XUD 7 models)

6.4B ... and topping up the engine oil (BX model)

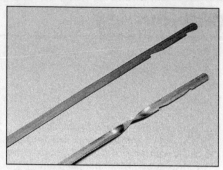

6.2B Minimum and maximum level cut-outs on the two types of dipstick

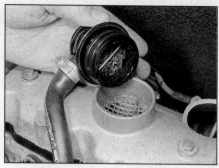

6.4A Removing the filler cap ...

applicable **(see illustrations)**. Allow time for the oil to run down to the sump before rechecking the level on the dipstick. Refit the filler cap and dipstick on completion.

5 All engines use some oil, depending on the degree of wear and the pattern of use. Oil which is not being lost through external leaks is entering the cylinders and being burnt, however, the diesel engine is not so prone to this problem as its petrol counterpart since there is no inlet vacuum to suck oil past piston rings and inlet valve stems.

7 Lights, wipers and horn - check

1 Check the operation of all external lights. Use the reflection from a garage door or showroom window, to check brake and reverse lamps. Make sure that all direction indicators are working, including when hazard warning switch is on. Replace bulbs and fuses as necessary.

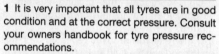

2 Turn on the wipers and check that the glass is cleared without smearing. Replace wiper blades, if the rubbers are worn or damaged.
3 Sound the horn (during sociable hours). If it does not work, check the fuse, the wiring connections and the earth connections.

8 Tyre pressure and condition - check

1 It is very important that all tyres are in good condition and at the correct pressure. Consult your owners handbook for tyre pressure recommendations.
2 Having a tyre failure at any speed is highly dangerous. Tyre wear is influenced by driving style. Harsh braking and acceleration, or fast cornering, will all produce more rapid tyre wear. As a general rule, the front tyres wear out faster than the rears. Interchanging the tyres from front to rear ("rotating" the tyres) may result in more even wear. However, if this is completely effective you may have the expense of replacing four tyres at once!
3 Remove any nails or stones embedded in the tread before they penetrate the tyre to cause deflation. If removal of a nail does reveal that the tyre has been punctured, refit the nail so that its point of penetration is marked. Then immediately change the wheel and have the tyre repaired, or replaced by a tyre dealer.
4 Regularly check the tyres for damage in the form cuts or bulges, especially in the sidewalls. Periodically remove the wheels and clean any dirt or mud from the inside and outside surfaces. Examine the wheel rims for signs of rusting, corrosion or other damage. Light alloy wheels are easily damaged by

"kerbing" whilst parking. Steel wheels may also become dented or buckled. A new wheel is very often the only way to overcome severe damage.
5 New tyres should be balanced when they are fitted, but it may become necessary to re-balance them as they wear, or if the balance weights fitted to the wheel rim, should fall off.
6 Unbalanced tyres will wear more quickly, as will the steering and suspension components.
7 Unbalanced wheels cause vibration, particularly at a certain speed (typically around 50 mph). If this vibration is only felt through the steering, it is likely that just the front wheels will need balancing. If however, the vibration is felt through the whole car, the rear wheels could also need balancing. Wheel balancing should be carried out by a tyre dealer or garage.
8 Check the security of the roadwheels. Ensure that all the bolts are tightened to their correct torque.

9 Washer fluid level - check

Ensure that the washer fluid is always topped-up after use. Modern screenwash additives not only prevent the fluid from freezing during winter months, but also reduces smearing, noticeable during night time driving at any time of year.

Clear the washer jets with a pin, if they become blocked. Ensure that the jets are directed toward the windscreen and not over the roof, to the vehicle behind.

6 000 miles or 6 months service

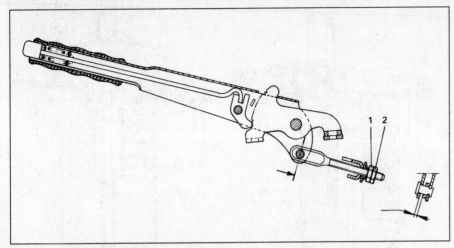

10.4 Handbrake adjustment nut (1) and locknut (2) on Visa Van models
There should be clearance at point arrowed

10 Handbrake - adjustment

Visa models

1 Chock the front wheels then jack up the rear of the vehicle and support on axle stands (see "*Jacking and vehicle support*").
2 Fully depress the footbrake pedal several times.
3 Apply the handbrake lever to the third notch. Turn each rear wheel separately and check that there is a slight resistance to movement, indicating that the brake shoes are just touching the drums.
4 If necessary adjust the cable with the handbrake lever still on the third notch. On Van models loosen the locknut on the primary cable, turn the adjustment nut as required, then tighten the locknut **(see illustration)**. On Saloon models turn the outer cable adjusters where they emerge from the vehicle floor. Check that there is equal resistance to both rear wheels.
5 Apply the handbrake lever to the fifth notch and check that both rear wheels are locked.
6 Lower the vehicle to the ground.

BX models

7 Handbrake adjustment on these models is automatic. The adjustment takes place when the handbrake travel reaches 12 to 15 notches.
8 If a new cable is being fitted, refer to the main manual, for details.

11 Hydraulic circuit - check

1 On Visa models the braking system is similar to that for petrol engine models, but there is insufficient vacuum for a vacuum servo unit. A vacuum pump, belt-driven from the camshaft, is therefore employed. The vacuum servo unit and master cylinder are located on the left-hand side of the bulkhead. A cross-tube mounted inside the passenger compartment links the brake pedal to the vacuum servo unit.
2 On BX models the braking system is virtually identical to that on petrol-engined models.
3 Check the hydraulic circuits pipes and hoses, for leaks, corrosion and damage. Pay particular attention to the areas around the connections. Replacement details can be found in the relevant main manual.
4 Ensure that all retaining clips are secure.

12 Hydraulic system fluid (BX models) - check

1 The hydraulic fluid reservoir is located on the left hand side of the bulkhead. It has a fluid level indicator built into it for easy checking. With the engine idling, open the bonnet and check that the yellow indicator float is between the two red rings **(see illustration)**. The ground clearance lever, inside the vehicle, should be fully rearwards in the maximum height position.
2 The difference between the maximum and minimum levels is approximately 0.45 litre.
3 The fluid level indication is only accurate after the vehicle has stabilised at the maximum ride height.
4 If topping-up is necessary, first clean the filler cap and the surrounding area, then remove the cap **(see illustration)**.
5 Using genuine green LHM fluid, top-up the reservoir until the indicator float reaches the upper red mark. Then refit the cap and switch off the engine.
6 In an emergency, automatic transmission fluid (or thin engine oil, i.e. SAE 10/20), may be used. However the system must be completely drained and replaced with new LHM fluid at the earliest opportunity. Do not use oils that could damage the rubber components of the system.
7 Refer to the main manual, for details on fluid renewal.

1

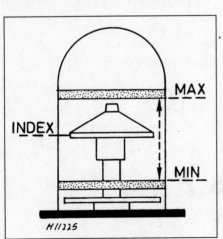

12.1 LHM fluid level indicator located on the reservoir

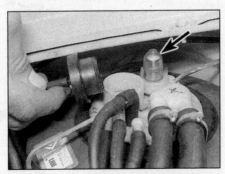

12.4 Filler cap removal from the hydraulic fluid reservoir
Fluid level indicator location is arrowed

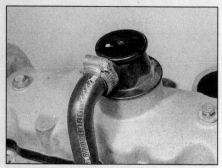

14.1 Oil filler cap / breather (BX model)

13 Steering gear and driveshaft - check

1 Check all swivel and ball joints for signs of excessive wear and replace worn or leaking components.
2 Ensure that the steering gear gaiters, driveshaft gaiters and balljoint rubbers show no signs of damage.
3 Check the fixings of all nuts and bolts on the steering gear and related components.
4 Replacement details, along with torque specifications can be found in the relevant main manual.

14 Oil filler cap (where applicable) - clean

Note: *This procedure is only applicable to models with the cap fitted to the valve cover.*
1 Pull the oil filler cap from the top of the valve cover then loosen the clip and disconnect the crankcase ventilation hose **(see illustration)**.
2 Clean the wire mesh filter in paraffin and allow to dry. If it is blocked with sludge, however, renew the cap complete.
3 Refit the hose to the filler cap and fit the cap to the valve cover.

15 Water in fuel filter - drain

1 Position a small container beneath the filter.
2 Loosen the bleed screw on the bottom of the filter and allow any water to drain into the container. Where fitted, also loosen the air bleed screw on the filter head or inlet union bolt **(see illustration)**.
3 Tighten the lower bleed screw when fuel free of water flows. Retighten the air bleed screw where fitted.
4 Prime the fuel injection system as described in Chapter 4.

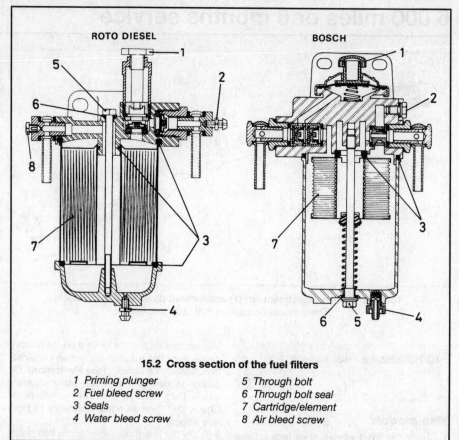

15.2 Cross section of the fuel filters

1 Priming plunger	5 Through bolt
2 Fuel bleed screw	6 Through bolt seal
3 Seals	7 Cartridge/element
4 Water bleed screw	8 Air bleed screw

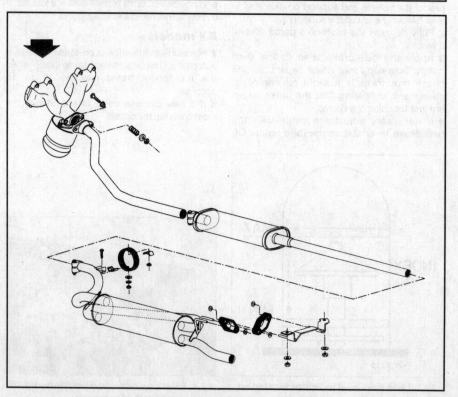

16.1 Exhaust system for Visa models

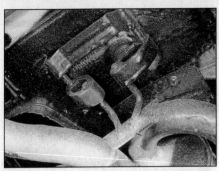

16.3 Central exhaust mounting rubbers

17.5 Unscrewing the oil filter with a strap wrench

17.6 Tighten the oil filter by hand only

17.7 Topping-up the engine oil (Visa)

16 Exhaust system - examination

1 Inspect the exhaust system periodically for leaks, corrosion and damage, and check the security and condition of the mountings **(see illustration)**. Small leaks are more easily detected if an assistant temporarily blocks the tailpipe with a wad of cloth whilst the engine is idling.

2 Proprietary pastes and bandages are available for the repair of holes and splits. They work well in the short term, but renewal of the section concerned will probably prove more satisfactory in the long run.

3 Check the rubber mountings for deterioration, and renew them if necessary **(see illustration)**.

17 Engine oil and filter - renewal

1 The engine oil should be replaced when hot (i.e. just after a run) with the vehicle parked on level ground.

2 Position a drain pan of adequate capacity beneath the sump. Wipe clean around the drain plug then unscrew it using a hexagon key and allow the oil to drain. The oil may be very hot, take precautions to avoid scalding.

3 Remove the oil filler cap and allow the oil to drain for at least 15 minutes.

4 Check and if necessary renew the drain plug washer then wipe the sump, refit the drain plug and tighten it.

5 Position the drain pan beneath the oil filter on the front of the cylinder block. Using a strap wrench, unscrew the filter and remove it **(see illustration)**. If a strap wrench is not available a screwdriver can be driven through the filter and used as a lever to remove it.

6 Wipe clean the filter seat on the cylinder block or oil cooler (as applicable). Smear a little clean engine oil on the sealing ring of the new oil filter then screw on the filter until it just touches the seat. Hand tighten the oil filter by a further two-thirds of a turn **(see illustration)**. Do not use any tools to tighten the filter.

7 Fill the engine with the correct grade and quantity of oil **(see illustration)**.

8 Start the engine and allow it to idle. Check that the oil pressure warning light goes out and also check that there is no oil leakage from the oil filter.

9 Switch off the engine and recheck the oil level.

10 Put the old oil into a sealed container and dispose of it safely. Do not pour old engine oil down a drain. Contact your local authority for further details.

1

12 000 miles or 12 months service

18.3 Checking tension of alternator drivebelt

18.5A Alternator pivot bolt

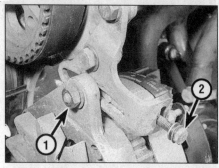

18.5B Alternator adjustment locknut (1) and adjustment bolt (2)

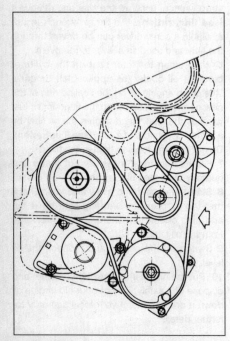

18.9 Drivebelt run - later models with air conditioning
Arrow shows tension checking point

18 Drivebelt tension - checking and adjusting

Checking

1 To ensure maximum life from either the alternator, or the vacuum pump (if applicable), the drivebelts need to be at the correct tension.
2 Refer to Section 20, for details on adjustment to the vacuum pump drivebelt.
3 There should be approximately 6.0 mm deflection on the alternator drivebelt, when moderate thumb pressure is applied midway between the pulleys **(see illustration)**.
4 Check the condition of the belt. If the belt is

cracked, frayed or found to be slipping, it needs to be replaced.
5 To remove the belt, loosen the pivot bolt and adjustment locknut **(see illustrations)**.
6 Unscrew the adjustment bolt to release the tension. The drivebelt can now be removed from the pulleys.
7 Refitting is a reversal of removal.

Adjusting

8 To adjust the tension, first check that the belt is correctly fitted over the pulleys. With the alternator mountings loose, tighten the adjustment bolt to tension the belt. As mentioned previously the belt should be able to move by approximately 6.0 mm, with moderate thumb pressure midway between the pulleys. Tighten the mounting bolts to the correct torque.

19.4 Idle speed adjustment screw (arrowed) on the Roto-diesel injection pump

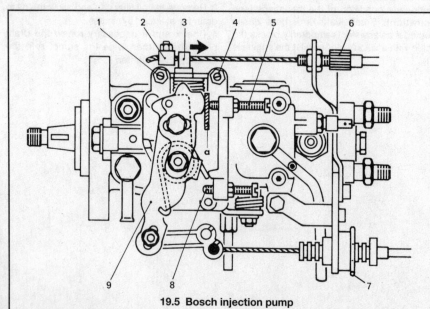

19.5 Bosch injection pump

1 *Fast idle adjustment screw*
2 *Cable end stop*
3 *Fast idle lever*
4 *Idling adjustment screw*
5 *Anti-stall adjustment screw*

6 *Fast idle cable adjustment ferrule*
7 *Accelerator cable adjustment ferrule*
8 *Engine maximum speed adjustment screw*
9 *Accelerator lever*
a *Shim*

Later models with air conditioning

9 During 1988, the three-pulley drivebelt system previously used was replaced by a five-pulley system, as shown **(see illustration)**.
10 With the new system, drivebelt tension is adjusted by movement of the bottom idler wheel. Tension is checked at the longest belt run, ie between the alternator and compressor pulleys.

19 Idle speed - checking and adjustment

Checking

1 The usual type of tachometer (rev counter), which works from ignition system pulses, cannot be used on diesel engines. A diagnostic socket is provided for use of Citroën test equipment, but this will not normally be available to the home mechanic. If it is not felt that adjusting the idle speed "by ear" is satisfactory, one of the following alternatives may be used:
a) Purchase or hire of an appropriate tachometer
b) Delegation of the job to a Citroën dealer or other specialist
c) Timing light (strobe) operated by a petrol engine running at the desired speed. If the timing light is pointed at a mark on the camshaft pump pulley the mark will appear stationary when the two engines are running at the same speed (or multiples of that speed). The pulley will be rotating at half the crankshaft speed but this will not affect the adjustment, (in practice it was found impossible to use this method on the crankshaft pulley due to the acute viewing angle)
2 Before making adjustments warm up the engine to normal operating temperature.
3 Check that the engine idles at the specified speed.

Adjustment

4 If adjustment is necessary on the Roto-diesel pump, loosen the locknut on the fast idle lever

then turn the adjustment screw as required and retighten the locknut **(see illustration)**.
5 If adjustment is necessary on the Bosch pump, first loosen the locknut and unscrew the anti-stall adjustment screw until it is clear of the accelerator lever. Loosen the locknut and turn the idle speed adjustment screw as required then retighten the locknut **(see illustration)**.
6 Adjust the anti-stall adjustment screw as described in Chapter 4.
7 Stop the engine and disconnect the instrument as appropriate.

20 Vacuum pump (Visa models) - check

Oil level

1 With the vehicle on level ground, unscrew the filler/level plug and check that the oil level is up to the bottom of the hole **(see illustration)**. If not, top-up with the correct grade of oil then refit and tighten the plug.

Drivebelt

2 Depress the drivebelt midway between the pulleys. If the deflection is not as given in the Specifications, loosen the pivot and adjustment bolts, reposition the vacuum pump, then tighten the bolts.

21 Rear brake shoes - inspection, removal and refitting

Visa models

Inspection

1 Jack up the rear of the car and support on axle stands. Chock the front wheels. Remove the rear wheel.
2 Prise the dust cap from the centre of the drum.
3 Unscrew the hub nut, recover the washer and withdraw the brake drum. If difficulty is experienced due to the drum being excessively worn, insert a screwdriver through a wheel bolt

hole and prise the spring tensioned sector from the automatic adjustment lever **(see illustration)**.
4 Examine the shoes for oil contamination or wear. If any shoe (or shoes), need replacing, only replace in complete axle sets.

Removal

5 Prise the rubber plug from the rear of the backplate then insert a screwdriver and actuate the handbrake lever so that the cable can be disengaged.
6 Note the position of the top and bottom return springs. Using a pair of pliers, unhook them from the brake shoes.
7 Using pliers, depress the anti-rattle spring cups, turn them through 90° and remove them, together with the springs. Extract the pins from the rear of the backplate.
8 Withdraw the brake shoes from the backplate.
9 Disengage the strut and detach the self-adjusting levers from the leading shoe.

Refitting

10 Refitting is a reversal of removal, but before fitting the return springs, actuate the self-adjusting mechanism to set the brake shoes to slightly less than the internal diameter of the brake drum **(see illustration)**.
11 Before refitting the drum, ensure that the bearings and the space between them are greased.
12 Refit the drum on the stub axle, followed by the washer and a new hub nut.
13 Tighten the hub nut to the specified torque then lock the collar into the stub axle groove using a round-ended drift.
14 Tap the dust cap into position.
15 Refit the rear wheel and lower the car to the ground. Apply the footbrake pedal several times to reset the automatic adjuster.

21.10 Rear brake shoes on Saloon models
1 Leading shoe
2 Trailing shoe
3 Upper return spring
4 Lower return spring
5 Anti-rattle springs
6 Handbrake cable (disconnected to show end fitting)
7 Self-adjusting mechanism
8 Handbrake lever
9 Strut

20.1 View of vacuum pump with air cleaner removed showing filler/level plug (arrowed)

21.3 Method of releasing the brake shoes on Visa models

22 Clutch pedal and cable - lubrication

1 Lubricate the clutch pedal pivot with grease.
2 Also grease the operating rods and/or cable ends where they connect with the operating levers.
3 Removal of the air filter will enable easier access to the clutch cable at the transmission end.

23 Fuel filter - removal and refitting

Note: *Although not essential, it is always beneficial to change the fuel filter just before winter, regardless of mileage.*

Except C15 Van models

Removal

1 This job may be carried out leaving the filter head *in situ*. However due to limited access and the possibility of spilling fuel over the engine, it is recommended that the filter head is removed, together with the cartridge.
2 Unscrew the union bolts and disconnect the inlet and outlet fuel unions from the filter head **(see illustration)**. Recover the union washers.

3 Unbolt the filter head from the bracket and withdraw it, together with the cartridge **(see illustration)**.
4 With the assembly in a container to catch spilled fuel, unscrew the through-bolt. On the Roto-diesel filter this will release the end cap and enable the cartridge and seals to be removed **(see illustrations)**. On the Bosch filter remove the chamber followed by the element and seals. The Purflux filter fitted to some models is similar to the Bosch filter.

Refitting

5 Clean the filter head and end cap or chamber.
6 Locate the new seals in position then fit the new cartridge or element using a reversal of the removal procedures.
7 Finally prime the fuel injection system as described in Chapter 4.

C15 Van models

Note: *If the fuel is allowed to escape out of the fuel filter housing onto the engine, it will find its way into the clutch (manual transmission models) and possibly damage the linings.*

Removal

8 On C15 Van models from early 1993, the fuel filter is modified. The coolant-heated filter base is no longer fitted. The fuel filter is relocated in a housing on the cylinder head, above the thermostat and cylinder head coolant outlet housing. The new housing has a water detector and a water drain plug in its base. There is an external hand-priming bulb, and a double valve return system.
9 To remove the filter, first drain the housing by loosening the drain plug. A plastic tube should be attached to the drain plug, so that the fuel can be directed into a suitable container **(see illustration)**.
10 With the fuel drained, unscrew the cover bolts, remove the cover and lift out the filter.

Refitting

11 If the filter is to be refitted, check the sealing rubber before reversing the removal procedure. Removal of the water detector is straightforward **(see illustrations)**.

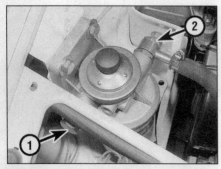

23.2 Inlet (1) and outlet (2) unions on the Bosch fuel filter

23.3 Removing the Roto-diesel filter head and cartridge

23.4A Unscrew the through bolt . . .

23.4B . . . and remove the Roto-diesel filter cartridge

23.9 Draining the fuel from the fuel filter housing

23.11A Unscrew the cover bolts . . .

23.11B . . . remove the cover . . .

23.11C . . . and remove the filter

23.11D Checking the sealing rubber

23.11E Disconnecting the wiring plug . . .

23.11F . . . and removing the water detector (arrowed)

1

30 000 miles or 2 years service

24.2 Expansion tank and filler cap on Visa models

24 Coolant - draining, flushing and filling

Note: *The coolant should be renewed at the first 12 000 miles (20 000 km) from new, or from when the engine is renewed. This is necessary to flush out corrosive elements that can build up to high levels during the early life of the engine. Thereafter renew as described in the maintenance schedule.*

Draining

1 Allow the engine to cool for at least 10 minutes after switching off.

24.14A Bleed screws (arrowed) on the thermostat housing

2 Depress the filler cap and slowly turn it anti-clockwise until it can be removed. If the engine is hot cover the cap with a thick cloth before removing it as a precaution against scalding **(see illustration)**.

3 Position a container beneath the left-hand side of the radiator then unscrew the drain plug and allow the coolant to drain.

> **HAYNES HiNT**
>
> *If there is no drain plug fitted, disconnect the drain pipe on the left-hand side of the radiator or disconnect the bottom hose from the right-hand side.*

4 When the radiator is completely drained refit the drain plug, pipe or hose then drain the block by unscrewing the drain plug located on the rear of the engine at the flywheel end. Refit the drain plug on completion.

Flushing

5 If the coolant is contaminated with rust and scale the complete system should be flushed as follows.

6 Drain the system as described in the previous Section.

7 Remove the thermostat as described in Chapter 3.

8 If not already done disconnect the bottom hose from the radiator.

9 Insert a garden hose into the thermostat housing so that the water runs through the engine in the reverse direction to normal flow and comes out of the bottom hose. Continue until the water emerges clean.

10 Run the water through the radiator in the normal direction of flow by inserting the garden hose in the top hose. In severe cases of contamination it may be helpful to remove the radiator and reverse-flush it.

11 Chemical descalers or flushing agents should only be used as a last resort, in which case follow the instructions given by the

manufacturers.

12 When flushing is complete, refit the thermostat and reconnect the hoses.

Filling

13 Make sure that the drain plugs are secure and that all hoses are in good condition and their clips tight.

14 Loosen or remove the bleed screws located on the thermostat housing cover, on the radiator on BX models and, on Visa models only, the expansion tank return pipe **(see illustrations)**.

15 Fill slowly with coolant through the filler neck and at the same time keep an eye on the bleed screw holes. When coolant free of air bubbles emerges refit and tighten the bleed screws.

16 Top up the radiator or expansion tank until it is full to the filler cap seating. There still remains air in the system which must be purged as follows.

17 Start the engine and run at a fast idle speed for several minutes. Stop the engine.

18 Top up the coolant level as follows. On Visa models top-up to the level plate visible through the filler neck. On BX models withdraw the black plastic tube from the radiator filler neck and note the coolant level on the "threaded" section **(see illustration)**. The bottom of the tube indicates the minimum level and the upper limit of the "threaded" section indicates the maximum level. Top up to the maximum level, then refit the tube.

19 Fit the filler cap.

20 Start the engine and run to normal operating temperature indicated by the electric cooling fan(s) cutting in then out after a few minutes.

21 Stop the engine and allow to cool for at least 1 hour.

22 Recheck the coolant level as described in paragraph 18 and top-up as necessary.

24.14B Bleed screw (arrowed) on the radiator (BX models)

24.14C Bleed screw (arrowed) on the expansion tank return pipe (Visa models)

24.18 Removing the coolant level tube on BX models

36 000 miles service

25 Transmission fluid level (manual transmission models) - check

Pre-1987 models

Note: *There is no oil level plug on pre-1987 models. The only way of making sure the level is correct is to drain and refill the transmission. Having done this, it makes sense to use new oil for refilling.*

1 Jack up the front of the vehicle and support on axle stands (see "*Jacking and vehicle support*"). Chock the rear wheels.

2 Two drain plugs are provided on early models - one for the transmission and one for the differential **(see illustration)**. On later models the transmission drain plug is deleted and it is important not to confuse the reverse gear shaft clamping screw with a drain plug.

3 Unscrew the drain plug(s) and drain the oil into a suitable container. On completion refit and tighten the drain plug(s).

4 There is no provision for a level plug so the correct quantity of oil must be measured before refilling the transmission through the filler plug hole.

5 Lower the vehicle to the ground.

1987-on models

6 On models built from 1987, an oil filler/level plug is fitted in the transmission end cover. Access is easiest through the left-hand wheel arch **(see illustration)**. The vehicle should be parked on level ground for this check.

7 Having gained access to the oil level plug, clean around the plug before removing it. Check the oil level; with the vehicle level, the oil level must be up to the bottom of the plug hole.

8 Top-up if necessary with the specified oil **(see illustration)**. Add the oil slowly; the oil level is correct when the oil just begins to flow from the plug hole. Allow a few minutes for the oil level to stabilise, then refit and tighten the filler/level plug. Check for leaks if regular topping-up is required.

25.2 Differential drain plug (arrowed)

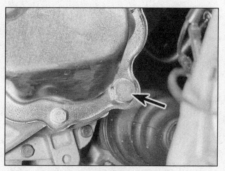

25.6 Manual transmission filler/level plug (arrowed) in end cover

25.8 Topping-up the transmission oil

1

48 000 miles service

26 Timing belt - renewal

 HAYNES HiNT *If the timing belt breaks in service, extensive damage may be caused to the engine. Renewal at or before the specified interval is strongly recommended.*

Refer to Chapter 2.

Notes

Chapter 2
Engine repair procedures

Contents

Degrees of difficulty

Easy, suitable for novice with little experience | **Fairly easy,** suitable for beginner with some experience | **Fairly difficult,** suitable for competent DIY mechanic | **Difficult,** suitable for experienced DIY mechanic | **Very difficult,** suitable for expert DIY or professional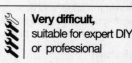

Specifications

General

Type	Four-cylinder, in-line, four-stroke, overhead camshaft, compression-ignition, mounted transversely and inclined 30° to rear. Transmission mounted on left-hand end of engine.
Codes:	
Visa, BX and C15	XUD 7 - 161A
BX Turbo	XUD 7TE/L - A8A
BX non-Turbo	XUD 9 - 162(B) or D9B - XUD 9A/L
Engine size:	
XUD 7	1765 cc
XUD 9	1905 cc
Number of cylinders	4
Bore and stroke:	
XUD 7 and XUD 7TE	80.0 x 88.0 mm
XUD 9 and XUD 9A	83.0 x 88.0 mm
Compression ratio:	
XUD 7	23.0 : 1
XUD 7TE	22.0 : 1
XUD 9	23.5 : 1
XUD 9A	23.0 : 1
Compression pressures (engine hot, cranking speed):	
Minimum	18 bar
Normal	25 to 30 bar
Maximum difference between any two cylinders	5 bar
Maximum torque (ISO):	
XUD 7	110 Nm at 2200 rpm
XUD 7TE	180 Nm at 2100 rpm
XUD 9	118 Nm at 2000 rpm
XUD 9A	120 Nm at 2000 rpm
Maximum power (ISO):	
XUD 7	43.5 kW at 4600 rpm
XUD 7TE	66.0 kW at 4300 rpm
XUD 9	47.0 kW at 4600 rpm
XUD 9A	51.0 kW at 4600 rpm

Maximum speed:
Except XUD 7TE models:
   No load .... 5100 rpm
   Laden .... 4600 rpm
XUD 7TE models:
   No-load .... 4800 rpm
   Loaded .... 4300 rpm
Firing order .... 1-3-4-2 (No 1 at flywheel end)

Cylinder block

Cylinder bore diameter:
XUD 7 and XUD 7TE .... 80.000 to 80.018 mm
   or 80.030 to 80.048 mm
XUD 9 and XUD 9A .... 83.000 to 83.018 mm
   or 83.030 to 83.048 mm

Pistons and piston rings

Piston diameter:
XUD 7 and XUD 7TE .... 79.93 ± 0.008 mm
   or 76.96 ± 0.008 mm
XUD 9 and XUD 9A .... 82.930 ± 0.009 mm
   or 82.960 ± 0.009 mm
Piston ring end gaps (fitted):
   Top compression .... 0.20 to 0.40 mm
   2nd compression .... 0.15 to 0.35 mm
   Oil scraper .... 0.10 to 0.30 mm
Connecting rod small-end bush inner diameter .... 25.007 to 25.020 mm
Maximum weight difference between any two pistons .... 2.5 g
Maximum piston protrusion difference between any two pistons ..... 0.12 mm

Crankshaft

Endfloat .... 0.07 to 0.32 mm
Maximum journal/crankpin out-of-round .... 0.007 mm

Cylinder head

Warp limit .... 0.07 mm subject to camshaft turning freely
Refinishing limit (see text) .... 0.40 mm
Swirl chamber protrusion .... 0 to 0.03 mm

Valves

Seat angle (inclusive):
Except XUD 7TE models:
   Inlet .... 120°
   Exhaust .... 90°
XUD 7TE models:
   Inlet and exhaust .... 90°
Valve recess below cylinder head:
   Inlet .... 0.50 to 1.05 mm
   Exhaust .... 0.90 to 1.45 mm

Valve clearances (cold):	**Inlet**	**Exhaust**
XUD7 161-A	0.10 to 0.25 mm	0.25 to 0.40 mm
XUD9 D9B and XUD9 162	0.15 to 0.25 mm	0.35 to 0.45 mm
XUD7 A8A	0.15 ± 0.08 mm	0.30 ± 0.08 mm

Valve timing:
XUD 7 models (at 1.0 mm clearance):
   Inlet opens .... 8° BTDC
   Inlet closes .... 40° ABDC
   Exhaust opens .... 56° BBDC
   Exhaust closes .... 12° ATDC
XUD 7TE models (at 0.8 mm clearance):
   Inlet opens .... 4° 30' BTDC
   Inlet closes .... 20° ABDC
   Exhaust opens .... 39° BBDC
   Exhaust closes .... 4° ATDC
XUD 9A models (at 0.8 mm clearance):
   Inlet opens .... 4° BTDC
   Inlet closes .... 35° ABDC
   Exhaust opens .... 43° BBDC
   Exhaust closes .... 0° (TDC)

Camshaft
Endfloat .... 0.07 to 0.16 mm

Lubrication system
Oil pressure
  Except XUD 7TE models (at engine temperature of 90°C/194°F):
    Minimum .... 2.5 bar at 800 rpm
    Maximum .... 3.5 to 5.0 bar at 4000 rpm
  XUD 7TE models (at 80°C/170°F) .... 3.4 bars at 2000 rpm
Oil pressure switch operating pressures:
  On .... 0.58 to 0.44 bar
  Off .... 0.8 bar maximum

Oil pump
Type .... Two gear
Pressure relief valve opens .... 4.0 bar
Gear endfloat .... 0.12 mm
Clearance between gear lobes and housing .... 0.064 mm

Torque wrench settings

	Nm	lbf ft
Big-end bearing cap	50	37
Camshaft bearing cap	18	13
Camshaft sprocket	35	26
Crankshaft pulley bolt:		
Stage 1	40	30
Stage 2	plus 60° or to 150	plus 60° or to 111
Cylinder head bolts:		
Pre-September 1986:		
Stage 1	30	22
Stage 2	60	44
Stage 3 Loosen ¼ turn then	60	44
Stage 4 (after 10 mins at 3000 rpm). Loosen ¼ turn then	70	52
From September 1986 on (refer to text):		
Stage 1	30	22
Stage 2	70	52
Stage 3	Angle-tighten a further 120°	
Engine mounting, left hand:		
Centre nut	35	26
Small nuts	18	13
Centre stud to transmission	50	37
Engine mounting bracket, right-hand lower	18	13
Engine mounting bracket, right-hand upper:		
To engine	35	26
To mounting rubber	28	21
Flywheel/driveplate	50	37
Front housing	11	8
Injection pump bracket	20	15
Lower link mounting	35	26
Main bearing cap	70	52
Oil cooler	68	50
Oil gallery plug	28	21
Oil pressure switch	30	22
Oil pump cover	9	7
Oil pump mounting	13	10
Pump pulley to camshaft	35	26
Sump	19	14
Sump oil drain bracket	3	2.2
Timing belt intermediate roller	18	13
Timing belt tensioner	18	13
Timing cover, lower	12	9
Valve cover	2	1.5

1 Description - general

The engine is of four-cylinder overhead camshaft design, mounted transversely and inclined 30° to the rear, with the transmission mounted on the left-hand side. Both the block and the cylinder head are of cast iron.

A toothed timing belt drives the camshaft, injection pump and water pump. Bucket tappets are fitted between the camshaft and valves, and valve clearance adjustment is by means of selective shims.

The camshaft is supported by three bearings machined directly in the cylinder head.

The crankshaft runs in five main bearings of the usual shell type. Endfloat is controlled by thrustwashers either side of No 2 main bearing.

The pistons are selected to be of matching weight, and incorporate fully floating gudgeon pins retained by circlips.

The oil pump is chain driven from the front of the crankshaft. An oil cooler is fitted to the 1.9 engine.

During 1988, a 1765 cc Turbo diesel (the XUD 7TE),was introduced to the BX range of models.

2 Compression and leakdown test - description and interpretation

Note: *A compression tester specifically designed for diesel engines must be used for this test*

Compression test

Description

1 When engine performance is down, or if misfiring occurs which cannot be attributed to the ignition or fuel systems, a compression test can provide diagnostic clues as to the engine's condition. If the test is performed regularly, it can give warning of trouble before any other symptoms become apparent.

2 A compression tester specifically intended for diesel engines must be used, because of the higher pressures this type of engine produces. The tester is connected to an adapter that screws into the glow plug or injector hole. It is unlikely to be worthwhile buying such a tester for occasional use, but it may be possible to borrow or hire one. If not, have the test performed by a garage, or dealer.

3 Unless specific instructions to the contrary are supplied with the tester, observe the following points:
a) *The battery must be in a good state of charge, the air filter must be clean, and the engine must be at normal operating temperature*
b) *All the injectors or glow plugs should be removed before starting the test. If removing the injectors, also remove the fire shield washers, otherwise they may be blown out*
c) *The stop solenoid must be disconnected, to prevent the engine from running or fuel from being discharged*

4 There is no need to hold the accelerator pedal down during the test, because the diesel engine air inlet is not throttled.

5 The actual compression pressures measured are not so important as the balance between cylinders. Values are given in the Specifications.

6 The cause of poor compression is less easy to establish on a diesel engine than a petrol driven one. The effect of introducing oil into the cylinders ('wet testing') is not conclusive, because there is a risk that oil will sit in the swirl chamber or in the recess on the piston crown instead of passing to the rings. However, the following can be used as a rough guide to diagnosis.

Interpretation

7 All cylinders should produce very similar pressures. Any difference greater than that specified indicates the existence of a fault. Note that the compression should build up quickly in a healthy engine. Low compression on the first stroke, followed by gradually increasing pressure on successive strokes, indicates worn piston rings. A low compression reading on the first stroke, which does not build up during successive strokes, indicates leaking valves or a blown head gasket (a cracked head could also be the cause). Deposits on the undersides of the valve heads can also cause low compression.

8 A low reading from two adjacent cylinders is almost certainly due to the head gasket having blown between them. The presence of coolant in the engine oil will confirm this.

9 If the compression reading is unusually high, the cylinder head surfaces, valves and pistons are probably coated with carbon deposits. If this is the case, the cylinder head should be removed and decarbonised.

Leakdown test

Description

10 A leakdown test measures the rate at which compressed air fed into the cylinder is lost. It is an alternative to a compression test, and in many ways is better, since the escaping air provides easy identification of where pressure loss is occurring (piston rings, valves or head gasket).

11 The equipment needed for leakdown testing is unlikely to be available to the home mechanic. If poor compression is suspected, have the test performed by a suitably equipped garage.

3 Major operations possible with the engine in the vehicle

The following operations can be carried out without having to remove the engine from the car:
a) *Timing belt - removal and refitting*
b) *Camshaft - removal and refitting*
c) *Cylinder head - removal and refitting*
d) *Camshaft oil seals - renewal*
e) *Crankshaft oil seals - renewal*
f) *Sump - removal and refitting*
g) *Oil pump - removal and refitting*
h) *Pistons and connecting rods - removal and refitting*
i) *Flywheel/driveplate - removal and refitting*

For almost any job involving work on the top of the engine (for example valve clearance adjustment) the intercooler must be removed. This is described in Chapter 4.

4.11 Right-hand engine mounting bracket

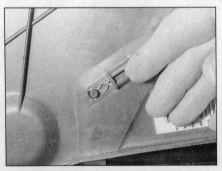
4.12A Timing cover front clip (early models) . . .

4.12B . . . and spring clips

4 Timing belt - removal, refitting and tensioning

Removal

1 The timing belt drives the camshaft, injection pump, and water pump from a toothed sprocket on the front of the crankshaft. If it breaks in service the pistons are likely to hit the valve heads and result in an expensive repair.

2 The timing belt should be renewed at the intervals specified in Chapter 1. However, if it is contaminated with oil or if it is at all noisy in operation (a "scraping" noise due to uneven wear) it should be renewed earlier. Where a Bosch injection pump is fitted, excessive play in the front bearing can wear the sides of the timing belt.

3 On Visa models apply the handbrake. On BX models chock the rear wheels and release the handbrake, as the handbrake operates on the front wheels.

4 On manual transmission models jack up the front right-hand corner of the vehicle until the wheel is just clear of the ground. Support the vehicle on an axle stand and engage 4th or 5th gear. This will enable the engine to be turned easily by turning the right-hand wheel. On automatic transmission models use an open-ended spanner on the crankshaft pulley bolt.

5 Remove the engine splash guard from under the right-hand front wheel arch.

6 Disconnect the battery negative lead.

7 Loosen the alternator pivot and adjustment bolts then unscrew the tension bolt until it is possible to slip the drivebelt from the pulleys.

8 With 4th or 5th gear selected on manual transmission models have an assistant depress the footbrake pedal, then unscrew the crankshaft pulley bolt. On BX models the handbrake may be applied instead of the footbrake pedal to hold the crankshaft stationary. On automatic transmission models unbolt the transmission cover and lock the starter ring gear. Note that the bolt is extremely tight.

9 Slide the pulley from the front of the crankshaft. Unbolt the bottom timing cover.

Using a twist drill to enter the TDC hole in the flywheel

10 Support the weight of the engine using a hoist or trolley jack.

11 Unscrew the nuts and remove the right-hand engine mounting bracket **(see illustration)**.

12 Pull up the front clip (early models), release the spring clips, and withdraw the two timing cover sections **(see illustrations)**. Note that the spring clip is not fitted to later models, which have a modified cover and fastenings.

13 Turn the engine by means of the front right-hand wheel or crankshaft pulley bolt until the three bolt holes in the camshaft and injection pump sprockets are aligned with the corresponding holes in the engine front plate.

14 Insert an 8.0 mm diameter metal dowel rod or drill through the special hole in the left-hand rear flange of the cylinder block by the starter motor. Then carefully turn the engine either way until the rod enters the TDC hole in the flywheel **(see Tool Tip)**.

15 Insert three M8 bolts through the holes in the camshaft and injection pump sprockets and screw them into the engine front plate finger-tight **(see illustration)**.

16 Loosen the timing belt tensioner pivot nut and adjustment bolt, then turn the bracket anti-clockwise to release the tension and retighten the adjustment bolt to hold the tensioner in the released position. If available use a ⅜ inch square drive extension in the hole provided to turn the bracket against the spring tension.

17 Mark the timing belt with an arrow to indicate its normal direction of turning then

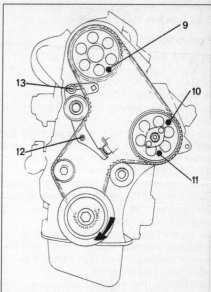

4.15 Holding camshaft and injection pump sprockets in position using M8 bolts

9, 10 and 11 M8 bolts
12 Tensioner pivot nut
13 Tensioner adjustment bolt

remove it from the camshaft, injection pump, water pump and crankshaft sprockets.

Refitting

18 Inspect the belt for cracks, fraying, and damage to the teeth. Pay particular attention to the roots of the teeth. If any damage is evident or if the belt is contaminated with oil it must be renewed and any oil leak rectified.

19 Begin refitting by locating the timing belt on the crankshaft sprocket, making sure that, where applicable, the rotation arrow is facing the correct way.

20 Hold the timing belt engaged with the crankshaft sprocket then feed it over the roller and onto the injection pump, camshaft, and water pump sprockets and over the tensioner roller. To ensure correct engagement, locate only a half width on the injection pump sprocket before feeding the timing belt onto the camshaft sprocket keeping the belt taut and fully engaged with the crankshaft

2

4.20A Fitting the timing belt over the injection pump sprocket . . .

4.20B . . . the camshaft sprocket . . .

4.20C . . . and the water pump sprocket

sprocket. Locate the timing belt fully onto the sprockets **(see illustrations)**.

Tensioning

21 With the pivot nut loose, slacken the tensioner adjustment bolt while holding the bracket against the spring tension. Slowly release the bracket until the roller presses against the timing belt. Retighten the adjustment bolt.

22 Remove the bolts from the camshaft and injection pump sprockets. Remove the metal dowel rod from the cylinder block.

23 Rotate the engine two complete turns in its normal direction. Do not rotate the engine backwards as the timing belt must be kept tight between the crankshaft, injection pump and camshaft sprockets.

24 Loosen the tensioner adjustment bolt to allow the tensioner spring to push the roller against the timing belt, then tighten both the adjustment bolt and pivot nut.

25 Recheck the engine timing as described in paragraphs 13 and 14 then remove the metal dowel rod.

26 Refit the three timing cover sections and secure with the special clip and spring clips.

27 Refit the right-hand engine mounting bracket and tighten the nuts.

28 Remove the trolley jack or hoist.

29 Slide the pulley onto the front of the crankshaft.

30 Apply three drops of locking fluid on the threads of the crankshaft pulley bolt then insert it and tighten to the specified torque while holding the crankshaft stationary using the method described in paragraph 8.

31 Refit the alternator drivebelt and tension it as described in Chapter 1.

32 Reconnect the battery negative lead.

5.5 Battery support bracket, also showing left-hand engine/transmission mounting

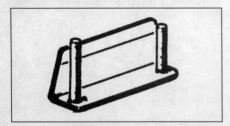

5.13 Citroën tool 7009-T1 for holding the tensioner plunger

33 Refit the engine splash-guard under the right-hand front wheel arch.

34 Lower the vehicle to the ground.

5 Timing belt tensioner - removal and refitting

Removal

1 On Visa models apply the handbrake. On BX models chock the rear wheels and release the handbrake.

2 On manual transmission models jack up the front right-hand corner of the vehicle until the wheel is just clear of the ground. Support the vehicle on an axle stand and engage 4th or 5th gear so that the engine may be rotated by turning the right-hand wheel. On automatic transmission models use an open-ended spanner on the crankshaft pulley bolt.

3 Support the weight of the engine using a hoist or trolley jack.

4 Unscrew the nuts and remove the right-hand engine mounting bracket.

Visa models

5 Remove the battery and the tray, then unbolt the support bracket **(see illustration)**.

6 Unscrew the nut from the left-hand engine mounting and remove the rubber mounting.

7 Move the engine and transmission to the left as far as possible and support it in this position.

All models

8 Pull up the special clip, release the spring clips and withdraw the two timing cover sections.

9 Turn the engine by means of the front right-hand wheel or crankshaft pulley bolt until the three bolt holes in the camshaft and injection pump sprockets are aligned with the corresponding holes in the engine front plate.

10 Insert an 8.0 mm diameter metal dowel rod or drill through the special hole in the left-hand rear flange of the cylinder block by the starter motor. Then carefully turn the engine either way until the rod enters the TDC hole in the flywheel.

11 Insert three M8 bolts through the holes in the camshaft and injection pump sprockets and screw them into the engine front plate finger-tight.

12 Loosen the timing belt tensioner pivot nut and adjustment bolt, then turn the bracket anti-clockwise until the adjustment bolt is in the middle of the slot and retighten the bolt. If available use a ⅜ inch square drive extension in the hole provided to turn the bracket against the spring tension.

13 A tool must now be obtained to hold the tensioner plunger in the mounting bracket. Citroën tool 7009-T1 **(see illustration)** is designed to slide in the two lower bolt holes of the mounting bracket and it should be quite easy to fabricate a similar tool out of sheet metal using long bolts instead of metal dowel rods.

14 Unscrew the two lower bolts then fit the

special tool. Grease the inner surface of the tool to prevent any damage to the end of the tensioner plunger.

15 Unscrew the pivot nut and adjustment bolt and withdraw the tensioner bracket, complete with roller.

16 Unbolt the engine mounting bracket noting that the uppermost bolt is on the inside face of the engine front plate.

17 Compress the tensioner plunger into the mounting bracket, remove the special tool then withdraw the plunger and spring.

Refitting

18 Refitting is a reversal of removal, but refer to Section 4, paragraphs 21 to 25 for details of the timing belt adjustment procedure.

6 Timing belt intermediate roller - removal and refitting

Removal

1 Follow the procedure given in paragraphs 1 to 12 of Section 5.

2 Remove the engine splash guard from under the right-hand front wheel arch.

3 Disconnect the battery negative lead on BX models.

4 Loosen the alternator pivot and adjustment bolts then unscrew the tension bolt until it is possible to slip the drivebelt from the pulleys.

5 With 4th or 5th gear selected on manual transmission models have an assistant depress the footbrake pedal, then unscrew the crankshaft pulley bolt. On BX models the handbrake may be applied instead of the footbrake pedal to hold the crankshaft stationary. On automatic transmission models unbolt the transmission cover and lock the starter ring gear.

6 Slide the pulley from the front of the crankshaft.

7 Unbolt the lower timing cover.

8 Remove the spacer from the stud for the upper timing cover sections. Note the position of the stud then unscrew and remove it.

9 Unscrew the remaining bolts securing the intermediate roller bracket to the cylinder block noting that the upper bolt also secures the engine mounting bracket.

10 Slightly loosen the remaining engine mounting bracket bolts then slide out the intermediate roller and bracket.

Refitting

11 Refitting is a reversal of removal, but note the following additional points:
 a) Tighten all bolts to the specified torque
 b) Apply three drops of locking fluid to the threads of the crankshaft pulley bolt before inserting it
 c) Tension the alternator drivebelt as described in Chapter 1
 d) Adjust the timing belt as described in Section 4, paragraphs 21 to 25

7.7 Crankcase ventilation hose (1.9 engine)

7.8A Unbolt the valve cover . . .

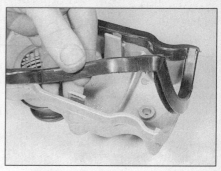

7.8B . . . and remove the gasket

7.9A Special lug (arrowed) for holding the camshaft

7.9B Removing the camshaft sprocket

7.13 Using a puller to remove the pump pulley from the camshaft

7.17 The DIST marking must be at the timing belt end

7.19A Fitting a camshaft end bearing cap

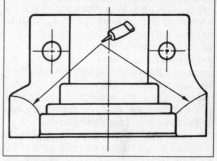

7.19B Areas on camshaft end bearing caps to apply sealing compound

2

7   Camshaft - removal and refitting

Removal

1 Follow the procedure given in paragraphs 1 to 12 of Section 5.

2 Remove the timing belt from the camshaft sprocket and tie it to one side without bending it excessively.

3 Unscrew the M8 bolt holding the camshaft sprocket in the timing position.

4 Where applicable, remove the oil filler cap/breather from the valve cover and position it to one side.

5 On BX models disconnect the battery negative lead and disconnect the air inlet hose from the inlet manifold and air cleaner.

6 Loosen the pivot and adjustment bolts of the hydraulic high pressure pump (BX models), or vacuum pump (Visa models), swivel the unit upwards, and disconnect the drivebelt from the pulleys.

7 On the 1.9 engine, disconnect the crankcase ventilation hose from the valve cover **(see illustration)**.

8 Unbolt and remove the valve cover. Remove the gasket **(see illustrations)**.

9 Hold the camshaft stationary with a spanner on the special lug between the 3rd and 4th cams or by using a lever in the sprocket holes then unscrew the camshaft sprocket bolt and withdraw the sprocket **(see illustrations)**. Recover the Woodruff key if it is loose. Do not rotate the camshaft otherwise the valves will strike the pistons of Nos 1 and 4 cylinders. If necessary turn the engine one quarter turn to position all the pistons halfway

down the cylinders to prevent any damage, however, release the timing belt from the injection pump sprocket first.

10 Mark the position of the camshaft bearing caps numbering them from the flywheel end and making the marks on the manifold side.

11 Progressively unscrew the nuts then remove the bearing caps.

12 Lift the camshaft and withdraw it through the front engine plate. Remove the oil seal from the timing end of the camshaft.

13 Hold the camshaft stationary with a spanner on the special lug between the 3rd and 4th cams, then unscrew the bolt and remove the pump pulley from the flywheel end of the camshaft. Use a puller if it is tight **(see illustration)**. Recover the Woodruff key if it is loose.

14 Remove the oil seal from the flywheel end of the camshaft.

7.20A Tightening the camshaft bearing cap nuts

7.20B Checking the camshaft endfloat

Using a socket and bolt to fit a camshaft oil seal

15 Clean all the components including the bearing surfaces in the cylinder head. Examine the components carefully for wear and damage, in particular check the surface of the cams for scoring and pitting. Renew components as necessary and obtain new oil seals.

Refitting

16 Begin reassembly by lubricating the cams and bearing journals with engine oil.
17 Locate the camshaft on the cylinder head, passing it through the engine front plate and with the tips of cams 4 and 6 facing downwards and resting on the bucket tappets. The cast DIST marking on the camshaft should be at the timing belt end of the cylinder head **(see illustration)** and the key slot for the camshaft sprocket should be facing upwards.
18 Fit the centre bearing cap the correct way round as previously noted then screw on the nuts and tighten them two or three turns.
19 Apply sealing compound to the end bearing caps on the areas as shown. Fit them in the correct positions and tighten the nuts two or three turns **(see illustrations)**.
20 Tighten all the nuts progressively to the specified torque making sure that cams 4 and 6 remain facing downwards **(see illustration)**. Check that the camshaft endfloat is as given in the Specifications using feeler blades **(see illustration)**. The only answer if it is not correct is to renew the cylinder head.
21 If the original camshaft is being refitted and it is known that the valve clearances are correct, go on to paragraph 22, otherwise check and adjust the valve clearances as described in Section 8. Note that as the timing belt is disconnected at this stage, the crankshaft must be turned one quarter turn either way from the TDC position so that all the pistons are halfway down the cylinders. This will prevent the valves striking the pistons when the camshaft is rotated. Release the timing belt from the injection pump sprocket while turning the engine as the timing bolts are still in position.
22 Smear the lips of the oil seals with oil then fit them over each end of the camshaft, open end first, and press them in until flush with the end faces of the end caps. Use an M10 bolt,

washers and a socket to press in the oil seals **(See Haynes Hint)**.
23 Fit the Woodruff key and pump pulley to the flywheel end of the camshaft, insert the bolt and tighten it while holding the camshaft stationary.
24 Fit the Woodruff key and camshaft sprocket to the timing end of the camshaft. Apply locking fluid to the threads then insert the bolt and tighten it to the specified torque while holding the camshaft stationary.
25 Refit the valve cover, together with a new gasket, and tighten the bolts.
26 Refit the crankcase ventilation hose.
27 Locate the drivebelt on the camshaft pulley and hydraulic pump (BX models), or vacuum pump pulley (Visa models). Press the pump downwards until the deflection of the belt midway between the two pulleys is approximately 5.0 mm under firm thumb pressure. Tighten the adjustment bolt followed by the pivot bolt.
28 On BX models reconnect the battery negative lead and the air inlet hose.
29 Refit the oil filler cap/breather.
30 Align the holes and refit the M8 timing bolt to the camshaft sprocket.
31 If the crankshaft was turned a quarter turn from TDC as in paragraphs 9 and 21, turn the crankshaft back the quarter turn so that pistons 1 and 4 are again at TDC. Do not turn the engine more than a quarter turn otherwise pistons 2 and 3 will pass their TDC positions and will strike valves 4 and 6.
32 Refit the TDC dowel rod to the flywheel.
33 Refit and adjust the timing belt, referring to Section 4, paragraphs 20 to 25. The remaining procedure is a reversal of removal.

8 Valve clearances - checking and adjustment

Checking

1 On Visa models apply the handbrake. On BX models chock the rear wheels and release the handbrake.
2 On manual transmission models jack up the front right-hand corner of the vehicle until the wheel is just clear of the ground. Support the vehicle on an axle stand and engage 4th or

5th gear so that the engine may be rotated by turning the right-hand wheel. On automatic transmission models use an open-ended spanner on the crankshaft pulley bolt.
3 Disconnect the battery negative lead.
4 Remove the oil filler cap/breather and position it to one side.
5 On BX models disconnect the air inlet hose from the inlet manifold and air cleaner.
6 Disconnect the crankcase ventilation hose from the valve cover.
7 Unbolt and remove the valve cover. Remove the gasket.
8 On a piece of paper draw the outline of the engine with the cylinders numbered from the flywheel end and also showing the position of each valve, together with the specified valve clearance. Above each valve draw two lines for noting (1) the actual clearance and (2) the amount of adjustment required.
9 Turn the engine until the inlet valve of No 1 cylinder (nearest the flywheel) is fully closed and the apex of the cam is facing directly away from the bucket tappet.
10 Using feeler blades measure the clearance between the base of the cam and the bucket tappet **(see illustration)**. Record the clearance on line (1).
11 Repeat the measurement for the other seven valves, turning the engine as necessary so that the cam lobe in question is always facing directly away from the particular bucket tappet.
12 Calculate the difference between each measured clearance and the desired value and record it on line (2). Since the clearance is different for inlet and exhaust valves make sure that you are aware which valve you are dealing with. The valve sequence from either end of the engine is:

Inlet - Exhaust - Exhaust - Inlet - Inlet - Exhaust - Exhaust - Inlet

13 If all the clearances are within tolerance, refit the valve cover using a new gasket if necessary. If any clearance measured is outside the specified tolerance, adjustment must be carried out as described below.

Adjustment

14 Remove the camshaft as described in Section 7.

8.10 Checking the valve clearances with feeler blades

8.15 Checking the shim thickness with a micrometer

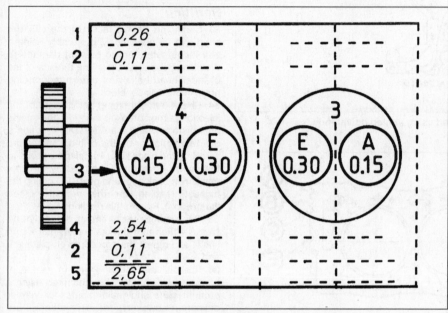

8.17 Example of valve shim thickness calculation
A Inlet E Exhaust

15 Withdraw the first bucket tappet and its shim. Be careful that the shim does not fall out of the tappet. Clean the shim and measure its thickness with a micrometer **(see illustration)**.
16 Refer to the clearance recorded for the valve concerned. If the clearance was more than the amount required the shim thickness must be increased by the difference recorded (2), if too small the thickness must be decreased.
17 Draw three more lines beneath each valve on the calculation paper as shown **(see illustration)**. On line (4) note the measured thickness of the shim then add or deduct the difference from line (2) to give the final shim thickness required on line (5).
18 Shims are available in thicknesses between 2.225 mm and 3.025 mm in steps of 0.025 mm, and between 3.100 mm and 3.550 mm in steps of 0.075 mm. Clean new shims before measuring or fitting them.
19 Repeat the procedure given in paragraphs 15 to 17 on the remaining valves keeping each tappet identified for position.
20 When reassembling, oil the shim and fit it

on the valve stem first with the size marking facing downwards then oil the bucket tappet and lower it onto the shim. Do not raise the tappet after fitting as the shim may become dislodged.
21 When all the tappets are in position with their shims, refit the camshaft referring to Section 7, but recheck the clearances to make sure they are correct.

9 Cylinder head - removal and refitting

Removal

1 On Visa models apply the handbrake. On BX models chock the rear wheels and release the handbrake.
2 On manual transmission models jack up the front right-hand corner of the vehicle until the wheel is just clear of the ground. Support the vehicle on an axle stand and engage 4th or 5th gear so that the engine may be rotated by

turning the right-hand wheel. On automatic transmission models use an open-ended spanner on the crankshaft pulley bolt.
3 Drain the cooling system as described in Chapter 1.
4 Disconnect the battery negative lead.
5 Remove the air cleaner as described in Chapter 4. On turbo models, remove the intercooler, as described in Chapter 4.
6 Support the weight of the engine using a hoist or trolley jack.
7 Unscrew the nuts and remove the right-hand engine mounting bracket.
8 Pull up the special clip, release the spring clips and withdraw the two timing cover sections.
9 Turn the engine by means of the front right-hand wheel or crankshaft pulley bolt until the three bolt holes in the camshaft and injection pump sprockets are aligned with the corresponding holes in the engine front plate.
10 Insert an 8.0 mm diameter metal dowel rod or a drill through the special hole in the left-hand rear flange of the cylinder block by the starter motor. Then carefully turn the engine either way until the rod enters the TDC hole in the flywheel
11 Insert three M8 bolts through the holes in the camshaft and injection pump sprockets and screw them into the engine front plate finger-tight.
12 Loosen the timing belt tensioner pivot nut and adjustment bolt, then turn the bracket anti-clockwise to release the tension and retighten the pivot nut to hold the tensioner in the released position. If available use a ⅜ inch square drive extension in the hole provided to turn the bracket against the spring tension.
13 Remove the timing belt from the camshaft sprocket and tie it to one side without bending it excessively.
14 Unscrew the M8 bolt holding the camshaft sprocket in the timing position. Also unscrew the tensioner adjustment bolt, and the two upper bolts from the engine mounting bracket.
15 At this stage the right-hand engine mounting bracket may be temporarily refitted and the hoist or trolley jack removed.
16 Disconnect the heater hose from the flywheel end of the cylinder head.
17 Disconnect the two small hoses from the thermostat housing then unbolt the housing from the cylinder head and position it to one side.
18 Remove the oil filler cap/breather and position it to one side. On BX models disconnect the air inlet hose from the inlet manifold.
19 If applicable, disconnect the turbo oil feed and return pipes. Refer to Chapter 4, for details.
20 Loosen the pivot and adjustment bolts of the hydraulic high pressure pump (BX models), or vacuum pump (Visa models), swivel the unit upwards, and disconnect the drivebelt from the pulleys.
21 Disconnect the crankcase ventilation hose from the valve cover.

2

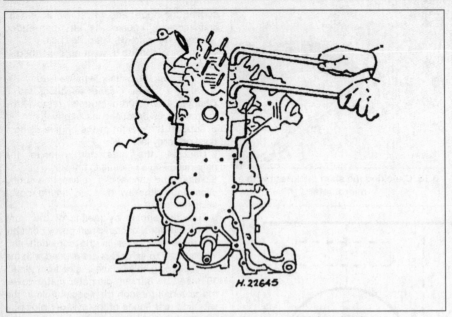

H.22645

9.30 Releasing the cylinder head using angled dowel rods

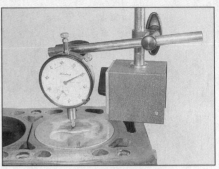

9.34 Checking the piston protrusion

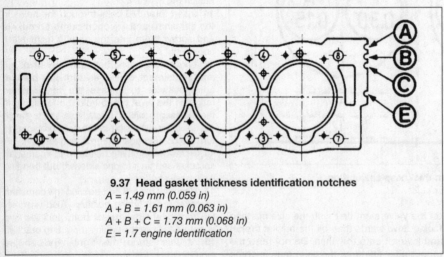

9.37 Head gasket thickness identification notches
A = 1.49 mm (0.059 in)
A + B = 1.61 mm (0.063 in)
A + B + C = 1.73 mm (0.068 in)
E = 1.7 engine identification

Refitting

33 Clean the gasket faces of the cylinder head and cylinder block, preferably using a soft blunt instrument to prevent damage to the mating surfaces. Clean the threads of the cylinder head bolts and the corresponding holes in the cylinder block.

34 Check that the timing belt is clear of the injection pump sprocket, then turn the engine until pistons 1 and 4 are at TDC. Position a dial test indicator on the cylinder block and zero it on the block face. Transfer the probe to the centre of piston 1 then slowly turn the crankshaft back and forth past TDC noting the highest reading on the indicator **(see illustration)**. Record this reading.

35 Repeat this measurement procedure on piston 4 then turn the crankshaft half a turn (180°) and repeat the procedure on pistons 2 and 3.

36 If a dial test indicator is not available, piston protrusion may be measured using a straight-edge and feeler blades or vernier calipers, however, these methods are inevitably less accurate and cannot therefore be recommended.

37 Ascertain the greatest piston protrusion measurement and use this to determine the correct cylinder head gasket from the following chart:

Piston protrusion	Gasket identification
0.54 to 0.65 mm	1 notch or 1 hole
0.65 to 0.77 mm	2 notches or 2 holes
0.77 to 0.82 mm	3 notches or 3 holes

22 Unbolt and remove the valve cover. Remove the gasket.

23 Unscrew the union nuts securing the injection pipes to the injectors and fuel injection pump, and remove the pipes as two assemblies.

24 Unbolt the left-hand engine lifting bracket.

25 Disconnect the wiring from the glow plugs.

26 Disconnect the fuel return pipes from the injection pump.

27 Hold the camshaft stationary with a spanner on the special lug between the 3rd and 4th cams or by using a lever in the sprocket holes, then unscrew the camshaft sprocket bolt and withdraw the sprocket. Recover the Woodruff key if it is loose. Do not rotate the camshaft otherwise the valves will strike the pistons of Nos 1 and 4 cylinders. If necessary release the timing belt from the injection pump sprocket and turn the engine one quarter turn in either direction to position

all the pistons halfway down the cylinders to prevent any damage.

28 Unscrew the exhaust manifold to downpipe bolts. Recover the springs.

29 Progressively unscrew the cylinder head bolts in the reverse order to that shown for tightening (refer to paragraph 41). Remove the washers.

30 Release the cylinder head from the cylinder block and location dowel by rocking it. The Citroën tool for doing this consists simply of two metal dowel rods with 90° angled ends **(see illustration)**.

31 Lift the cylinder head from the block and remove the gasket.

32 Do not dispose of the old gasket until a new one has been obtained. The correct thickness of gasket is determined after measuring the protrusion of the pistons at TDC.

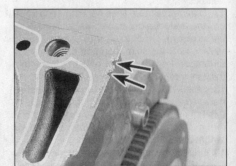

9.39 Cylinder head gasket identification notches (arrowed)

9.41A Cylinder head bolt with spiral grooving on its shank

9.41C Angle-tightening a cylinder head bolt, using a commercially-available angle gauge

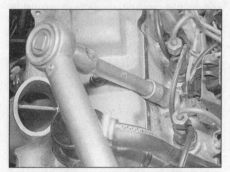

9.70 Retightening the cylinder head bolts

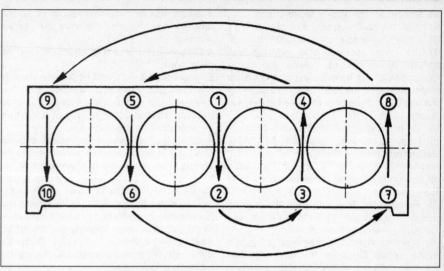

9.41B Cylinder head bolt tightening sequence

Note that the notch on the centre line of the gasket **(see illustration)** identifies the gasket for use only on the 1.7 engine (type XUD 7) and has no significance for the gasket thickness. The head gasket for the turbo engine is identified by having two notches on the centre-line.

38 Turn the crankshaft clockwise (viewed from the timing belt end) until pistons 1 and 4 pass bottom dead centre (BDC) and start to rise, then position them halfway up their bores. Pistons 2 and 3 will also be at their mid-way positions, but descending their bores.

39 Fit the correct gasket the right way round on the cylinder block with the identification notches or holes at the flywheel/driveplate end **(see illustration)**. Make sure that the location dowel is in place at the timing end of the block.

40 Lower the cylinder head onto the block.
41 Models produced after September 1986 are fitted with revised cylinder head bolts and have a different tightening procedure. The later (angle-tightened) type, bolts can be identified by having a coarse spiral grooving on the upper shank - early-type bolts have a plain shank **(see illustration)**. Grease the threads and contact faces of the cylinder head bolts, then insert them, together with their washers, and tighten them in the sequence shown **(see illustration),** in stages as given in Specifications. If using the angle tightening method in the final Stage, retightening after warm-up is not necessary **(see illustration)**.
42 Recheck the valve clearances, referring to Section 8 and adjust them as necessary. Do this even if the clearances have been adjusted with the cylinder head removed, as there may be minor differences.
43 Lubricate the exhaust manifold-to-downpipe contact surfaces with heat resistant grease, then reconnect them and fit the bolts, together with the springs, cups and self-locking nuts. On 1.9 engines the bolts incorporate a shoulder to ensure that the springs are compressed correctly. However, on 1.7 engines, tighten the nuts progressively until approximately four threads are visible and the springs are compressed to 22.0 mm in length.
44 Check that the Woodruff key is in place on the camshaft then fit the camshaft sprocket and bolt. Tighten the bolt to the specified torque while holding the camshaft stationary with a spanner on the special lug between the 3rd and 4th cams.
45 Turn the camshaft until the tips of cams 4 and 6 (counting from the flywheel end) are facing downwards.
46 Turn the crankshaft a quarter turn clockwise until pistons 1 and 4 are at TDC, and fit the TDC dowel rod to the flywheel. Do

not turn the crankshaft anti-clockwise otherwise pistons 2 and 3 will pass their TDC positions and will strike valves 4 and 6.
47 Align the hole and refit the M8 timing bolt to the camshaft sprocket.
48 Refit the valve cover, together with a new gasket.
49 Apply locking fluid to the threads then refit and tighten the two upper bolts to the right-hand engine mounting bracket. Also refit the tensioner adjustment bolt and tighten it. Loosen the tensioner pivot nut.
50 Refit and adjust the timing belt, referring to Section 4, paragraphs 20 to 25.
51 Reconnect the fuel return pipes to the injection pump.
52 Reconnect the glow plug wiring.
53 Refit the left-hand engine lifting bracket.
54 Refit the injection pipes and tighten the union nuts.
55 Reconnect the crankcase ventilation hose to the valve cover.
56 Locate the drivebelt on the camshaft pulley and hydraulic pump (BX models) or vacuum pump (Visa models) pulley. Press the pump downwards until the deflection of the belt midway between the two pulleys is approximately 5.0 mm under firm thumb pressure. Tighten the adjustment bolt followed by the pivot bolt.
57 On BX models reconnect the air inlet hose to the inlet manifold.
58 Refit the oil filler cap/breather.
59 Clean the thermostat housing mating faces then refit it, together with a new gasket, and tighten the bolts. Refit the two small hoses.
60 Reconnect the heater hose to the cylinder head.
61 Refit the timing cover sections.
62 Refit the right-hand engine mounting bracket and tighten the nuts. Remove the hoist or trolley jack.
63 Refit the air cleaner (Chapter 4).

2

64 Reconnect the battery negative lead.

65 Refill the cooling system (Chapter 1).

66 Lower the vehicle to the ground.

67 On Turbo models, after refitting and before initial start-up, prime the turbo lubrication circuit by disconnecting the stop solenoid lead at the fuel pump, and cranking the engine on the starter for three ten-second bursts.

68 On pre-September 1986 models carry out the following including paragraphs 69 and 70. Before retightening the head bolts, run the engine at 3000 rpm for 10 minutes then switch off the ignition and let the engine cool for at least 3½ hours.

69 Remove the filler cap from the cooling system expansion tank to release any remaining pressure, then refit it.

70 Working on each cylinder head bolt in turn in the correct sequence first loosen the bolt 90° then retighten to the final torque given in the Specifications **(see illustration)**.

---

10 Cylinder head - dismantling, overhaul and reassembly

Dismantling

1 With the head removed as described in the previous Section remove the camshaft, referring to Section 7.

2 Withdraw the bucket tappets, together with their respective shims, keeping them all identified for location **(see illustration)**.

3 Disconnect the remaining leak off pipes and unscrew the injectors. Remove the special washers.

4 Disconnect the wiring and unscrew the glow plugs.

5 Unscrew the nuts and bolts, and remove the inlet and exhaust manifolds from the cylinder head. Remove the exhaust manifold gaskets. The turbocharger, if applicable, may be removed with the manifolds.

6 Using a valve spring compressor, depress one valve spring retainer to gain access to the collets. The valves are deeply recessed, so the end of the compressor may need to be extended with a tube or box section with a "window" for access. Remove the collets and release the compressor. Recover the retainer, large and small valve springs, and the spring seat, then withdraw the valve from the cylinder head **(see illustrations)**. Repeat the procedure to remove the other seven valves, keeping each valve and components identified for position. Remove the timing probe blank if necessary.

7 Dismantling of the cylinder head is now complete. Refer to Section 11 for decarbonisation procedures.

Overhaul

8 Clean all the components and examine them for wear. Obtain new gaskets for the cylinder head, manifolds, valve cover and thermostat housing. Inspect the head for cracks or other damage.

9 Check the head gasket face for distortion (warp) using a straight-edge and feeler blades diagonally and along the edge **(see illustration)**. Do not position the straight-edge over the swirl chambers, as they may be proud of the cylinder head face. Distortion more than that specified may be corrected by machining ("skimming") within a specified limit. This is a specialist's job; the valve seats and swirl chambers must also be machined, and washers fitted under the valve springs. A head that cannot be reclaimed by machining, or any head in which the camshaft does not turn freely, must be renewed.

10 Inspect the valve seats and swirl chambers for burning or cracks **(see illustration)**. Both can be renewed but the work should be entrusted to a specialist.

11 Using a dial test indicator check that the swirl chamber protrusion is within the limits given in the Specifications **(see illustrations)**.

12 Check each valve for straightness, freedom from burning or cracks, and for an acceptable fit in its guide. Excessive play in the guide may be caused by wear in either component. Measure the valve stem with a micrometer, or try the fit of a new valve, if available, to establish whether it is the valve or the guide that is worn.

13 The valve guides can be renewed, but this is a job for a specialist.

14 Minor surface pitting or carbon build-up on the valve heads and seats may be removed by grinding, but if refacing or recutting is required, consideration must be given to the final height of the valve head in relation to the cylinder head surface. A dial test indicator will be required to check that the

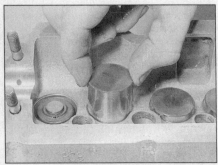

10.2 Removing the bucket tappets

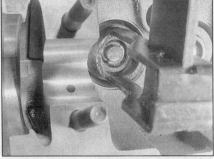

10.6A Depress the retainer with a valve spring compressor and remove the collets, retainer . . .

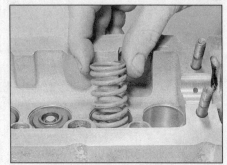

10.6B . . . large valve spring . . .

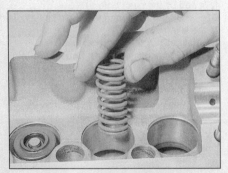

10.6C . . . small valve spring . . .

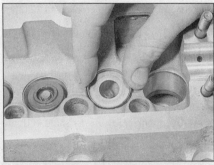

10.6D . . . spring seat . . .

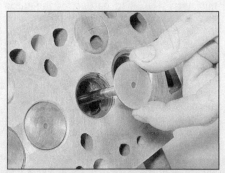

10.6E . . . and valve

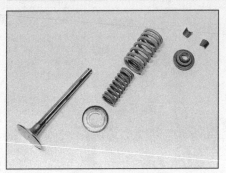

10.6F Valve components

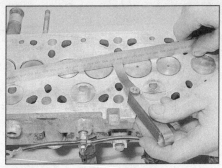

10.9 Checking the head gasket face for distortion

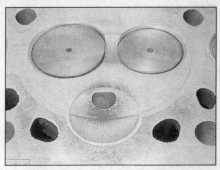

10.10 This swirl chamber shows the initial stages of cracking and burning

10.11A Zero the dial test indicator . . .

10.11B . . . then check the swirl chamber protrusion

10.14 Checking the valve head height

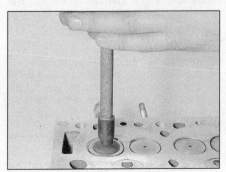

10.16 Grinding in the valves

valve head is within the specified limits **(see illustration)**.

15 New or refaced valves and seats should be ground together as follows (the coarse paste may be omitted if the fit is already good).

16 Invert the head and support it securely. Smear a little coarse grinding paste around the sealing area of the valve head. Insert the valve in its guide and grind it to the seat using a valve grinding stick and rubber sucker. The stick is held between the hands and rotated first in one direction then in the opposite direction **(see illustration)**. Lift the valve occasionally to redistribute the grinding paste.

17 Wipe the paste from the valve and seat occasionally to check progress. When the sealing faces are unbroken and all pitting is removed, repeat the procedure using fine grinding paste.

18 After all the valves have been ground in,

clean away all traces of grinding paste, first with a paraffin-soaked rag then with clean dry rags, finally with compressed air if available. Do not overlook the valve guides. It will be obvious that even a small quantity of grinding paste remaining in the engine could cause extremely rapid wear.

19 Examine the valve springs for signs of fatigue and if possible compare their length with a new spring. It is worth renewing all the springs if the engine has completed a high mileage.

20 Examine the tappets and their bores for scoring or other damage.

21 Examine the camshaft bearing surfaces in the cylinder head and bearing caps. Also examine the camshaft, referring to Section 7.

22 Inspect the studs for the manifolds and camshaft bearing caps. Renew them if necessary by using a proprietary stud extractor, or lock two nuts together on the exposed threads. Studs that have come out by mistake should be cleaned up and refitted using thread locking fluid.

Reassembly

23 Begin reassembly by oiling a valve stem and inserting it into its guide. With the cylinder head on its side, fit the spring seat followed by the two springs (either way up) and the retainer.

24 Compress the springs with the compressor and fit the collets. A smear of grease on the collets will hold them in place on the valve stem groove. Carefully release the compressor and remove it.

25 Repeat the procedure to fit the other

seven valves. Refit the timing probe blank if removed.

26 Refit the inlet and exhaust manifolds with new gaskets and progressively tighten the nuts.

27 Insert and tighten the heater plugs to the specified torque (Chapter 4). Reconnect the wiring.

28 Insert and tighten the injectors with their washers to the specified torque (Chapter 4). Reconnect the leak off pipes.

29 Oil and insert the bucket tappets, together with their respective shims, making sure that they are fitted in the correct locations, and with the size markings downwards. Make a note of the shim thickness fitted at each position, if not already done, for reference when checking the valve clearances.

30 Refit the camshaft, referring to Section 7.

11 Cylinder head and pistons - decarbonisation

Decarbonisation

1 With the cylinder head removed as described in Section 9, the carbon deposits should be removed from the valve heads and surrounding surfaces of the head. Use a blunt scraper or wire brush and take care not to damage the valve heads.

2 Where a more thorough job is to be carried out, the cylinder head should be dismantled as described in the previous Section so that the valves may be ground in and the parts

2

Holding the camshaft sprocket stationary with a home made tool

cleaned, brushed and blown out after the manifolds have been removed. Also clean the manifolds, particularly the exhaust manifold where an accumulation of carbon is most likely.

3 Before grinding-in a valve, remove the carbon and deposits completely from its head and stem. With an inlet valve this is usually simply a matter of scraping off the carbon with a blunt knife and finishing with a wire brush. With an exhaust valve the deposits are much harder to remove. One method of cleaning valves quickly is to mount them in the chuck of an electric drill using a piece of card or foil to protect the surface of the stem. A scraper or wire brush may then be used carefully to remove the carbon.

4 An important part of the decarbonising operation is to remove the carbon deposits from the piston crowns. To do this, turn the crankshaft so that two pistons are at the top of their stroke and press some grease between these pistons and the cylinder walls. This will prevent carbon particles falling down into the piston ring grooves. Cover the other two bores and the cylinder block internal oil and water channels with newspaper taped down securely.

5 Using a blunt scraper remove all the carbon from the piston crowns, taking care not to score the soft alloy. Thoroughly clean the combustion spaces that are recessed in the piston crowns.

6 Remove the newspaper then rotate the crankshaft half a turn and repeat the cleaning

12.8 Socket, bolt and washer for fitting the camshaft oil seals

operation on the remaining two pistons. Wipe away the grease from the top of the bores.

7 Finally clean the top surface of the cylinder block.

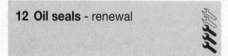

12 Oil seals - renewal

Note: *The procedures described here are for renewal with the engine in the vehicle - with the engine removed, the steps taken to gain access may be ignored.*

Camshaft (timing belt end)

1 Follow the procedure given in paragraphs 1 to 12 of Section 5.

2 Remove the timing belt from the camshaft sprocket and tie it to one side without bending it excessively.

3 Unscrew the M8 bolt holding the camshaft sprocket in the timing position.

4 Hold the camshaft sprocket stationary using a large screwdriver (or similar tool), through two of the holes. A tool may be made out of flat metal bar and two long bolts **(see Haynes Hint)**. Alternatively a strap wrench as used for removing oil filters may be used to hold the sprocket.

5 Unscrew the bolt and withdraw the sprocket from the camshaft. Do not rotate the camshaft otherwise the valves will strike the pistons of Nos 1 and 4 cylinders. Recover the Woodruff key if it is loose.

6 Pull out the oil seal using a hooked instrument.

12.18 Camshaft oil seal flush with the end face of the cylinder head

7 Clean the oil seal seating.

8 Smear the lip of the new oil seal with oil then fit it over the end of the camshaft, open end first, and press it in until flush with the end face of the cylinder head. Use an M10 bolt, washers and a socket to press it in **(see illustration)**.

9 Fit the Woodruff key (if removed) and the camshaft sprocket to the camshaft, insert the bolt and tighten it while holding the camshaft stationary.

10 Refit the M8 timing bolt to the camshaft sprocket.

11 Refit and adjust the timing belt, referring to Section 4, paragraphs 20 to 25. The remaining procedure is a reversal of removal.

Camshaft (flywheel end)

12 Remove the air cleaner.

13 Remove the inlet ducting as necessary.

14 Loosen the pivot and adjustment bolts of the hydraulic high pressure pump (BX models), or vacuum pump (Visa models), swivel the unit upwards, and disconnect the drivebelt from the pulleys.

15 Unscrew the centre bolt and remove the pump pulley from the camshaft. If the centre bolt is very tight it will be necessary to remove the timing covers and hold the camshaft sprocket stationary while the bolt is loosened (to prevent damage to the timing belt). Recover the Woodruff key if it is loose.

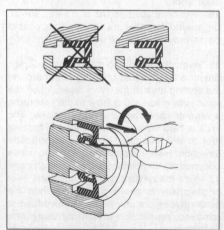

12.26 Fitting the timing belt end oil seal to the crankshaft with a plastic protector

12.33A Fitting the flywheel end oil seal to the crankshaft with a plastic protector

12.33B Correct fitting of the crankshaft flywheel end oil seal

13.4A Crossmember front bolt (arrowed) . . .

13.6 Removing the sump

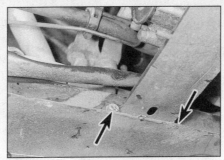

13.4B . . . and rear bolts (arrowed) on BX models

27 Refit the Woodruff key and timing belt sprocket.
28 Refit the timing belt, referring to Section 4.

Crankshaft (flywheel end)

29 Remove the flywheel/driveplate as described in Section 16.
30 Using vernier calipers measure the fitted depth of the oil seal and record it.
31 Pull out the oil seal using a hooked instrument. Alternatively drill a small hole in the oil seal and use a self-tapping screw to remove it.
32 Clean the oil seal seating and crankshaft flange.
33 Dip the new oil seal in engine oil, locate it on the crankshaft open end first, and press it in squarely to the previously noted depth using a metal tube. A piece of thin plastic is useful to prevent damage to the oil seal. When fitted note that the outer lip of the oil seal must point outwards; if it is pointing inwards use a piece of bent wire to pull it out **(see illustrations)**.
34 Refit the flywheel/driveplate, referring to Section 16.

13 Sump - removal and refitting

Removal

1 Chock the rear wheels then jack up the front of the car and support on axle stands (see "*Jacking and vehicle support*").
2 Position a container beneath the engine. Unscrew the drain plug and allow the oil to drain from the sump.
3 Wipe clean the drain plug and refit it.
4 On BX models unbolt the crossmember beneath the sump **(see illustrations)**.
5 Note the location of the sump bolts **(see illustration)**, then unscrew them.
6 Remove the sump and gasket **(see illustration)**. The sump will probably be stuck in position in which case it will be necessary to cut it free using a thin knife.

Refitting

7 Clean all remains of gasket from the sump and block and wipe dry.

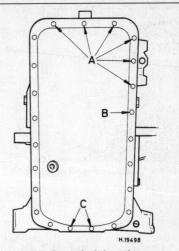

13.5 Sump bolt locations
A 6 socket-head bolts
B 15 bolts (16 mm length)
C 2 bolts (14 mm length)

8 Apply a little sealing compound where the front housing abuts the block on both sides.
9 Position a new gasket on the sump then lift the sump into position and insert the bolts in their correct locations.
10 Tighten the bolts evenly to the specified torque.
11 Refit the crossmember on BX models.
12 Lower the car to the ground and refill the engine with the correct quantity and grade of oil.

14 Oil pump - removal, inspection and refitting

Note: *From July 1987, the oil pump spacer and location dowel are no longer fitted. The height of the pump is increased to compensate. A new pump may be fitted in place of an old one, provided that the spacer and dowel are discarded. Thicker washers must be fitted under the heads of the oil pump bolts. On A8A engines, a thin spacer is still fitted between the oil pump and the block.*

Removal

1 Remove the timing belt as described in Section 4.
2 Slide the timing belt sprocket from the crankshaft and recover the Woodruff key if it is loose.
3 Remove the sump as described in Section 13.
4 Unscrew the bolts and remove the front oil seal housing. Remove the gasket.
5 Unscrew the three bolts securing the oil pump to the crankcase. Identify them for position as all three are of different lengths.
6 Withdraw the L-shaped spacer from beneath the oil pump, if applicable.

16 Pull out the oil seal using a hooked instrument.
17 Clean the oil seal seating.
18 Smear the lip of the new oil seal with oil then fit it over the end of the camshaft, open end first, and press it in until flush with the end face of the cylinder head **(see illustration)**. Use a bolt, washers and a socket to press it in.
19 Refit the Woodruff key (if removed) and the pump pulley to the camshaft and tighten the centre bolt.
20 Locate the drivebelt on the camshaft pulley and pump pulley then press the pump downwards until the deflection of the belt midway between the two pulleys is approximately 5.0 mm under firm thumb pressure. Tighten the adjustment bolt followed by the pivot bolt.
21 Refit the air cleaner.
22 Refit the inlet ducting.

Crankshaft (timing belt end)

23 Remove the timing belt as described in Section 4.
24 Slide the timing belt sprocket from the crankshaft and recover the Woodruff key if it is loose.
25 Note the fitted depth then pull the oil seal from the housing using a hooked instrument. Alternatively drill a small hole in the oil seal and use a self-tapping screw to remove it.
26 Clean the housing and crankshaft then dip the new oil seal in engine oil and press it in (open end first) to the previously noted depth. A piece of thin plastic is useful to prevent damage to the oil seal **(see illustration)**.

2

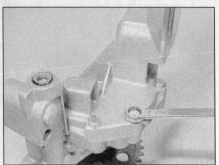

14.9A Unscrew the oil pump bolts . . .

14.9B . . . separate the halves . . .

14.9C . . . and remove the relief valve
spring . . .

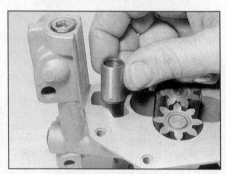

14.9D . . . and plunger

7 Remove the location dowel (if fitted) and disengage the oil pump sprocket from the chain. Withdraw the oil pump.
8 Remove the chain and sprocket from the nose of the crankshaft and recover the Woodruff key if it is loose.

9 Remove the six bolts which hold the two halves of the oil pump together. Separate the halves, being prepared for the release of the relief valve spring and plungers **(see illustrations)**.
10 If necessary remove the strainer by prising

off the cap, then clean all components **(see illustrations)**.

Inspection

11 Inspect the gears and the housings for wear and damage. Check the endfloat of the gears using a straight-edge and feeler blades, also check the clearance between the tip of the gear lobes and the housing **(see illustrations)**. If any of these clearances exceeds the specified limit, renew the pump. Note that except for the relief valve spring and plunger, individual components are not available.
12 If the pump is to be renewed it is wise to renew the chain and the crankshaft sprocket also.

Refitting

13 Lubricate the gears with engine oil then reassemble the oil pump in reverse order and tighten the six bolts evenly to the specified torque.
14 Locate the Woodruff key on the nose of the crankshaft and refit the sprocket, teeth end first. Engage the chain with the sprocket.
15 Prise the oil seal from the front housing. Refit the housing to the cylinder block, together with a new gasket, and tighten the bolts evenly to the specified torque.
16 Fit a new oil seal to the housing, referring to Section 12.
17 Check that the location dowel is fitted to the block. Engage the oil pump sprocket with the chain and slide the L-shaped spacer into position, making sure that its open end engages the dowel.

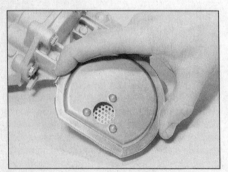

14.10A Removing the oil pump cap . . .

14.10B . . . and strainer

14.11A Oil pump rotors and housing

14.11B Checking the rotor endfloat

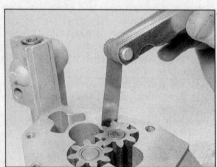

14.11C Checking the rotor side clearance

14.18 Tightening the oil pump mounting
bolts (longest bolt arrowed)

15.5 Removing a big-end bearing cap

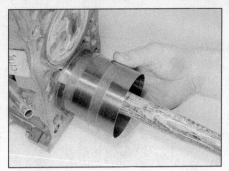

15.13 Using a hammer handle to tap the piston through the ring compressor

15.14 Tightening the big-end bearing cap nuts

18 Insert the bolts in their correct locations. The longest bolt through the dowel and the next longest by the oil return hole. Tighten the bolts evenly to the specified torque **(see illustration)**.

19 Refit the sump, referring to Section 13.

20 Refit the Woodruff key and timing belt sprocket.

21 Refit the timing belt, referring to Section 4.

15 Pistons and connecting rods - removal and refitting

Removal

1 Remove the cylinder head as described in Section 9.

2 Remove the oil pump as described in Section 14.

3 If there is a pronounced wear ridge at the top of any bore, it may be necessary to remove it with a scraper or ridge reamer to avoid piston damage during removal. Such a ridge may indicate that reboring is necessary, which will entail new pistons in any case.

4 Check that each connecting rod and cap is marked for position and, if not, mark them with a centre punch on the oil filter side, number one at the flywheel end.

5 Turn the crankshaft to bring pistons 1 and 4 to BDC (bottom dead centre). Unscrew the nuts from No 1 piston big-end bearing cap, then take off the cap and recover the bottom half bearing shell **(see illustration)**.

6 Using a hammer handle push the piston up

through the bore and remove it from the block. Loosely refit the shell bearings and cap to ensure correct reassembly.

7 Remove No 4 piston in the same manner then turn the crankshaft 180° to bring pistons 2 and 3 to BDC (bottom dead centre) and remove them.

8 If new piston rings are to be fitted to old bores, the bores must be deglazed to allow the new rings to bed-in properly. Protect the big-end journals by wrapping them in masking tape, then use a piece of coarse emery paper to produce a cross-hatch pattern in each bore. A flap wheel in an electric drill may be used, but beware of spreading abrasive dust. When deglazing is complete wash away all abrasive particles and unwrap the big-end journals.

Refitting

9 Begin refitting by laying out the assembled pistons and rods in order, with the bearing shells, connecting rod caps and nuts.

10 Arrange the piston ring gaps 120° from each other.

11 Clean the bearing shells, caps and rods then press the shells into position so that the locating tangs engage in the grooves.

12 Oil the bores, pistons, crankpins and shells. Fit a piston ring compressor to No 1 piston. With Nos 1 and 4 crankpins at BDC insert No 1 piston in the bore nearest the flywheel, making sure that the clover leaf cut-out on the piston crown is towards the oil filter side of the engine.

13 Using a hammer handle tap the piston through the ring compressor and into the bore **(see illustration)**. Guide the connecting rod

onto the crankpin and fit the cap, together with its shell bearing, making sure it is the correct way round.

14 Fit the nuts and tighten them to the specified torque **(see illustration)**. Turn the crankshaft to check for free movement.

15 Repeat the procedure to fit the other three pistons.

16 Refit the oil pump, referring to Section 14.

17 Refit the cylinder head, referring to Section 9.

16 Flywheel/driveplate - removal and refitting

Removal

1 Either remove the engine and transmission and separate them (Sections 19, 20 and 21), or remove the transmission alone as described in the appropriate main manual.

2 On manual transmission models make alignment marks then slacken the clutch pressure plate bolts progressively and remove the pressure plate and driven plate **(see illustration)**.

3 Hold the flywheel/driveplate stationary with a screwdriver or bar inserted between the teeth of the starter ring gear and the transmission location dowel, then unscrew and remove the bolts and lift the flywheel/driveplate from the crankshaft. Alignment marks are not required as there is a location dowel on the crankshaft flange. Obtain new bolts for reassembly.

2

16.2 Removing the clutch pressure plate and driven plate

16.6A Apply locking fluid to the flywheel bolts . . .

16.6B . . . and tighten them to the specified torque

17.2A Home-made tool for unscrewing the engine mounting rubber

17.2B Engine mounting rubber showing slots

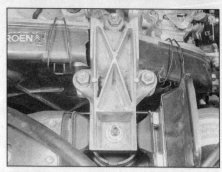

17.3 Right-hand engine mounting bracket (BX models)

17.12A Lower engine mounting and torque link (Visa models)

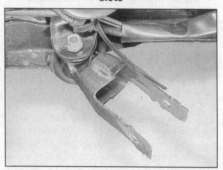

17.12B Lower engine mounting torque link (BX models) - top view with engine removed

Refitting

4 Begin refitting by cleaning the mating surfaces of the crankshaft and flywheel/driveplate.
5 Locate the flywheel/driveplate on the crankshaft dowel.
6 Apply locking fluid to the threads of the bolts, insert them, and tighten them to the specified torque while holding the flywheel/driveplate stationary **(see illustrations)**.
7 On manual transmission models refit the clutch driven and pressure plates.
8 Refit the transmission and the engine, if removed.

17 Engine/transmission mountings - removal and refitting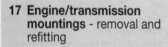

Right-hand mounting

Removal

1 Support the engine with a hoist or with a trolley jack and block of wood beneath the sump.
2 Make up a tool similar to that shown, to engage with the slots in the rim of the rubber **(see illustrations)**. Assuming that the rubber is being renewed, the new component can be used as a guide when making the tool. Unscrew the old rubber from the body using the tool.
3 Unscrew the nuts and remove the right-hand mounting bracket, noting the location of any shims **(see illustration)**.

Refitting

4 Refitting is a reversal of removal. Tighten the rubber firmly to the body using the tool, to the specified torque. With the weight of the engine on the mounting, the clearance between the mounting bracket and each rubber stop should be 1.0 ± 0.7 mm. If necessary adjust the clearance by means of shims positioned under the stops.

Left-hand mounting

Removal

5 Support the transmission with a hoist or with a trolley jack and block of wood.
6 Remove the air cleaner and trunking.
7 Remove the battery and battery tray.
8 Unscrew the nut and remove the rubber mounting. Also unscrew the nuts or bolts and remove the mounting bracket.
9 If necessary unscrew the mounting stud from the transmission casing.

Refitting

10 Refitting is a reversal of removal, but before fitting the mounting stud, clean the threads and apply a little locking fluid. Tighten the nuts and bolts to the specified torque.

Lower mounting

Removal

11 Jack up the front of the car and support on axle stands (see "*Jacking and vehicle support*").
12 Unscrew and remove both bolts from the torque link and withdraw the link **(see illustrations)**.

Refitting

13 Drive or press the mounting from the housing.
14 Drive or press the new mounting into position then refit the torque link and tighten the bolts to the specified torque.
15 Lower the car to the ground.

18 Engine, methods of removal - general

General

The engine is removed together with the transmission by lifting upwards from the engine compartment. On BX models the engine and transmission are lifted at a very steep angle and a hoist with sufficient height will therefore be necessary.

It is possible to remove the transmission alone from under the vehicle, after which it would, in theory, be possible to remove the engine from above. However, this method is not recommended as it involves the extra work of disconnecting the transmission which, if required is best carried out with the engine and transmission removed from the vehicle.

19 Engine and transmission (Visa models) - removal and refitting

Removal

1 Remove the bonnet.
2 Apply the handbrake then jack up the front of the vehicle and support on axle stands (see "*Jacking and vehicle support*").
3 Drain the cooling system as described in Chapter 1.
4 Unscrew the drain plug from the rear of the differential housing drain the oil into a container, then refit and tighten the drain plug.
5 Remove the bolts securing the front track control arms to the stub axle carriers.
6 Using a lever between the anti-roll bar and track control arm, lever the balljoints from the bottom of the stub axle carriers.
7 Have an assistant pull the left-hand wheel

19.18 Gearchange control rods (Visa models)

outwards while the left-hand driveshaft is levered from the differential side gear.

8 Loosen the two nuts retaining the right-hand driveshaft intermediate bearing in the bracket bolted to the rear of the cylinder block and turn the bolt heads through 90° to release the bearing.

9 Have an assistant pull the right-hand wheel outwards while the right-hand driveshaft is removed from the differential side gear.

10 Unbolt the intermediate bearing bracket from the cylinder block, also unscrew and remove the bolt securing the torque link to the underbody.

11 Tie the right-hand driveshaft and intermediate bearing bracket towards the rear.

12 Remove the battery and tray, and unbolt the support.

13 Drain the engine oil if required.

14 Remove the air cleaner, together with the inlet hoses and the hose to the oil separator.

15 Unscrew and remove the exhaust manifold-to-downpipe bolts, together with the springs and collars.

16 Disconnect the coolant hoses from the engine.

17 Unbolt the securing clamp and remove the cooling system expansion tank.

18 Disconnect the gearchange control rods **(see illustration)**. Also disconnect the reverse cable where fitted.

19 Disconnect the vacuum hose from the brake vacuum servo unit.

20 Refer to Chapter 7 and remove the brake master cylinder.

21 Disconnect the fuel supply and return hoses from the injection pump.

22 Disconnect the wiring from the following components:
 a) Starter motor
 b) Oil pressure switch
 c) Alternator
 d) Water temperature switch
 e) Glow plugs
 f) Stop solenoid on the injection pump
 g) Diagnostic socket
 h) Transmission earth cable
 i) Reverse lamp switch

23 Disconnect the speedometer cable from the transmission.

24 Disconnect the clutch cable.

25 Disconnect the accelerator cable from the injection pump.

26 Connect a hoist to the engine lifting brackets so that the engine and transmission may be lifted in a horizontal position. Take the weight of the assembly.

27 Unscrew the nuts and remove the right-hand engine mounting bracket.

28 Unscrew the nut from the left-hand engine mounting and remove the rubber mounting. Also unbolt the support bracket.

29 Position a piece of hardboard over the radiator to protect it when the engine is being removed.

30 Raise the engine and transmission assembly, making sure that the surrounding components in the engine compartment are not damaged. When clear of the front panel withdraw the assembly and lower it to the ground.

31 If the vehicle must be moved with the engine and transmission out, reconnect the track control arms and balljoints to the stub axle carriers and support the driveshafts with wire so that they can rotate without damage.

Refitting

32 Refitting is the reversal of the removal procedure, but note the following additional points:
 a) Use a final drive oil seal protector (Chapter 6) when inserting the right-hand driveshaft. Remove the protector when the driveshaft is fitted
 b) Refill the transmission and engine with oil
 c) Adjust the accelerator and fast idle cables, referring to Chapter 4
 d) Tighten the exhaust manifold-to-downpipe bolts, referring to Section 9, paragraph 43
 e) Refit the engine/transmission mountings, referring to Section 17
 f) Adjust the clutch cable
 g) Refill the cooling system (Chapter 1)
 h) Check the injection pump timing if necessary

20 Engine and transmission (BX models) - removal and refitting

Removal

Note: The procedure described here is for manual transmission models. The procedure for automatic transmission models is similar.

1 Remove the bonnet.

2 Chock the rear wheels and release the handbrake.

3 Jack up the front of the vehicle and support on axle stands (see "Jacking and vehicle support"). Remove the front wheels.

4 Place the ground clearance control to minimum height. Loosen the hydraulic pressure regulator release screw one and a half turns to release the pressure from the hydraulic system. Do not remove the screw otherwise the sealing ball will fall out.

5 Drain the cooling system as described in Chapter 1.

6 Unscrew the drain plugs from the transmission and differential housing and drain the oil/fluid into a container, then refit and tighten the drain plugs. Also drain the engine oil if required.

7 Unscrew the nut from the left-hand front suspension lower balljoint. Using a balljoint separator tool release the suspension arm.

8 Unscrew the nut from the top of the left-hand link rod for the front anti-roll bar, then lower the suspension arm **(see illustration)**.

9 Have an assistant pull the left-hand wheel outwards while the left-hand driveshaft is levered from the differential side gear.

10 On models manufactured before July 1984 the left-hand differential side gear must be supported using a dowel, preferably wooden. If this precaution is not taken, the side gears may become misaligned when the right-hand driveshaft is removed.

11 Remove the right-hand driveshaft completely.

12 Unscrew and remove the exhaust manifold-to-downpipe bolts, together with the springs and collars **(see illustration)**.

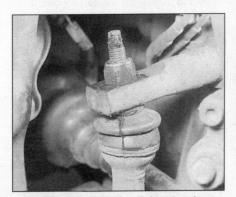

20.8 Front anti-roll bar link rod and nut

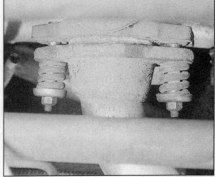

20.12 Exhaust manifold-to-downpipe bolts, springs and collars

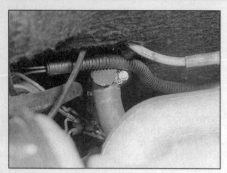

20.13 Heater hose connection at the bulkhead

20.14A Disconnecting the gearchange lower rod . . .

20.14B . . . upper rod . . .

20.14C . . . and rear rod (BX models)

13 Disconnect the heater hoses from the engine and bulkhead **(see illustration)**.
14 Disconnect the gearchange control rods, including the rearmost rod from the intermediate lever **(see illustrations)**. Turn

both intermediate levers so that they are parallel with the steering gear. Disconnect the reverse cable where applicable.
15 Remove the battery, air cleaner and the supporting lug **(see illustrations)**.
16 Remove the radiator as described in Chapter 3, and disconnect the top hose from the thermostat housing **(see illustration)**.
17 Disconnect the clutch cable and recover the pushrod.
18 Disconnect the speedometer cable at the bulkhead **(see illustration)**.
19 Disconnect the battery earth cable from the transmission **(see illustration)**.
20 Disconnect the accelerator cable from the injection pump.
21 Pull apart the wiring connectors located beneath the battery support bracket **(see illustration)**.
22 Disconnect the supply wiring from No 2 glow plug.

23 Where applicable disconnect the tachometer wiring from the harness.
24 Disconnect the fuel supply and return hoses from the injection pump **(see illustration)**.
25 Unbolt and remove the fuel filter.
26 Disconnect the high pressure pump suction pipe and the return pipe from the fluid reservoir and plug the open holes to prevent the ingress of dust and dirt. Release the pipe from the clip **(see illustration)**.
27 On manual steering models disconnect the fluid return pipe from the pressure regulator, also disconnect the coiled fluid supply pipe and release it from the clips **(see illustration)**. Plug all pipe ends.
28 On power steering models disconnect the overflow return pipe from the pressure regulator, also disconnect the fluid supply pipe from the output distributor. Unbolt the pressure regulator and output distributor and

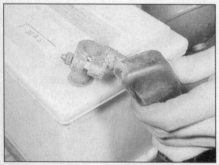

20.15A Disconnecting the battery leads

20.15B Removing the battery clamp

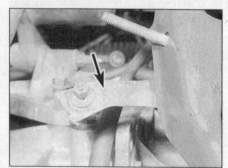

20.15C Air cleaner supporting lug (arrowed)

20.16 Disconnecting the top hose from the thermostat housing

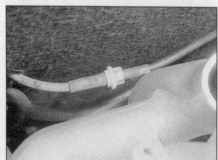

20.18 Speedometer cable connection at the bulkhead

20.19 Battery earth cable on the transmission

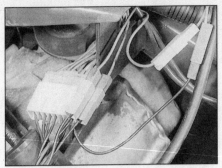

20.21 Engine harness wiring connectors beneath the battery support bracket

20.24 Injection pump fuel supply hose (arrowed)

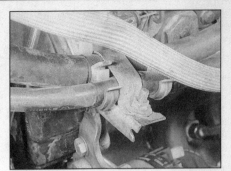

20.26 Hydraulic pipe retaining clip (BX models)

20.27 Hydraulic pressure regulator (arrowed) with return pipe port plugged (BX models)

20.30 Engine lower mounting and torque link (BX models)

20.31 Left-hand engine mounting (BX models)

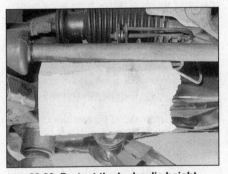

20.33 Protect the hydraulic height corrector with a piece of hardboard

20.34 Lifting the engine and transmission assembly - note the support plate (arrowed) for the left-hand mounting

tie the assembly to the electric cooling fan.

29 Connect a hoist to the engine lifting brackets so that the engine and transmission assembly will assume an angle of 45° when lifted (with the engine uppermost). Take the weight of the assembly.

30 Unscrew and remove the front bolt from the torque link beneath the engine **(see illustration)**.

31 Unscrew the nut from the left-hand engine mounting and remove the rubber mounting **(see illustration)**. To prevent the mounting stub subsequently falling below the mounting bracket it is advisable though not essential, to position a loose fitting metal plate on the stud and refit the nut.

32 Unscrew the nuts and remove the right-hand engine mounting bracket.

33 Place a piece of hardboard over the

hydraulic height corrector to the right of the torque link to protect the dust cover **(see illustration)**.

34 Raise the engine and transmission assembly, making sure that the surrounding components in the engine compartment are not damaged **(see illustration)**. When clear of the front panel withdraw the assembly and lower it to the ground.

35 If the vehicle must be moved with the engine and transmission out, reconnect the left-hand front suspension lower balljoint, also temporarily refit the right-hand driveshaft. Support the driveshafts with wire so that they can rotate without damage. Note that the wheel bearings can be damaged if the vehicle is moved without the driveshafts in position.

Refitting

36 Refitting is the reversal of the removal procedure, but note the following additional points:

a) Use a final drive oil seal protector (Chapter 6) when inserting the right-hand driveshaft. Remove the protector when the driveshaft is fitted

b) Refill the transmission and engine with oil

c) Adjust the accelerator and fast idle cables, referring to Chapter 4

d) Refit the engine/transmission mountings, referring to Section 17

e) On manual transmission models adjust the clutch cable

f) Refill the cooling system (Chapter 1)

g) Prime the hydraulic high pressure pump as described in the BX main manual

h) Check the injection pump timing if necessary

37 On turbo models, prime the turbo lubrication circuit before start-up by disconnecting the stop solenoid lead at the fuel pump and cranking the engine on the starter for three ten-second bursts.

21 Engine and transmission - separation

1 With the engine and transmission removed from the vehicle clean away all external dirt.

2 Slacken the bolts and remove the TDC sensor **(see illustration)**. Remove the bolts

2

21.2 Removing the TDC sensor

21.3 Reversing lamp switch and wiring

21.4 Transmission bottom cover

21.6A Extended hexagon for pump adjustment link (BX models)

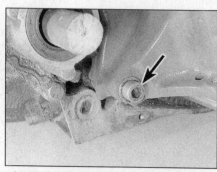

21.6B Socket-headed rear transmission bolt (arrowed)

21.7A Removing the hydraulic pressure pump (BX models)

21.7B Hydraulic line and bracket (BX models)

and withdraw the sensor holder.

3 Disconnect the wiring and unbolt the starter motor using a hexagon key. Also disconnect the wiring from the reversing lamp switch (see illustration).

4 Unbolt the bottom cover from the transmission (see illustration).

5 On automatic transmission models unscrew the bolts securing the torque converter to the driveplate. Turn the engine as required to bring the bolt heads into view.

6 Note the location of the hydraulic pressure pump (BX) or vacuum pump (Visa), the coolant tube, the hydraulic line, and the transmission retaining bolts. The pump adjustment link is attached to an extended hexagon, and the rearmost transmission bolt has a socket head (see illustrations).

7 Remove the drivebelt and unbolt the hydraulic pressure pump or vacuum pump

bracket. Where applicable unbolt the bracket for the hydraulic line (see illustrations).

8 Support the engine then unscrew the bolts and lift the transmission from the engine. On automatic transmission models make sure that the torque converter is kept in full engagement with the transmission. On BX models the hydraulic pressure regulator may remain attached to the transmission.

22 Engine overhaul - preparation

Note: *Many components are specific to Turbo models. Although the parts may appear to be the same they are not all interchangeable.*

1 Clean the engine thoroughly using a

water-soluble grease solvent or similar product. Keep dirt and water out of vulnerable components such as the fuel injection pump and the alternator.

2 When possible the engine should be dismantled on a workbench or strong table. If an engine dismantling stand is available, so much the better. Avoid working directly on a concrete floor, as grit presents a serious problem. If there is no alternative to working on the floor, cover it with an old piece of lino or carpet.

3 As well as the usual selection of tools, have available some wooden blocks for propping up the engine. A notebook and pencil will be needed, as will a couple of segmented boxes or a good supply of plastic bags and labels.

4 A waterproof marker pen is useful for making alignment marks, without having to use to punches or chisels, however, take care that the marks are not erased during cleaning.

5 Whenever possible, refit nuts, washers etc. to the components from where they were removed. This makes reassembly much simpler.

6 Spills of oil, fuel and coolant are bound to occur during dismantling. Have rags and newspapers handy to mop up the mess.

7 Do not throw away old gaskets immediately, but save them for comparison with new ones or for use as patterns if new gaskets have to be made.

8 Before starting reassembly, make sure that all parts are clean and that the new components required have been obtained. A full set of oil seals and gaskets must be bought - refer to Section 9 for selection of the correct head gasket.

9 Renew any nuts, bolts or studs with damaged threads.

10 A dial test indicator and stand (preferably magnetic) will be needed, also an oil can filled with clean engine oil to lubricate working parts as they are assembled.

11 Small quantities of grease, thread locking compound, anti-seize compound and various types of sealant will be called for.

12 Have available a good quantity of lint-free rags for wiping excess oil off hands and engine parts.

23.2A Removing the front timing cover section . . .

23.2B . . . and the rear timing cover section

23.3A Diagnostic socket wiring connector

23.3B Temperature sensors and wiring

23.4 Diagnostic socket and mounting bolt

23.5 Removing the pump pulley from the flywheel end of the camshaft

23 Engine overhaul - dismantling

Note: *Refer to Section 22, before this procedure.*

1 If not already done, drain the engine oil.

2 Pull up the special clip, release the spring clips, and withdraw the two timing cover sections **(see illustrations)**.

3 Disconnect the wiring from the following components and identify each wire for location:

a) *Alternator*
b) *Oil pressure switch*
c) *Diagnostic socket (if fitted)* **(see illustration)**
d) *Temperature sensor(s)* **(see illustration)**
e) *Oil level sensor*

4 Unbolt and remove the diagnostic socket and bracket where fitted **(see illustration)**.

5 Unscrew the bolt and withdraw the pump pulley from the flywheel end of the camshaft **(see illustration)**. If it is tight due to corrosion, use a two or three-legged puller to remove it. Recover the Woodruff key.

6 Note the location of the fuel pipes from the injection pump to the injectors then unscrew the union nuts and remove the pipe assemblies. Cover the pipe ends, the injectors and the injection pump outlets to prevent entry of dust and dirt. Small plastic bags and elastic bands are ideal for this **(see illustrations)**.

23.6A Fuel pipe locations (arrowed)

23.6B Small plastic bags can be used to protect the injectors from dust and dirt

23.8A Engine lifting bracket

23.8B Lower rear engine mounting bracket - also supports right-hand driveshaft

2

7 Pull the leak-off hoses from the injectors

8 Unbolt the engine lifting bracket from the cylinder head. Also unbolt the lower rear engine mounting bracket **(see illustrations)**.

9 Remove the alternator (Chapter 5) and bracket.

10 Unscrew the oil filter cartridge using a strap wrench if necessary.

11 On the 1.9 engine disconnect the hoses from the oil cooler. Unscrew the centre stud and remove the oil cooler from the block. Disconnect the oil cooler hoses.

12 Disconnect the bottom hose from the water pump inlet.

13 Disconnect the crankcase ventilation hoses from the valve cover and sump inlet. Remove the clip and slide the oil separator from the dipstick tube.

14 Remove the oil filler cap and ventilation hose if fitted.

15 Unscrew the bolts and remove the inlet manifold from the cylinder head. There are no gaskets.

16 Unscrew the nuts and withdraw the exhaust manifold and gaskets from the studs, complete with turbo, if applicable.

17 Slacken the bolt and remove the clamp from the end of the fast idle cable. Unscrew the locknut and remove the fast idle outer cable from the bracket on the injection pump.

18 Unscrew and remove the oil level sensor from the cylinder block, if fitted **(see illustrations)**. Unscrew the oil temperature sensor, if fitted. This can be found just above the oil filter.

19 Unscrew and remove the oil pressure switch **(see illustration)**.

20 Unbolt the thermostat housing from the cylinder head, complete with the fast idle thermo-unit and temperature sensor(s) **(see**

illustrations).

21 Unbolt the water pump inlet and remove the gasket. Also unbolt the coolant tube from the cylinder block **(see illustrations)**.

22 Unscrew the nuts securing the inlet bracket to the sump. Remove the bracket and gasket **(see illustrations)**.

23 Have an assistant hold the flywheel/driveplate stationary with a screwdriver or bar inserted between the teeth of the starter ring gear and the transmission location dowel, then unscrew the crankshaft pulley bolt. Slide the pulley from the front of the crankshaft **(see illustration)**.

24 Unbolt the bottom timing cover **(see illustration)**.

25 Turn the engine by the flywheel/driveplate until the three bolt holes in the camshaft and injection pump sprockets are aligned with the corresponding holes in the engine front plate.

26 Insert an 8.0 to 8.5 mm diameter metal dowel rod or twist drill through the special hole in the left-hand rear flange of the cylinder block. Then carefully turn the engine either way until the rod enters the TDC hole in the flywheel/driveplate.

27 Insert three M8 bolts through the holes in the camshaft and injection pump sprockets and screw them into the engine front plate finger tight.

28 Loosen the timing belt tensioner pivot nut and adjustment bolt, then turn the bracket anti-clockwise to release the tension and retighten the adjustment bolt to hold the tensioner in the released position.

29 Mark the timing belt with an arrow to indicate its normal direction of turning then

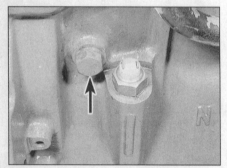

23.18A Oil level sensor location in the cylinder block. Coolant drain plug (arrowed) is adjacent

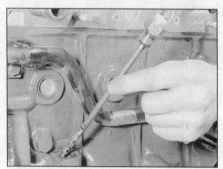

23.18B Removing the oil level sensor

23.19 Removing the oil pressure switch

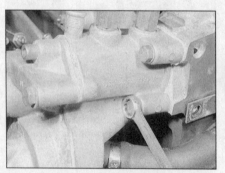

23.20A Unscrew the bolts . . .

23.20B . . . and remove the thermostat housing

23.21A Removing the water pump inlet

23.21B Coolant tube mounting on the rear of the cylinder block

23.21C Coolant tube mounting on the front of the cylinder block

23.23 Removing the crankshaft pulley

23.24 Bottom timing cover (arrowed)

23.31A Unscrew the nut . . .

23.31B . . . and remove the injection pump sprocket

23.36 Injection pump mounting bracket

23.37 Removing the tensioner arm and roller

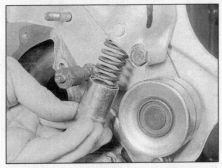

23.38 Removing the tensioner plunger and spring

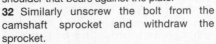

23.39A Right-hand engine mounting bracket

23.39B Timing belt intermediate roller and bracket

23.40 Removing the engine front plate

remove it from the camshaft, injection pump, water pump, and crankshaft sprockets.

30 Unbolt and remove the valve cover. Remove the gasket.

31 With the injection pump sprocket held stationary by the timing bolts, unscrew the central nut to release the sprocket from the pump shaft taper. Remove the timing bolts and the pump sprocket with its nut and puller, and recover the Woodruff key if it is loose **(see illustrations)**. The puller is incorporated in the sprocket by means of the plate bolted over the nut, and the nut has an outer shoulder that bears against the plate.

32 Similarly unscrew the bolt from the camshaft sprocket and withdraw the sprocket.

33 Slide the sprocket from the crankshaft and recover the Woodruff key if it is loose.

34 Unscrew the bolts and remove the water pump from the cylinder block. Remove the gasket.

35 Mark the injection pump in relation to the mounting bracket. Unscrew the nuts and bolt and withdraw the injection pump.

36 Unbolt and remove the mounting bracket **(see illustration)**.

37 Unscrew the timing belt tensioner adjustment bolt and pivot nut. A tool may now be used to hold the tensioner plunger as described in Section 5 while the tensioner arm and roller is removed. However, it is possible to remove the arm and roller by keeping the arm pressed against the plunger **(see illustration)**.

38 Remove the plunger and spring **(see illustration)**.

39 Unscrew the bolts and remove the engine mounting bracket and the timing belt intermediate roller and bracket **(see illustrations)**.

40 Unbolt the engine front plate **(see illustration)**.

41 Progressively unscrew the cylinder head bolts in the reverse order to that shown in illustration 9.41B. Remove the washers.

42 Release the cylinder head from the cylinder block and location dowel by rocking

23.46 Withdrawing the oil pump spacer

23.47 Removing the oil pump

23.48 Removing the crankshaft front oil seal housing

23.49A Slide off the oil pump sprocket . . .

23.49B . . . and remove the Woodruff key

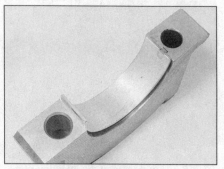

23.56 Main bearing cap and lower half bearing shell

23.57A Lift out the crankshaft . . .

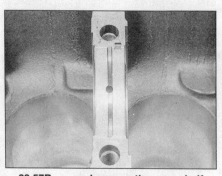

23.57B . . . and remove the upper half bearing shells

it. Lift the head from the block and remove the gasket.

43 Remove the clutch if applicable then hold the flywheel/driveplate stationary with a screwdriver or bar inserted between the teeth of the starter ring gear and the transmission location dowel. Then unscrew and remove the bolts and lift the flywheel/driveplate from the crankshaft.

44 Invert the engine and unbolt the sump. Remove the gasket.

45 Unscrew the three bolts securing the oil pump to the crankcase. Identify them for position as all three are of different lengths.

46 Withdraw the L-shaped spacer from beneath the oil pump (if fitted) **(see illustration)**.

47 Remove the location dowel (if fitted), and disengage the oil pump sprocket from the chain. Withdraw the oil pump **(see illustration)**.

48 Unscrew the bolts and remove the front oil seal housing **(see illustration)**. Remove the gasket.

49 Remove the oil pump chain followed by the sprocket. Recover the Woodruff key if it is loose **(see illustrations)**.

50 Check that each connecting rod and cap is marked for position and, if not, mark them with a centre punch on the oil filter side, number one at the flywheel end.

51 Position the cylinder block either on its side or on the flywheel end.

52 Turn the crankshaft to bring pistons 1 and 4 to BDC (bottom dead centre). Unscrew the nuts from No 1 piston big-end bearing cap then take off the cap and recover the bottom half bearing shell.

53 Using a hammer handle push the piston up through the bore and remove it from the

block. Loosely refit the shell bearings and cap to ensure correct reassembly.

54 Remove No 4 piston in the same manner then turn the crankshaft 180° to bring pistons 2 and 3 to BDC and remove them.

55 The main bearing caps should be numbered 1 to 5 from the flywheel end. If not, mark them accordingly. Also note the fitted depth of the rear oil seal.

56 Invert the engine then unbolt and remove the main bearing caps. Recover the lower half bearing shells keeping them with their respective caps **(see illustration)**. Also recover the thrustwashers.

57 Lift out the crankshaft. Discard the rear oil seal. Recover the upper half bearing shells and keep them together with their respective caps, however, identify them as the upper shells **(see illustrations)**. Also recover and identify the upper thrustwashers.

24 Engine overhaul - reassembly

Note: *Refer to Section 22, before this procedure.*

1 Position the block upside down on the bench. Wipe clean the main bearing shell seats in the block and caps.

2 Wipe any protective coating from the new bearing shells. Fit the top half main bearing shells (with the oil grooves) to their seats in the block. Make sure that the locating tangs on the shells engage with the recesses in the seats.

24.3 No 2 main bearing and thrustwashers

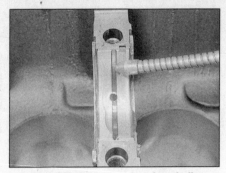
24.4 Oiling the main bearing shells

24.8 Fitting No 5 main bearing cap

24.9 Applying thread locking fluid to the No 1 main bearing cap joint face

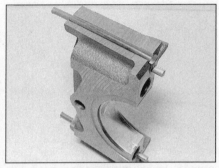
24.10A Sealing strips fitted to No 1 main bearing cap

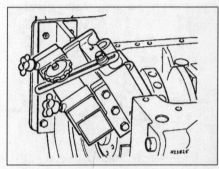
24.10B Using the special tool to fit No 1 main bearing cap

24.11A Slide the No 1 main bearing cap and metal strips into position . . .

24.11B . . . insert the bolts . . .

24.11C . . . then carefully pull out the metal strips

24.12 Tightening the main bearing bolts

3 Fit the thrustwashers on each side of No 2 main bearing, grooved side outwards. Use a smear of grease to hold them in position (see illustration).
4 Lubricate the top half shells and lower the crankshaft into position (see illustration).
5 Fit the plain bottom half main bearing shells to their caps, making sure that the locating tangs engage with the recesses. Oil the shells.
6 Fit the thrustwashers on each side of No 2 main bearing cap using a smear of grease to hold them in position.
7 Before fitting the caps check that the crankshaft endfloat is within the specified limits using a dial test indicator on the crankshaft nose.
8 Fit the main bearing caps Nos 2 to 5 to their correct locations (see illustration) and the right way round (the bearing shell tang locations in the block and caps must be on the same side). Insert the bolts loosely.
9 Apply a small amount of thread locking fluid to the No 1 main bearing cap face on the block around the sealing strip holes (see illustration).

10 Press the sealing strips in the grooves on each side of No 1 main bearing cap (see illustration). It is now necessary to obtain two thin metal strips of 0.25 mm thickness or less to prevent the strips moving when the cap is being fitted. Citroën garages use the tool shown (see illustration) which acts as a clamp, however, metal strips can be used provided all burrs that may damage the sealing strips are first removed.
11 Oil both sides of the metal strips and hold them on the sealing strips. Fit the No 1 main bearing cap, insert the bolts loosely, then carefully pull out the metal strips with a pair of pliers in a horizontal direction (see illustrations).
12 Tighten the main bearing bolts evenly to the specified torque (see illustration).
13 Check that the crankshaft rotates freely - there must be no tight spots or binding.

24.14 Fitting the crankshaft rear oil seal with a plastic protector

24.23 Checking the crankshaft turning torque

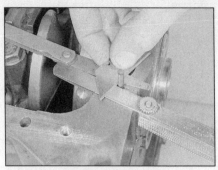

24.24 Cutting the sealing strips on No 1 main bearing cap

24.25 Fitting the chain to the oil pump sprocket

24.26 Tightening the front oil seal housing bolts

24.30A Apply sealing compound here . . .

24.30B . . . then fit the new sump gasket

14 Dip the new rear oil seal in engine oil, locate it on the crankshaft open end first, and press it squarely to the previously noted depth using a metal tube slightly less than 102 mm diameter. A piece of thin plastic is useful to prevent damage to the oil seal **(see illustration)**. Make sure that the outer lip of the oil seal points outwards and if necessary use a piece of bent wire to pull it out.

15 Position the cylinder block either on its side or on the flywheel end.

16 Lay out the assembled piston and rods in order with the bearing shells, connecting rod caps and nuts.

17 Check that the piston ring gaps are arranged 120° from each other.

18 Clean the bearing shells, caps and rods then press the shells into position so that the locating tangs engage in the grooves.

19 Oil the bores, pistons, crankpins and shells. Fit a piston ring compressor to No 1

piston. With Nos 1 and 4 crankpin at BDC insert No 1 piston in the bore at the flywheel end, making sure that the clover leaf cut-out on the piston crown is towards the oil filter side of the engine.

20 Using a hammer handle tap the piston through the ring compressor and into the bore. Guide the connecting rod onto the crankpin and fit the cap, together with its shell bearing, making sure it is the correct way round.

21 Fit the nuts and tighten them to the specified torque. Turn the crankshaft to check for free movement.

22 Repeat the procedure to fit the other three pistons.

23 Temporarily refit the pulley bolt to the nose of the crankshaft then, using a torque wrench, check that the torque required to turn the crankshaft does not exceed 41 Nm (30 lbf ft) **(see illustration)**. Any excessive tightness

must be investigated before proceeding.

24 Using feeler blades and a knife, cut the sealing strips on No 1 main bearing cap to 1.0 mm above the sump gasket mating surface **(see illustration)**.

25 Fit the Woodruff key to the groove in the crankshaft and refit the oil pump sprocket, teeth end first. Engage the chain with the sprocket and tie it up or to one side so that it remains engaged **(see illustration)**.

26 Prise the oil seal from the front housing. Check that the two dowels are located in the front of the cylinder block then refit the front housing, together with a new gasket, and tighten the bolts evenly to the specified torque **(see illustration)**.

27 Check that the dowel is fitted to the bottom of the block. Engage the oil pump sprocket with the chain and slide the L-shaped spacer under the pump, making sure that its open end engages the dowel.

28 Insert the oil pump bolts in their correct location, the longest bolt through the dowel and the next longest by the oil return hole. Tighten the bolts evenly to the specified torque.

29 Dip the front oil seal in engine oil then press it into the front housing until flush with the outer face.

30 Apply a little sealing compound where the front housing abuts the block on both sides. Position a new gasket on the block and refit the sump **(see illustrations)**. Note the correct location of the bolts as shown, in illustration 13.5. Tighten the bolts evenly to the specified torque. Remove the sump drain plug, renew the washer, then refit and tighten the plug.

31 Locate the flywheel/driveplate on the crankshaft dowel.

32 Apply locking fluid to the threads of the bolts, insert them, and tighten them to the specified torque while holding the flywheel/driveplate stationary with a screwdriver or bar inserted between the teeth of the starter ring gear and the transmission location dowel.

33 Position the cylinder block upright on the bench.

34 Check that the cylinder head bolt holes in the block are clear preferably using an M12 x 1.5 tap **(see illustration)**.

35 Locate the correct cylinder head gasket

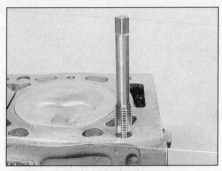

24.34 Cleaning the cylinder head bolt holes with a tap

24.35 Head gasket fitted to cylinder block with location dowel arrowed

24.38 Lowering the cylinder head onto the block

24.39 Tighten the cylinder head bolts to the specified torque

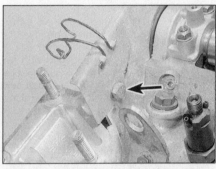

24.41 Inner bolt location for the engine mounting bracket (arrowed)

24.42A Turn the tensioner bracket anti-clockwise . . .

24.42B . . . and tighten the bolt to hold the tensioner in the released position

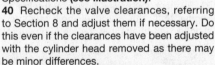

24.46 Fitting the sprocket to the crankshaft

24.47 Tightening the camshaft sprocket bolt with the timing bolt in position

(see Section 9) on the block the right way round with the identification notches or holes at the flywheel/driveplate end. Check that the location dowel is fitted **(see illustration)**.

36 Turn the crankshaft clockwise (from timing belt end) until pistons 1 and 4 pass BDC and begin to rise. Then position them halfway up their bores. Pistons 2 and 3 will also be at their mid-way positions, but descending their bores. The Woodruff key groove on the nose of the crankshaft will be at the 9 o'clock position.

37 Check that the camshaft is set to TDC with the Woodruff key position facing upwards and the tips of cams 4 and 6 resting on the bucket tappets.

38 Lower the cylinder head onto the block **(see illustration)**.

39 Grease the threads and contact faces of the cylinder head bolts, then insert them and tighten them in the sequence shown in

illustration 9.41B in three stages as given in Specifications **(see illustration)**.

40 Recheck the valve clearances, referring to Section 8 and adjust them if necessary. Do this even if the clearances have been adjusted with the cylinder head removed as there may be minor differences.

41 Refit the engine front plate followed by the timing belt intermediate roller and bracket, and the engine mounting bracket. Tighten all the bolts. Do not forget the mounting bracket bolt on the inside face of the engine front plate **(see illustration)**.

42 Insert the timing belt tensioner spring and plunger in the mounting bracket. Press the tensioner arm against the plunger and refit the bracket and roller onto the pivot stud. Alternatively compress the plunger with the tool described in Section 5. Fit the adjustment bolt and pivot nut, and tighten the bolt with the tensioner in the released position (ie

spring compressed) **(see illustrations)**.

43 Refit the injection pump mounting bracket and tighten the bolts.

44 Refit the injection pump, align the previously made marks then tighten the nuts followed by the bolt.

45 Refit the water pump together with a new gasket and tighten the bolts to the specified torque (Chapter 3).

46 Locate the Woodruff key in the groove then slide the sprocket onto the front of the crankshaft **(see illustration)**.

47 Fit the camshaft sprocket to the camshaft. Apply locking fluid to the threads then insert and tighten the bolt to the specified torque. The sprocket may be held stationary by fitting the timing bolt through the special hole **(see illustration)**.

48 Unbolt the special puller from the injection pump sprocket. Check that the Woodruff key is in place then refit the sprocket and tighten

2

24.48 Tightening the injection pump sprocket bolt with the timing bolts in position

24.60 Bottom timing cover fitted

the nut **(see illustration)**.
49 Bolt the special puller onto the sprocket **(see illustration)**.
50 Refit the valve cover, together with a new gasket, and tighten the bolts.
51 Insert the three M8 timing bolts through the holes in the camshaft and injection pump sprockets and screw them into the engine front plate fingertight.
52 Insert an 8.0 to 8.5 mm diameter metal dowel rod through the special hole in the left-hand rear flange of the cylinder block. Then turn the crankshaft slowly clockwise (from the timing belt end) until the rod enters the TDC hole in the flywheel/driveplate. It is only necessary to turn the crankshaft a quarter turn as Nos 1 and 4 pistons are already halfway up their bores. Do not turn the crankshaft more than this otherwise pistons 2

24.49 Tightening the special puller to the injection pump sprocket

and 3 will strike valves 4 and 6.
53 Locate the timing belt on the crankshaft sprocket making sure where applicable that the rotation arrow is facing the correct way.
54 Hold the timing belt engaged with the crankshaft sprocket then feed it over the roller and onto the injection pump, camshaft, and water pump sprockets and over the tensioner roller. To ensure correct engagement locate only a half width on the injection pump sprocket before feeding the timing belt onto the camshaft sprocket, keeping the belt taut and fully engaged with the crankshaft sprocket. Locate the timing belt fully onto the sprockets.
55 With the pivot nut loose, slacken the tensioner adjustment bolt while holding the bracket against the spring tension, then slowly release the bracket until the roller presses against the timing belt. Retighten the adjustment bolt **(see illustration)**.
56 Remove the bolts from the camshaft and injection pump sprockets. Remove the metal dowel rod from the cylinder block.
57 Rotate the engine two complete turns in its normal direction. Do not rotate the engine backwards as the timing belt must be kept tight between the crankshaft, injection pump and camshaft sprockets.
58 Loosen the tensioner adjustment bolt to allow the tensioner spring to push the roller against the timing belt, then tighten both the adjustment bolt and pivot nut.
59 Recheck the engine timing by turning the engine until the sprocket bolt holes are aligned, and check that the metal dowel rod

24.55 Tightening the tensioner adjustment bolt

can be inserted into the flywheel/driveplate.
60 Refit the bottom timing cover and tighten the bolts **(see illustration)**.
61 Fit the pulley to the front of the crankshaft over the Woodruff key.
62 Apply locking fluid to the threads of the pulley bolt. Then insert it and tighten to the specified torque while an assistant holds the flywheel/driveplate stationary with a screwdriver inserted between the teeth of the starter ring gear and the transmission location dowel. Note that after tightening to the initial torque, the bolt must be angle tightened a further 60° that is the equivalent of one flat on the bolt head. Alternatively mark the flat extremities on the socket together with a starting datum on the pulley **(see illustrations)**.
63 Locate a new gasket on the side of the sump, refit the inlet bracket, and tighten the nuts evenly.
64 Refit the water pump inlet together with a new gasket and tighten the bolts.
65 Bolt the coolant tube to the cylinder block and fit the hoses.
66 Refit the thermostat housing, together with a new gasket, and tighten the bolts.
67 Insert the oil pressure switch in the block and tighten.
68 Insert the oil level sensor and tighten.
69 Refit the fast idle cable to the injection pump, referring to Chapter 4.
70 Refit the exhaust manifold, together with new gaskets, and tighten the nuts evenly.
71 Refit the inlet manifold and tighten the bolts evenly. There are no gaskets.

24.62A Apply locking fluid to the crankshaft pulley bolt before fitting it

24.62B Tightening the crankshaft pulley bolt

24.62C Markings necessary in order to angle-tighten the crankshaft pulley bolt by 60°

24.73 Oil separator located on the dipstick tube (1.9 engine)

24.75A Oil cooler . . .

24.75B . . . and coolant hose connections

24.81 Tightening the pump pulley bolt on the camshaft

72 Refit the oil filler cap and ventilation hose if fitted.

73 Slide the oil separator onto the dipstick tube **(see illustration)** and secure with the clip. Reconnect the crankcase ventilation hoses to the valve cover and sump inlet.

74 Reconnect the bottom hose to the water pump inlet.

75 On the 1.9 engine reconnect the oil cooler hoses and refit the oil cooler, tightening the centre stud to the specified torque **(see illustrations)**.

76 Smear a little engine oil on the sealing ring of the oil filter cartridge then refit it and tighten by hand only.

77 Refit the alternator (Chapter 5).

78 Refit the engine lifting bracket to the cylinder head, also refit the lower rear engine mounting bracket.

79 Reconnect the leak off hoses to the injectors.

80 Refit the fuel pipe assemblies to the injectors and injection pump and tighten the union nuts to the specified torque (Chapter 4).

81 Slide the pump pulley onto the flywheel end of the camshaft. Insert the bolt and tighten it to the specified torque **(see illustration)**.

82 Where applicable refit the diagnostic socket and bracket and tighten the bolt.

83 Reconnect the wiring harness to the following components:
 a) Alternator
 b) Oil pressure switch
 c) Diagnostic socket (if fitted)
 d) Temperature sensor(s)
 e) Oil level sensor

84 Refit the two timing cover sections and press down the special clip and spring clips to secure.

85 Refit the clutch on manual transmission models.

25 Engine overhaul examination and renovation - general

1 With the engine completely dismantled, all components should be cleaned and examined as detailed in the appropriate Sections of this Chapter.

2 Most components can be cleaned with rags, a soft brush and paraffin, or some other solvent. Do not immerse parts with oilways in solvent since it can be very difficult to remove and if left will contaminate the oil. Clean oilways and water channels with a piece of wire and blow through with compressed air if available.

3 When faced with a borderline decision whether to renew a particular part, take into consideration the expected future life of the engine and the degree of trouble or expense that will be caused if the part fails before the next overhaul.

4 If extensive overhauling is required, estimate the likely cost and compare it with the cost of a complete reconditioned engine. The difference may not be great, and the reconditioned engine will have a guarantee.

26 Engine components - overhaul

Cylinder block and bores

Overhaul

1 Check the cylinder block casting for any damage or cracking.

2 If necessary unscrew the two plugs from the rear of the block and from the flange beneath the oil filter location, and clean the oil gallery. Refit and tighten the plugs on completion. The water channels may be cleaned by removing the inspection plate from the rear of the block. On Turbo models,

remove the piston cooling jets. Clean them and inspect them for damage or wear and replace them if necessary.

3 Check the core plugs for signs of leakage and if necessary renew them. It may be possible to remove the old plugs by drilling a small hole and using a self-tapping screw to pull them out. Alternatively, use a hammer to drive a chisel through the old plugs and prise them out. Clean the seating then apply a little sealing compound and tap the new plug into position with the flat face of a hammer. Spread the core plug by striking the centre with a ball face hammer.

4 If cracks in the block are suspected it may be necessary to have it crack-tested professionally. There are various ways of doing this, some involving special dyes and chemicals, some using ultrasonic or electromagnetic radiation.

5 Bore wear is indicated by a wear ridge at the top of the bore. For accurate assessment a bore micrometer is required, however, a rough measurement can be made by inserting feeler blades between a piston (without rings) and the bore wall. Compare the clearance at the bottom of the bore, which should be unworn, with that just below the wear ridge. No wear limits are specified, but out-of-round or taper more than 0.1 mm would normally be considered grounds for a rebore. Scuffs, scores and scratches must also be taken into account.

6 If reboring is undertaken the machine shop will normally obtain the oversize pistons and rings at the same time.

7 Where the degree of wear does not justify a rebore, the fitting of proprietary oil control rings may be considered.

Crankshaft and bearings

Overhaul

8 Check the crankshaft for damage or excessive wear.

9 Examine the bearing shells for wear and scratches on the working surfaces. New shells should be fitted in any case, unless the old ones are obviously in perfect condition and are known to have covered only a nominal mileage **(see illustration)**. Refitting used shells is false economy.

10 Examine the bearing journals on the

26.9 Big-end bearing shell

crankshaft for scoring or other damage, which if present will probably mean that regrinding or renewal is necessary. If a micrometer is available, measure the journals in several places to check for out-of-round and taper. No limits are specified but typically 0.025 mm is the maximum acceptable.

11 Note that the crankshaft may already have been reground, and that the makers only specify one stage of regrinding.

12 Main and big-end bearing clearances can be measured using Plastigage thread. The journal and bearing shell are wiped dry before placing the thread across the journal. After tightening the bearing cap onto the Plastigage it is removed and a special gauge used to determine the running clearance. The makers do not specify any clearances but typically it would be between 0.025 and 0.050 mm.

13 Check the crankshaft endfloat using a feeler blade between the No 2 thrustwashers and crankshaft web. If this is more than the specified amount obtain new thrustwashers. Alternatively a dial gauge on the end of the crankshaft may be used for the check **(see illustration)**.

Pistons, piston rings and connecting rods

Overhaul

14 The piston rings may be removed from each piston with the aid of some old feeler blades or similar thin metal strips. Carefully spread the top ring just far enough to slide the blades in between the ring and the piston, then remove the ring and blades together **(see**

Haynes Hint). Be careful not to scratch the piston with the ends of the ring.

15 Repeat the process to remove the second and third rings, using the blades to stop the rings falling into the empty grooves. Note that the third ring incorporates an expander. Always remove the rings from the top of the piston. Keep each set of rings with its piston if the old rings are to be re-used.

16 Measure the end gaps of the rings by fitting them, one at a time, to their bores. Check the gaps with the rings either at the extreme top or bottom of the bores, where the wear is minimum, using feeler blades **(see illustration)**.

17 If the rings are renewed the bores must be deglazed as described in Section 15.

18 Examine the pistons for damage, in particular for burning on the crown and for scores or other signs of "picking-up" on the skirts and piston ring lands. Scorch marks on the sides show that blow-by has occurred.

19 If the pistons pass this preliminary inspection clean all the carbon out of the ring grooves using a piece of old piston ring. Protect your fingers - piston rings are sharp. Do not remove any metal from the ring grooves.

20 Roll each ring around its groove to check for tight spots. Any excessive clearance not due to worn rings must be due to piston wear and, unless the piston can be machined to accept special rings, renewal is required.

21 If renewing pistons without reboring make sure that the correct size is obtained. Piston class is denoted by either an "A1" mark or no mark at all on the centre of the crown. The identical code appears also on the corner of the cylinder block at the timing belt end. The piston weight class is stamped on the crown and must be identical on all pistons in the same engine.

22 To separate a piston from its connecting rod, prise out the circlips and push out the gudgeon pin **(see illustrations)**. Hand pressure is sufficient to remove the pin. Identify the piston and rod to ensure correct reassembly.

23 Wear between the gudgeon pin and the connecting rod small-end bush can be cured by renewing both the pin and bush. Bush

renewal, however, is a specialist job because press facilities are required and the new bush must be reamed accurately.

24 New gudgeon pins and circlips are supplied when buying new pistons. The connecting rods themselves should not be in need of renewal unless seizure or some other major mechanical failure has occurred.

25 Reassemble the pistons and rods. Make sure that the pistons are fitted the right way round - the clover leaf cut-out on the crown must face the same way as the shell bearing cut-out in the connecting rod. Oil the gudgeon pins before fitting them **(see illustrations)**. When assembled, the piston should pivot freely on the rod.

26 Fit the piston rings using the same technique as for removal. Fit the bottom ring first and work up. When fitting the oil control ring first insert the expander then fit the ring with its gap positioned 180° from the expanders gap. Arrange the gaps of the upper two rings 120° either side of the oil control ring gap. Make sure that No 2 ring is fitted the correct way round **(see illustration)**.

Flywheel/driveplate

Overhaul

27 Examine the clutch mating surface of the flywheel for scoring or cracks. Light grooving or scoring may be ignored. Surface cracks or deep grooving can sometimes be removed by specialist machining, provided not too much metal is taken off, otherwise the flywheel must be renewed.

28 Inspect the flywheel/driveplate for damage or cracks and renew it if necessary.

29 Inspect the starter ring gear for damaged or missing teeth. It is not possible to obtain a genuine Citroën ring gear separate from the flywheel/driveplate, and if damaged it may therefore be necessary to renew the complete flywheel/driveplate. However, some motor factors may be able to supply one, in which case the old ring gear should be drilled and split with a cold chisel to remove it. The new ring gear must be heated then quickly tapped onto the flywheel/driveplate and allowed to cool naturally. The temperature to which the ring gear must be heated is critical - too little heat and the ring gear may not fit or may even jam halfway on. Too much heat and the

26.13 Checking the crankshaft endfloat

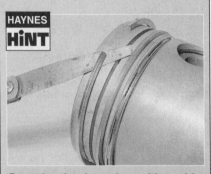

Removing the piston rings with an old feeler blade

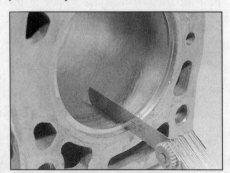

26.16 Measuring the piston ring end gaps

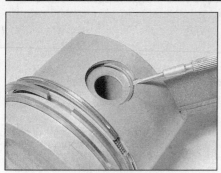

26.22A Prising out the gudgeon pin circlip

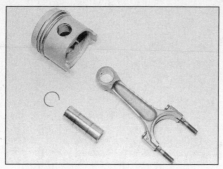

26.22B Piston and connecting rod components

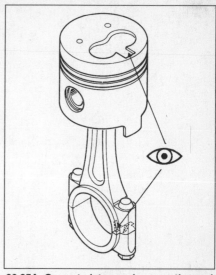

26.25A Correct piston and connecting rod assembly

temper of the metal may be lost causing it to wear rapidly in use. The correct temperature is normally attached to the new ring gear, however, the average DIY mechanic may prefer to leave the job to a garage or engineering works.

30 The makers recommend that the flywheel/driveplate bolts only are renewed at overhaul, however, it would be prudent to also renew the cylinder head bolts especially if they have been tightened more than once.

27 Engine and transmission - reconnection

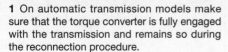

1 On automatic transmission models make sure that the torque converter is fully engaged with the transmission and remains so during the reconnection procedure.
2 Support the engine then lift the transmission into position. On manual transmission models turn the unit as required until the splined input shaft enters the clutch driven plate.
3 Push the transmission onto the location dowels and insert the bolts in their correct locations as previously noted. Tighten the bolts to the specified torque (Chapter 6).
4 Refit the hydraulic pressure pump or vacuum pump bracket and tighten the bolts. Refit the adjustment link. Slip the drivebelt over the pulleys then swivel the pump to tension the drivebelt and tighten the link bolt and pivot bolt. When correctly tensioned the

belt deflection under firm thumb pressure mid-way between the pulleys should be approximately 5.0 mm.
5 Where applicable, refit the hydraulic line bracket and tighten the bolt.
6 On automatic transmission models align the driveplate and torque converter bolt holes, and insert and tighten the bolts.
7 Refit the bottom cover and tighten the bolts.
8 Refit the starter motor, tighten the bolts, and reconnect the wiring.
9 Refit the TDC sensor and holder and tighten the bolts. When the TDC sensor is fitted new it incorporates three legs that are 1.0 mm long and these automatically set the sensor 1.0 mm from the flywheel/driveplate. When fitting an old sensor the legs should be filed off - the unit can then be fully inserted until it touches the flywheel/driveplate and then withdrawn by 1.0 mm before tightening the bolts.

28 Initial start-up after engine overhaul - general

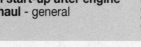

1 Check that the oil, coolant and fuel have all been replenished and that the battery is well charged.
2 On early models fitted with a Roto-diesel fuel filter unscrew the pump plunger.
3 Switch on the ignition to energise the stop solenoid then actuate the pump on the fuel filter until resistance is felt. Retighten the plunger where necessary.
4 Fully depress the accelerator pedal, turn

the ignition key to position "M" and wait for the preheating warning light to go out.
5 Start the engine. Additional cranking may be necessary to bleed the fuel system before the engine starts.
6 Once started keep the engine running at a fast tickover. Check that the oil pressure light goes out, then check for leaks of oil, fuel and coolant.
7 On pre-September 1986 models, if all is well, continue to run the engine at 3000 rpm for 10 minutes then switch off the ignition and let the engine cool for at least 3½ hours.
8 Remove the filler cap from the cooling system expansion tank to release any remaining pressure, then refit it.
9 Working on each cylinder head bolt in turn in the correct sequence first loosen the bolt 90° then retighten to the final torque given in the Specifications.
10 If many new parts have been fitted, the engine should be treated as new and run in at reduced speeds and loads for the first 600 miles (1000 km) or so. After this mileage it is beneficial to change the engine oil and oil filter.
11 Have the injection pump timing and idling speed checked and adjusted as described in Chapter 4.

2

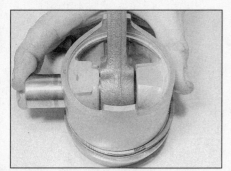

26.25B Pushing the gudgeon pin into the piston

26.25C Clover leaf cut-out on the piston crown

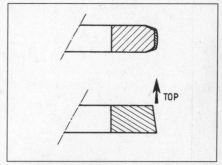

26.26 Piston ring cross sections

Notes

Chapter 3
Cooling system

Contents

Degrees of difficulty

Easy, suitable for novice with little experience	Fairly easy, suitable for beginner with some experience	Fairly difficult, suitable for competent DIY mechanic	Difficult, suitable for experienced DIY mechanic	Very difficult, suitable for expert DIY or professional

Specifications

General

System type	Pressurised, front-mounted radiator (with integral expansion tank on BX models), coolant pump and thermostat. Electric cooling fan(s)

Thermostat:
  Pre 1987 models:
    Starts to open at .... 82°C
  1987-on models:
    except BX Turbo and C15 Vans .... 88°C
    BX Turbo .... 83°C
    C15 Van .... 89°C
Radiator cap pressure .... 1 bar
Temperature warning switch operating temperature .... 103 to 107°C
Emergency temperature warning switch (yellow connector)
operating temperature .... 110 to 114°C
Cooling fan(s):
  Except BX Turbo and C15:
    1st speed cuts in at .... 86 to 90°C
    2nd speed cuts in at .... 90 to 94°C
  BX Turbo:
    1st speed cuts in at .... 93°C
    2nd speed cuts in at .... 97°C
  C15 Van:
    1st speed cuts in at .... 88°C
    2nd speed cuts in at .... 92°C

Torque wrench settings	Nm	lbf ft
Water pump	12	9

1 Description - general

The cooling system is pressurised with a front-mounted radiator and a water pump driven by the engine timing belt. The thermostat is located on the flywheel end of the cylinder block, and enables the engine to achieve a fast warm-up period by initially restricting the coolant flow within the engine and heater circuits. Thereafter, the coolant flows through the radiator to provide additional cooling. The main engine temperature control is provided by one or two electric cooling fans mounted in front of the radiator. Visa models have two separate fans and BX models a single twin-speed fan. In both cases a twin action sensor in the radiator activates the fan(s) according to the coolant temperature **(see illustrations)**.

Essential to the operation of the system is the expansion tank, integral with the radiator on BX models or separate on Visa models. This tank provides a reservoir to allow for expansion and contraction of the coolant with changes in temperature. It also incorporates a filler/pressure relief valve cap.

The radiator is of the crossflow type, with plastic side tanks. A temperature warning switch is provided on the water outlet from the cylinder head to warn the driver of excessive temperature. An additional warning switch is also provided on BX models which operates at the "emergency" temperature and causes the warning lamp to remain on permanently as against the flashing warning lamp activated at the lower temperature.

The basic cooling system on BX Turbo models is similar to that described for other BX models, except for the addition of a remote expansion tank. The radiator is specific to Turbo models, as are the water pump and radiator cooling fans **(see illustration)**.

From 1989 model year to early 1993, on Visa (and C15) models, the remote expansion tank is no longer fitted. The cooling system filler/pressure cap is now on the radiator, at the right-hand end. The radiator, hoses and surrounding components are modified **(see illustration)**.

At the same time, the electric fuel heater fitted to some models was discontinued. A coolant-fed fuel heater is fitted instead. This is mounted on the rear face of the engine block, at the timing belt end **(see illustration)**. If it has to be removed or disconnected for any reason, note the arrow showing the direction of fuel flow.

From early 1993, on the C15 models the fuel heater is no longer mounted on the rear of the engine block. Instead, the fuel is heated using a special filter housing on the front of the cylinder head (see Chapter 4 for more details) **(see illustration)**.

When the BX diesel is used for towing loads

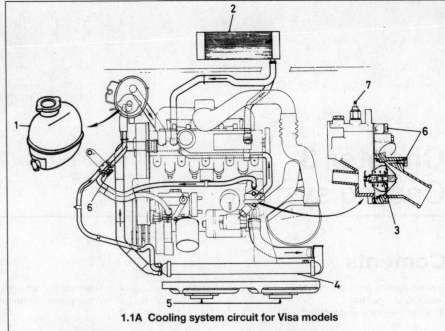

1.1A Cooling system circuit for Visa models

1 Expansion tank	5 Electric cooling fans
2 Heater matrix	6 Bleed screws
3 Thermostat	7 Temperature warning switch
4 Radiator	

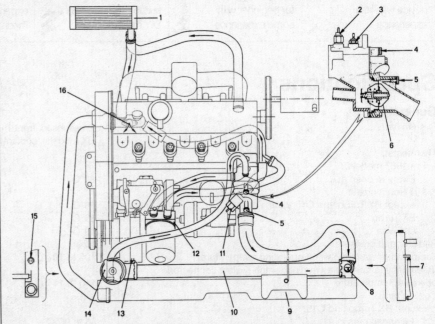

1.1B Cooling system circuit for BX models

1 Heater matrix	9 Electric cooling fan
2 Temperature warning switch	10 Radiator
3 Emergency temperature warning switch	11 Fast idle temperature sensor
4 and 5 Bleed screws	12 Oil cooler
6 Thermostat	13 Electric cooling fan thermal switch
7 Drain pipe	14 Filler cap
8 Radiator bleed screw	15 Low level warning switch
	16 Water pump inlet

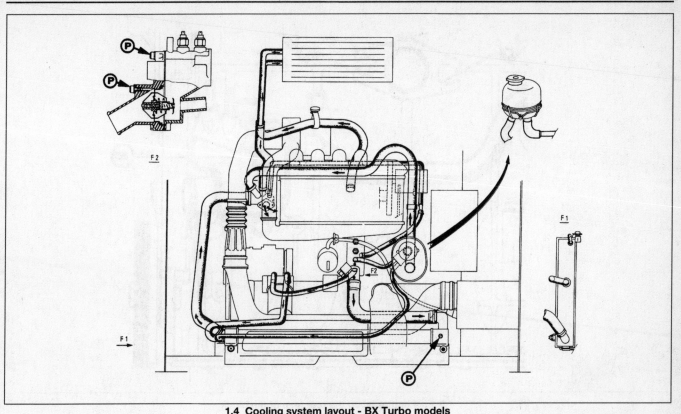

1.4 Cooling system layout - BX Turbo models
P Bleed screws

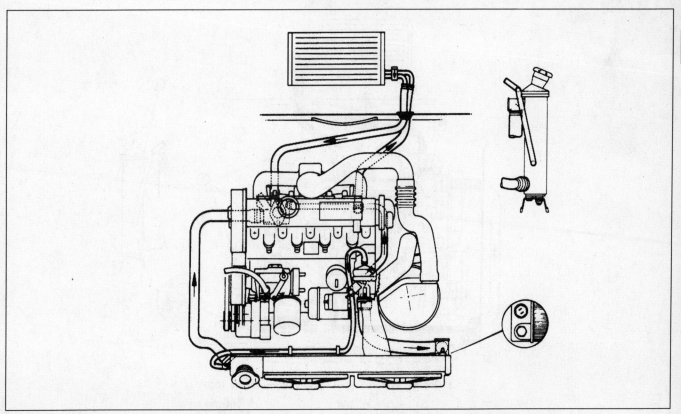

1.5 Cooling system layout - Visa/C15 Van, 1989 to early 1993

3

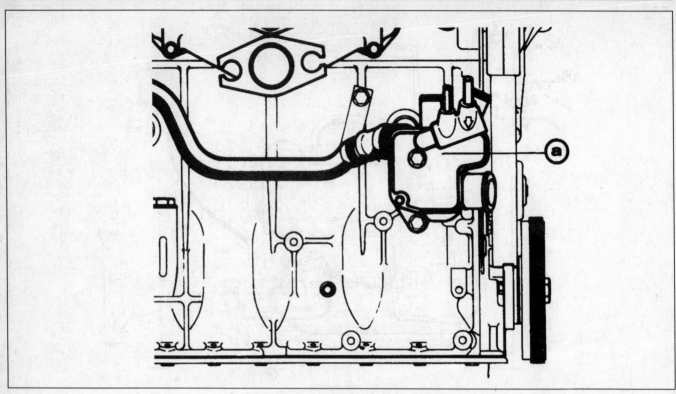

1.6 Fuel heater (a) on the rear face of the block

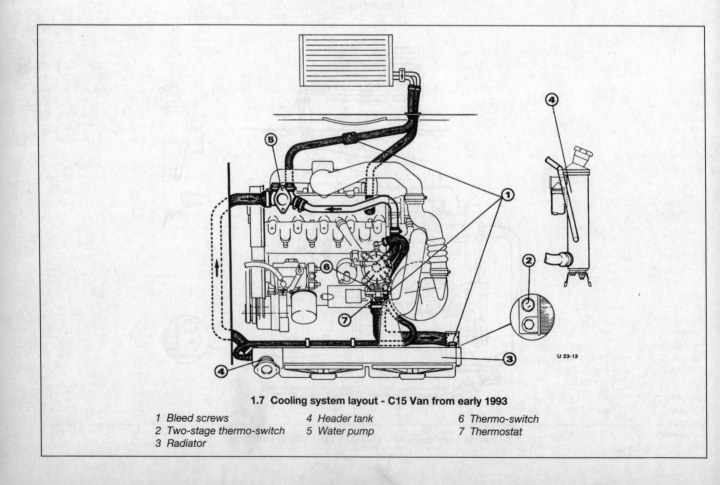

1.7 Cooling system layout - C15 Van from early 1993

1 Bleed screws	4 Header tank	6 Thermo-switch
2 Two-stage thermo-switch	5 Water pump	7 Thermostat
3 Radiator		

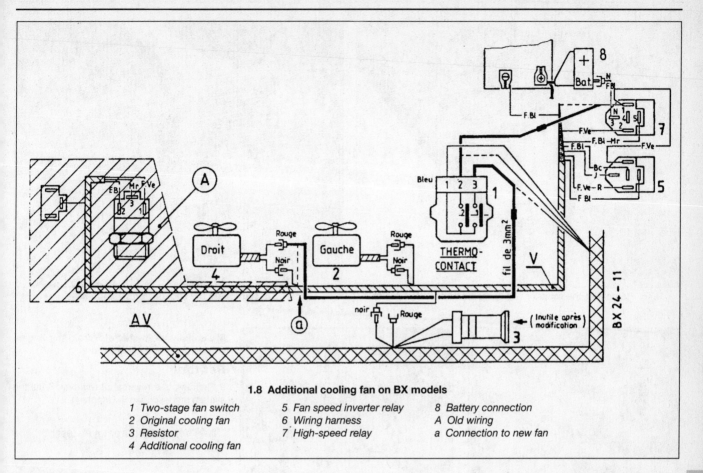

1.8 Additional cooling fan on BX models

1 Two-stage fan switch
2 Original cooling fan
3 Resistor
4 Additional cooling fan
5 Fan speed inverter relay
6 Wiring harness
7 High-speed relay
8 Battery connection
A Old wiring
a Connection to new fan

of more than 650 kg, Citroën recommend that an additional cooling fan is fitted to the radiator **(see illustration)**. All of the parts necessary to carry out the modification are obtainable from a Citroën dealer.

If the existing cooling fan control switch is fitted to the left-hand side of the radiator, it will also be necessary to obtain a new wiring harness.

2 Cooling system pressure - testing

1 In cases where leakage is difficult to trace a pressure test can prove helpful. The test involves pressurising the system by means of a hand pump and an adapter which is fitted to the expansion tank or radiator in place of the filler cap. The resourceful home mechanic may be able to improvise the apparatus using an old filler cap and a tyre valve, alternatively the test can be performed by a Citroën garage.
2 Fit the test equipment to the expansion tank or radiator then run the engine to normal operating temperature and switch it off.
3 Apply 1.4 bar pressure and check that this pressure is held for at least 10 seconds. If the pressure drops prematurely there is a leak in the cooling system which must be traced and rectified.

4 Besides leaks from hoses, pressure can also be lost through leaks in the radiator and heater matrix. A blown head gasket or a cracked head or block can cause an "invisible" leak, but there are usually other clues to this condition such as poor engine performance, regular misfiring, or combustion gases entering the coolant.
5 After completing the test, allow the engine to cool then remove the test equipment.
6 The condition of the filler cap must not be overlooked. Normally it is tested with similar equipment to that used for the pressure test. The release pressure is given in the Specifications and is also usually stamped on the cap itself. Renew the cap if it is faulty.

3 Radiator - removal and refitting

Removal

1 Drain the cooling system as described in Chapter 1.
2 Remove the air cleaner as described in Chapter 4.
3 Loosen the clips and disconnect the top hose, bottom hose, and bypass hose from the radiator.

4 On Visa models disconnect the bonnet release cable from its catch and unbolt the crossmember. Lift the crossmember from the top of the radiator.
5 Disconnect the wiring from the thermal switch on the right-hand side of the radiator. Also disconnect the coolant level warning switch (when fitted).
6 On Visa models remove the front grille panel then remove one headlamp unit and detach the fan cowl.
7 On BX models unscrew the bolts and lift the crossmember from the top of the radiator **(see illustrations)**.

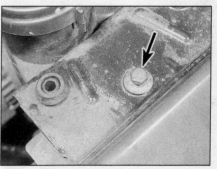

3.7A Radiator top crossmember retaining bolt – arrowed (BX models)

3

3.7B Removing the radiator top crossmember (BX models)

3.8 Removing the radiator on BX models

4.3A Unscrewing the thermostat housing
cover bolts

4.3B Removing the thermostat housing
cover gasket

4.4 Thermostat and retaining circlip

4.5 Removing the rubber seal from the
thermostat

8 Carefully lift the radiator from the engine
compartment (see illustration).

Refitting

9 Refitting is a reversal of removal. Refill the
system as described in Chapter 1.

4   Thermostat - removal, testing and refitting

Removal

1 Drain the cooling system as described in
Chapter 1.
2 Loosen the clip and disconnect the top
hose from the thermostat housing cover.
3 Unscrew the four bolts and remove the
thermostat housing cover from the cylinder
head water outlet. There is no need to
disconnect the fast idle cable. Remove the
gasket (see illustrations).
4 Using circlip pliers, extract the circlip from
the cover and lift out the thermostat (see
illustration).
5 If necessary pull the rubber seal from the
thermostat (see illustration).

Testing

6 To test the thermostat place it in a pan of
cold water and check that it is initially closed.
Heat the water and check that it commences
to open at the temperature given in Specifications. Continue to heat the water and check

5.5A Unscrew the bolts . . .

5.5B . . . and withdraw the water pump

5.5C Water pump showing impeller vanes

the fully open temperature and minimum travel. Finally allow the water to cool and check that it fully closes. Discard it if it is faulty.

Refitting

7 Refitting is a reversal of removal, but when inserting the thermostat in the cover, position the vent hole uppermost and also fit a new gasket. Refill the system as described in Chapter 1.

5 Water pump - removal and refitting

Removal

1 Disconnect the battery negative lead.
2 Remove the timing belt as described in Chapter 2.
3 Drain the cooling system as described in Chapter 1.
4 To provide additional working room loosen the clips and remove the bottom hose.
5 Unscrew the bolts and withdraw the water

pump from the cylinder block **(see illustrations)**. Remove the gasket.

Refitting

6 Clean the mating faces of the water pump and block.
7 Fit the water pump together with a new gasket, insert the bolts, and tighten them evenly to the specified torque.
8 Reconnect the bottom hose if removed.
9 Refit the timing belt as described in Chapter 2.
10 Reconnect the battery negative lead.
11 Refill the cooling system as described in Chapter 1.

3

Notes

Chapter 4
Fuel and exhaust systems

Contents

Degrees of difficulty

Easy, suitable for novice with little experience	**Fairly easy,** suitable for beginner with some experience	**Fairly difficult,** suitable for competent DIY mechanic 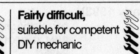	**Difficult,** suitable for experienced DIY mechanic	**Very difficult,** suitable for expert DIY or professional 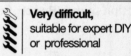

Specifications

General

System type	Rear-mounted fuel tank, injection pump with integral transfer pump, indirect injection
Firing order	1-3-4-2 (No 1 at flywheel end)
Fuel:	
Type	Commercial diesel fuel for road vehicles (DERV)
Tank capacity:	
Visa	43 litres
BX	52 litres

Injection pump (Roto-diesel)

Static advance	2.26 ± 0.05 mm BTDC (equivalent to 16° BTDC)
Dynamic advance:	
Visa	14 ± 1° BTDC at 800 rpm
BX17	14 ± 1° BTDC at 800 rpm
BX19 with injection pump code DPCR 844 3161 A	17 ± 1° BTDC at idle speed
BX19 with injection pump code DPCR 844 3261 C	14 ± 1° BTDC at idle speed
Maximum engine speed (no load)	5100 ± 100 rpm
Rotation	Clockwise from sprocket end

Injection pump (Bosch) - pre 1987 models

Static advance:	
Visa	0.72 ± 0.03 mm BTDC
BX17	0.80 ± 0.03 mm BTDC
BX19	0.57 ± 0.03 mm BTDC
Dynamic advance:	
Visa	14 ± 1° BTDC at 800 rpm
BX17	14 ± 1° BTDC at 800 rpm
BX19	13 to 14° BTDC at idle speed
Maximum engine speed	5100 ± 100 rpm
Fast idle speed (automatic transmission only)	1150 to 1250 rpm
Rotation	Clockwise from sprocket end

4

Injection pump (Bosch) - 1987-on models
Timing values at TDC (refer to text):

Engine code	Pump code	Timing value
XUD 7 (from October 1987)	VER 171-1	0.90 mm
XUD 7 (from early 1993)	VER R171-3	0.89 mm
XUD 9A (from April 1987 to April 1988)	VER 272-1	0.83 mm
XUD 9A (from April 1988)	VER 272-2	0.90 mm
XUD 7TE	-	0.80 mm

Injection pump (Bosch, in C15 Van from early 1993)
Type	523 (R171-3)
Static timing (pump ABDC)	0.89 mm
Idle speed	800 ± 50 rpm
Maximum engine speed	5150 ± 125 rpm
Fast idle speed	950 ± 50 rpm
Injector opening pressure (colour code)	130 bars (mauve)

Injection pump (Lucas, in C15 Van from early 1993)
Type	047 (R 8443B 930 A)
Static timing	"X" dimension marked on pump
Idle speed	800 ± 50 rpm
Maximum engine speed	5150 ± 125 rpm
Fast idle speed	950 ± 50 rpm
Injector opening pressure:	
Green collar	138 to 143 bars
Green collar and green spot	142 to 147 bars

Injection pump (Bosch, in BX models from early 1993)
Type	D9B XUD9A/L BVM XUD201 R425/1	D9B XUD9A/L BVA XUD201 R425/3
Static timing (pump ABDC)	1.07 mm	0.98 mm
Idling speed	750 to 800 rpm	750 to 800 rpm
Fast idle speed	900 to 1000 rpm	900 to 1000 rpm
Maximum engine speed (loaded)	4600 rpm	4600 rpm
Injector opening pressure (colour code)	130 bars (silver)	130 bars (silver)
Type	DJZ* XUD9/Y 518 R162/4 XUD200	AJZ* XUD7TE/Y R403
Static timing (pump ABDC)	0.77 mm	0.74 mm
Idling speed	750 to 800 rpm	750 to 800 rpm
Fast idle speed	900 to 1000 rpm	900 to 1000 rpm
Maximum engine speed (loaded)	4600 rpm	4300 rpm
Injector opening pressure (colour code)	130 bars (mauve)	155 bars (silver)

Not fitted to UK models

Injection pump (Lucas, in BX models from early 1993)
Type	161-A XUD7/L 052 R8444 B030A	A8A XUD7TE/L 056 R8443 B941A
Static timing	"X" dimension marked on pump	"X" dimension marked on pump
Dynamic timing	14° ± 1°	-
Anti-stall speed (with 3.0 mm diameter pin and 3.0 mm shim)	800 to 1000 rpm	800 to 1000 rpm
Maximum engine speed (loaded)	4600 rpm	4300 rpm
Injector opening pressure (colour code)	118 ± 5 bars	143 ± 5 bars

Injectors
Type	Pintle
Opening pressure:	
Roto-diesel	115 ± 5 bar
Bosch	130 ± 5 bar

Heater plug
Type	Champion CH 68

Turbocharger

Make	KKK or Garrett
Type:	
KKK	K14
Garrett	T2
Boost pressure	0.8 to 0.9 bars at full-load

Torque wrench settings

	Nm	lbf ft
Cylinder head blanking plug	30	22
Heater plug	22	16
Injection pump	18	13
Injection pump (Bosch) blanking plug	20	15
Injection pump sprocket nut	50	37
Injector:		
Bosch	90	66
Roto-diesel	130	96
Injector pipe union nuts	20	15
Turbocharger mounting bolts	45	33
Turbocharger oil feed pipe unions	20	15

1 Description - general

⚠️ **Warning: It is necessary to take certain precautions when working on the fuel system components, particularly the fuel injectors. Before carrying out any operations on the fuel system, refer to the precautions given in 'Safety first!' at the beginning of this manual, and to any additional warning notes at the start of the relevant Sections.**

The fuel system consists of a rear-mounted fuel tank, a fuel filter, a fuel injection pump, injectors and associated components. The exhaust system is similar to that used on petrol-engined vehicles.

Fuel is drawn from the tank by a vane-type transfer pump incorporated in the delivery head of the injection pump. Before reaching the pump the fuel passes through a fuel filter where foreign matter and water are removed. The injection pump is driven at half crankshaft speed by the timing belt. The high pressure required to inject the fuel into the compressed air in the swirl chambers is achieved by two opposed pistons forced together by rollers running on a cam ring. The fuel passes through a central rotor with a single outlet drilling which aligns with ports leading to the injector pipes and injectors. Fuel metering is controlled by a centrifugal governor that reacts to accelerator pedal position and engine speed. The governor is linked to the metering valve that moves the rotor sleeve to increase or decrease the amount of fuel transferred to the high pressure chamber. Injection timing is varied by turning the cam ring to suit the prevailing engine speed **(see illustration)**.

There are four precision-made injectors that inject a homogeneous spray of fuel into the swirl chambers located in the cylinder head.

The injectors are calibrated to open and close at critical pressures to provide efficient and even combustion. The injector needle is lubricated by fuel that accumulates in the spring chamber and is channelled to the injection pump return hose by leak-off pipes **(see illustration)**.

Preheater or "glow" plugs are fitted to each swirl chamber to facilitate cold starting. Additionally, a thermostatic sensor in the cooling system operates a fast idle lever to increase the idling speed and supply additional fuel when the engine is cold.

A stop solenoid cuts the fuel supply to the injection pump rotor when the ignition is switched off, and there is also a hand-operated stop lever for use in an emergency **(see illustration)**.

Servicing of the injection pump and injectors is very limited for the home mechanic, and any dismantling other than that described in this Chapter must be entrusted to a Citroën dealer or fuel injection specialist.

In 1987 the Bosch injection pump was modified to increase the length of the pump shaft front bearing. At the same time, the pump sprocket, timing belt tensioner roller and timing belt covers were modified. Old and new components are not interchangeable. Maintenance and adjustment procedures are unchanged.

Following the introduction of new EEC emission standards, all engines fitted to BX models from early 1993 are equipped with modified injection pumps. Details of the various components are as shown **(see illustration)**, and refer to the Specifications for data on the new injection pump.

On automatic transmission models, the injection pump incorporates an ALFB system that automatically adjusts the advance of injection according to the load on the engine. The advance is controlled by a solenoid valve located on the injection pump, and the solenoid valve is activated by a thermostatic switch located on the thermostat housing

(see illustration).

A turbocharger is fitted to the XUD 7TE engine. It increases engine efficiency by raising the pressure in the inlet manifold above atmospheric pressure. Instead of the air simply being sucked into the cylinders, it is forced in.

Energy for the operation of the turbocharger comes from the exhaust gas. The gas flows through a specially shaped housing (the turbine housing) and in so doing, spins the turbine wheel. The turbine wheel is attached to a shaft, at the end of which is another vaned wheel known as the compressor wheel. The compressor wheel spins in its own housing, and compresses the inducted air on the way to the inlet manifold **(see illustration)**.

Between the turbocharger and the inlet manifold the compressed air passes through an intercooler. This is an air-to-air heat exchanger, mounted over the engine and supplied with air ducted through the bonnet insulation. The purpose of the intercooler is to remove from the inducted air some of the heat it gained in being compressed. Removal of this heat further increases engine efficiency.

Boost pressure (the pressure in the inlet manifold) is limited by a wastegate, which diverts the exhaust gas away from the turbine wheel in response to a pressure-sensitive actuator. A pressure-operated switch operates a dashboard warning light in the event of excessive boost pressure developing.

The turbo shaft is pressure-lubricated by an oil feed pipe from the main oil gallery. The shaft "floats" on a cushion of oil. A drain pipe returns the oil to the sump.

Before starting any work involving the turbo, read the precautions in the following section, first.

4

1.2 Cutaway view of the Roto-diesel injection pump

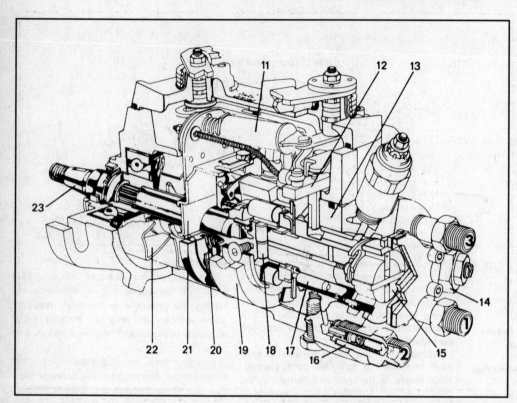

11 *MIN-MAX speed regulator*
12 *Fuel metering valve*
13 *Hydraulic head*
14 *Transfer pressure adjustment*
15 *Transfer pump*
16 *High pressure outlet and recirculation valve*
17 *Overload ram*
18 *Piston*
19 *Cam ring*
20 *Overleaf springs*
21 *Control lever*
22 *Centrifugal governor*
23 *Driveshaft*

1.3 Cross-section of the injectors

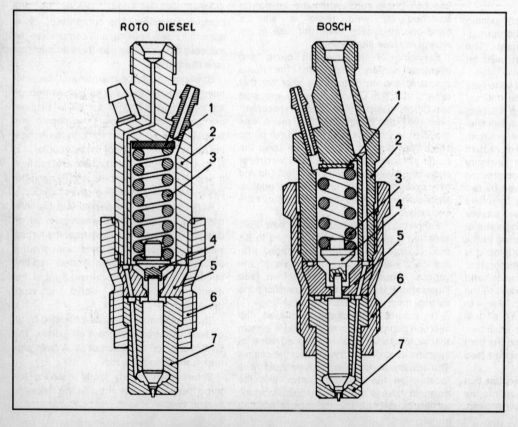

1 *Adjustment shim*
2 *Upper body*
3 *Spring*
4 *Pushrod*
5 *Spacer*
6 *Nut*
7 *Lower body and needle*

1.5 Roto-diesel injection pump

1 Manual stop lever
2 Fuel return to tank
3 Engine maximum speed
   adjustment screw
4 Stop solenoid
5 Fuel inlet
6 Timing inspection plug
7 Accelerator lever
8 Anti-stalling adjustment screw
9 Fast idle lever
10 Idling adjustment screw

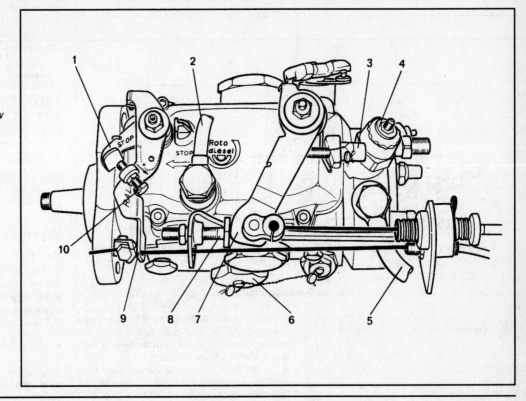

1.8 Bosch injection pump - BX models from early 1993

1 Cold engine low-load advance
   suppression device (ALFB)
   fitted to automatic transmission
   models
2 Stop lever
3 Load lever
4 Load lever position switch
5 Load lever position switch
   connector (2-way)
6 Electrical stop and ALFB
   connector (3-way)
7 Residual flow adjustment screw
8 Fast idle adjustment screw
9 Idle speed adjustment screw
10 Stop solenoid valve
11 Calibrated return banjo bolt
   (marked OUT)

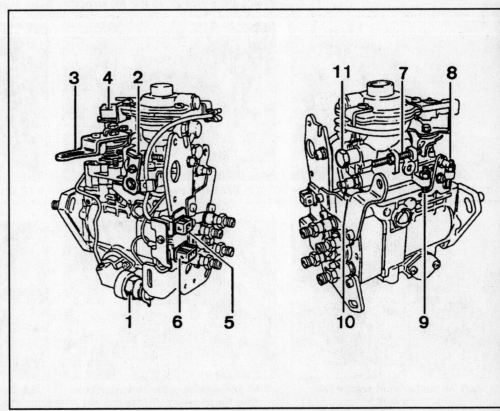

4

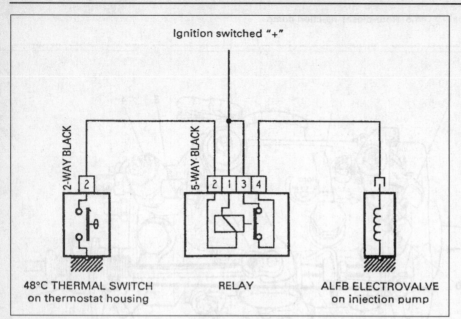

Ignition switched "+"

2-WAY BLACK

5-WAY BLACK

48°C THERMAL SWITCH
on thermostat housing

RELAY

ALFB ELECTROVALVE
on injection pump

1.9 ALFB wiring circuit

turbo spinning without lubrication.
5 Allow the engine to idle for several minutes before switching off after a high-speed run.
6 Observe the recommended intervals for oil and filter changing, and use a reputable oil of the specified quality.

  Neglect of oil changing, or use of inferior oil, can cause carbon formation on the turbo shaft and subsequent failure.

3 Air cleaner and element (non-Turbo models) - removal and refitting

Visa models

Removal

1 Unscrew and remove the through-bolt from the top of the air cleaner.
2 Release the spring clips and lift off the cover **(see illustration)**.
3 Remove the element and wipe clean the inside surfaces of the main body and cover.
4 Loosen the clips and disconnect the inlet ducting. Leave the bracket for the rear duct attached to the duct, but unbolt the bracket from the inlet manifold. Disconnect the ventilation hose from the oil separator **(see illustrations)**.
5 Unscrew the nut from the base of the main body then slide the body rearwards from the

2 Turbocharger - precautions

1 The turbocharger operates at extremely high speeds and temperatures. Certain precautions must be observed, to avoid premature failure of the turbo or injury to the operator.

2 Do not operate the turbo with any parts exposed. Foreign objects falling onto the rotating vanes could cause excessive damage and (if ejected) personal injury.
3 Do not race the engine immediately after start-up, especially if it is cold. Give the oil a few seconds to circulate.
4 Always allow the engine to return to idle speed before switching it off - do not blip the throttle and switch off, as this will leave the

1.11 View of the compressor wheel end of the turbocharger (KKK type)

3.2 Air cleaner element (Visa models)

3.4A Disconnecting the air duct from the inlet manifold

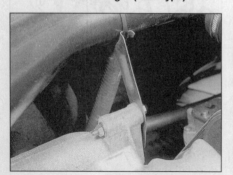

3.4B Air duct support bracket (Visa models)

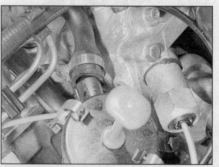

3.4C Disconnecting the ventilation hose from the oil separator (Visa models)

3.5 Removing the air cleaner from the mounting rubbers (Visa models)

3.7A Unscrew the wing nut . . .

3.7B . . . and lift off the air cleaner cover (BX models)

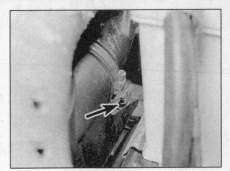

3.11A Air cleaner mounting nut - arrowed (BX models)

3.11B Air cleaner mounting rubbers - arrowed (BX models)

4.1 Unclipping the air intake tube

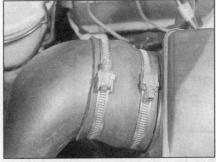

4.2 Two hose clips securing the stub hose

two mounting rubbers (see illustration).

Refitting

6 Refitting is a reversal of removal.

BX models

Removal

7 Unscrew the wing nut and lift the cover from the air cleaner (see illustrations).
8 Move the inlet duct to one side and remove the element. Wipe clean the inside surfaces of the main body and cover.
9 Check the sealing ring for the cover and renew it if necessary.
10 Loosen the clips and disconnect the inlet ducting.
11 Unscrew the nut securing the base of the main body to the bracket below the battery, then slide the body rearwards from the mounting rubbers in the bracket over the

radiator (see illustrations).

Refitting

12 Refitting is a reversal of removal.

4 Air cleaner and element (Turbo models) - removal and refitting

Removal

1 Unclip the rigid air inlet tube on the right-hand side of the engine bay (see illustration).
2 At the air cleaner end of the inlet tube, remove the stub hose that joins the tube to the air cleaner (see illustration).
3 Disconnect the crankcase ventilation hose (see illustration).
4 Release the spring clips which secure the

air cleaner body to its mounting.
5 Release the spring clips which secure the air cleaner lid.
6 Remove the air cleaner lid (see illustration). It is likely to be a tight fit, but by manipulating the lid and the air cleaner body at the same time, the lid can be removed.
7 Remove the element and clean out the housing. The housing can be removed by pulling it off its rubber mountings.

Refitting

8 Fit the new element. It can only be fitted one way up (see illustration).
9 Refit and secure the other disturbed components.

4

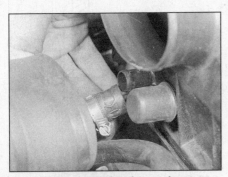

4.3 Disconnecting the crankcase ventilation hose

4.6 Removing the air cleaner lid

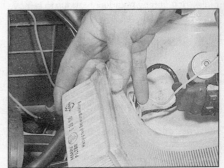

4.8 Fitting the air cleaner element

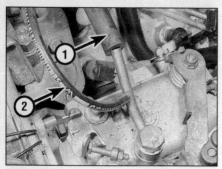

5.9 Main fuel return pipe (1) and injector leak off return pipe (2) (Roto-diesel)

5.10 Disconnecting the stop solenoid wire (Roto-diesel)

5.11 Injector pipe union nuts on the Roto-diesel injection pump

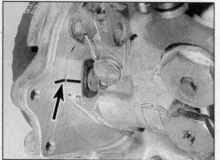
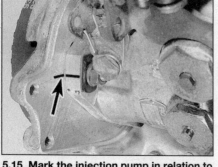

5.15 Mark the injection pump in relation to the mounting bracket (arrowed)

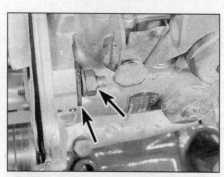

5.16A Injection pump mounting nut and plate (arrowed)

5.16B Injection pump mounting bolt (arrowed)

5 Injection pump (non-Turbo models) - removal and refitting

Removal

1 Disconnect the battery negative lead.
2 Cover the alternator with a plastic bag as a precaution against spillage of diesel fuel.
3 On Visa models apply the handbrake. On BX models chock the rear wheels and release the handbrake.
4 On manual transmission models, jack up the front right-hand corner of the vehicle until the wheel is just clear of the ground. Support the vehicle on an axle stand and engage 4th or 5th gear. This will enable the engine to be turned easily by turning the right-hand wheel. On automatic models the engine must be turned by using a spanner on the crankshaft pulley bolt. It may be advantageous to remove the heater plugs.
5 Pull up the special clip, release the spring clips, and withdraw the two timing cover sections.
6 Open the accelerator lever on the injection pump and disconnect the cable by passing it through the special slot. Disconnect the cable adjustment ferrule from the bracket.
7 Note the position of the end stop on the fast idle cable then loosen the screw and disconnect the inner cable. Unscrew the adjustment locknut and remove the cable and ferrule from the bracket.
8 Loosen the clip and disconnect the fuel

supply hose.
9 Disconnect the main fuel return pipe and the injector leak off return pipe from the union tube **(see illustration)**.
10 Disconnect the wire from the stop solenoid **(see illustration)**.
11 Unscrew the union nuts securing the injector pipes to the injection pump **(see illustration)**.
12 On BX models remove the clip securing the hydraulic pipes to the engine front plate.
13 Turn the engine by means of the front right-hand wheel or crankshaft pulley bolt until the two bolt holes in the injection pump sprocket are aligned with the corresponding holes in the engine front plate.
14 Insert two M8 bolts through the holes and hand tighten them. The bolts must retain the sprocket while the injection pump is removed thereby making it unnecessary to remove the timing belt.

5.18 Removing the injection pump from its mounting bracket

15 Mark the injection pump in relation to the mounting bracket using a scriber or felt tip pen **(see illustration)**. This will ensure the correct timing when refitting. If a new pump is being fitted transfer the mark from the old pump to give an approximate setting.
16 Unscrew the three mounting nuts and remove the plates. Unscrew and remove the rear mounting bolt and support the injection pump on a block of wood **(see illustrations)**.
17 Unscrew the sprocket nut until the taper is released from the sprocket. The nut acts as a puller, together with the plate bolted to the sprocket. From late 1992, the fuel injection pump sprocket bolt no longer incorporates a puller. To free the sprocket from the taper on the injection pump shaft, a flange must be

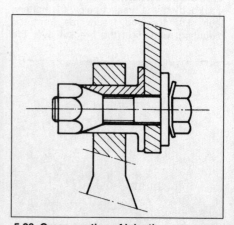

5.26 Cross-section of injection pump rear mounting

bolted to the sprocket before unscrewing the bolt. Ideally, a flange should be removed from an old sprocket and used to remove the new-type sprocket. Alternatively, a flange can be made up from steel plate.

18 Continue to unscrew the sprocket nut and withdraw the injection pump from the mounting bracket **(see illustration)**. Recover the Woodruff key from the shaft groove if it is loose.

Refitting

19 Begin refitting the injection pump by fitting the Woodruff key to the shaft groove (if removed).

20 Unbolt the puller plate from the injection pump sprocket.

21 Insert the injection pump from behind the sprocket, making sure that the shaft key enters the groove in the sprocket. Screw on the nut and hand tighten it.

22 Fit the mounting nuts, together with their plates, and hand tighten the nuts.

23 Tighten the sprocket nut to the specified torque then refit the puller plate and tighten the bolts.

24 Unscrew and remove the two bolts from the injection pump sprocket.

25 If the original injection pump is being refitted, align the scribed marks and tighten the mounting nuts. If fitting a new pump, the timing must be set as described in Sections 8 or 9, as applicable.

26 Refit the rear mounting bolt and special nut, tightening the nut slowly to allow the bush to align itself as shown **(see illustration)**.

27 On BX models refit the clip securing the hydraulic pipes.

28 Refit the injector pipes to the injection pump and tighten the union nuts.

29 Reconnect the wire to the stop solenoid.

30 Refit the fuel supply and return pipes.

31 Refit the fast idle cable and accelerator cable, and adjust them, referring to Sections 10 and 18.

32 Refit the two timing cover sections and secure with the spring clips.

33 Lower the vehicle to the ground and apply the handbrake (BX models).

34 Remove the plastic bag from the alternator and reconnect the battery negative lead.

35 Prime the fuel circuit by first switching on the ignition to energise the stop solenoid, then actuating the pump on the fuel filter until resistance is felt. On early models fitted with a Roto-diesel filter the pump plunger must first be unscrewed then retightened after priming.

36 Turn the ignition key to position M and wait for the preheating warning light to go out. Start the engine and adjust the idling speed, referring to Chapter 1.

6 Injection pump (Turbo models) - general, removal and refitting

General

1 The injection pump fitted to Turbo models is similar to that fitted to normally-aspirated models, but incorporates the following additional features.

Lucas CAV/Roto-diesel

2 An over-fuelling device varies the quantity of fuel injected in response to turbo boost pressure. Pressure is sensed through a hose connected to the inlet manifold **(see illustration)**.

3 An electromagnetic timing system advances injection timing when the engine is cold. The system is switched off by a contact activated by movement of the fast idle control lever **(see illustrations)**.

4 These additional devices cannot be checked or adjusted by the home mechanic.

Bosch

5 A richness limiter replaces the over-fuelling device just described, and a cold start accelerator replaces the electromagnetic timing system **(see illustrations)**.

6 The cold start accelerator receives its own coolant feed. Because it is a mechanical device, it must be disconnected when timing the pump.

Removal

7 Proceed as in Section 5, but additionally disconnect the boost pressure hose from the over-fuelling device or richness limiter.

8 On the Bosch pump, the coolant hoses must be disconnected from the cold start accelerator. If the cooling system is first depressurised by removing the expansion tank cap (system cold), and preparations made to plug the disconnected hoses, coolant loss can be kept to a minimum.

Refitting

9 Refit by reversing the removal operations. Check the pump timing if necessary as described in Sections 8 or 9, as applicable. Top-up the coolant level if necessary.

6.2 The overfuelling device - Lucas CAV/Rotor-diesel pump

6.3A Electromagnetic timing device (arrowed) - Lucas CAV/Roto-diesel pump

6.3B Electromagnetic timing contact on the fast idle lever

6.5A Richness limiter - Bosch pump

6.5B Cold start accelerator - Bosch pump

4

7 Injection pump dynamic timing (all models) - general

Dynamic timing is given for certain models in the Specifications. However, the specialist equipment necessary to check the timing dynamically is quite expensive, and will not normally be available to the home mechanic. Also, the setting-up procedure varies according to the type of equipment used, so it is important to refer to the equipment maker's instructions when connecting the equipment to the engine. Note that most dynamic checking testers are only accurate to approximately ±2°.

Dynamic timing should only be used within the limitations of the checking equipment. If the timing requires adjustment, then it must only be adjusted using the static timing method.

8 Injection pump static timing (Roto-diesel) - checking

Caution: The maximum engine speed and transfer pressure settings, together with timing access plugs, are sealed by the manufacturers at the factory using locking wire and lead seals. Do not disturb the wire if the vehicle is still within the warranty period otherwise the warranty will be invalidated. Also do not attempt the timing procedure unless accurate instrumentation is available.

Pre mid-1987 models

Checking

1 Disconnect the battery negative lead.
2 Cover the alternator with a plastic bag as a precaution against spillage of diesel fuel.
3 On Visa models apply the handbrake. On BX models chock the rear wheels and release the handbrake.
4 On manual transmission models jack up the front right-hand corner of the vehicle until the wheel is just clear of the ground. Support the vehicle on an axle stand and engage 4th or 5th gear. This will enable the engine to be

8.12 Roto-diesel injection pump with the timing plug removed

8.7 Removing the blanking plug from No 4 cylinder

turned easily by turning the right-hand wheel. On automatic transmission models use an open-ended spanner on the crankshaft pulley bolt.
5 Disconnect the wire and unscrew the heater plug from cylinder No 4 (timing belt end). Note that the engine is timed with No 4 piston at TDC compression (ie No 1 piston at TDC with valves "rocking").
6 Two dial test indicators are now necessary for checking the positions of the No 4 piston and the injection pump. Magnetic type stands will be found helpful or alternatively brackets may be made for fitting to appropriate positions on the engine.
7 Unscrew and remove the blanking plug from the cylinder head next to No 4 injector (see illustration).
8 Turn the engine forwards until pressure is felt in No 4 cylinder indicating that No 4 piston is beginning its compression stroke.
9 Position the dial test indicator over the blanking hole and fit the probe (see illustration).
10 Turn the engine forwards until the maximum lift of piston No 4 is registered on the dial test indicator. Turn the engine slightly back and forth to determine the exact point of maximum lift then zero the indicator.
11 On BX models remove the clip securing the hydraulic pipes to the engine front plate and move the pipes to one side.
12 Loosen the lower of the two large side plugs on the side of the injection pump. Position a small container beneath the plug then remove the plug and catch the escaping fuel in the container (see illustration).

8.13A Timing the Roto-diesel injection pump with a dial test indicator

8.9 Setting No 4 piston timing position with a dial test indicator

13 Inside the plug aperture there is a probe guide. Insert the probe and connect it to the dial test indicator directly over the hole (see illustration). Note that the end of the probe must be pointed in order to fully engage the groove in the pump rotor (see illustration).
14 Turn the engine backwards approximately ⅛th of a turn or until the No 4 piston has moved 4.0 mm down the cylinder. Now turn the engine slowly forwards while watching the dial test indicator on the injection pump. After the probe has reached the bottom of the timing groove then risen by 0.01 to 0.02 mm, check that the upper dial test indicator reads 2.26 ± 0.05 mm before TDC. If the timing is incorrect continue as follows.
15 Check the zero setting of the upper dial test indicator by repeating the procedure given in paragraph 10.
16 Turn the engine backwards approximately ⅛th of a turn or until No 4 piston has moved 4.0 mm down the cylinder. Now turn the engine slowly forwards until No 4 piston is 2.26 ± 0.05 mm before TDC.
17 Unscrew the union nuts and disconnect the injector pipes from the injection pump. Loosen the injection pump mounting nuts and bolt.
18 Turn the pump body until the probe is at the bottom of the timing groove in the rotor. Zero the dial test indicator. Now turn the pump clockwise (from the injector pipe end) until the probe has risen by 0.01 to 0.02 mm.
19 Tighten the mounting nuts and bolts making sure that there is no movement on the dial test indicator.
20 Recheck the timing as described in

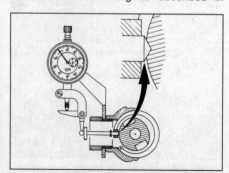

8.13B Checking the timing on the Roto-diesel fuel injection pump

8.26 Plastic disc on later Lucas CAV/Roto-diesel pump

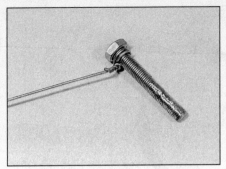

8.27 Home-made TDC setting tool

8.31 Removing the inspection plug from the pump

paragraph 14.

21 Remove the dial test indicators and refit the plugs. Reconnect the injector pipes and tighten the union nuts.

22 Refit the hydraulic pipe clip on BX models.

23 Refit the heater plug and connect the wire.

24 Lower the car to the ground and reconnect the battery negative lead. Remove the plastic bag from the alternator.

25 Prime the fuel system as described in Section 23.

From mid-1987

Checking

26 From mid-1987, a modified pump is fitted. The pump can be recognised by the presence of a white or blue plastic disc on its front face. A timing value is engraved on the disc **(see illustration)**.

27 The pump timing is now carried out at TDC. Only one dial test indicator is needed, but it will be necessary to make up a bent rod (8.0 mm diameter) or similar tool to enter the TDC setting hole. The tool made up in the workshop consisted of an M8 bolt with the threads filed away, attached to a piece of welding rod **(see illustration)**. Alternatively, the starter motor can be removed, and a twist drill or straight rod can be used (refer to Chapter 2, Section 23).

28 Prepare the engine as described in paragraphs 1 to 4.

29 Turn the engine to bring No 4 cylinder (timing belt end) to TDC on compression. To establish which cylinder is on compression, either remove No 4 cylinder heater plug and feel for pressure, or remove the valve cover and observe when No 1 cylinder valves are "rocking" (inlet opening and exhaust closing).

30 Insert the TDC setting tool into the hole, and turn the engine back and forth slightly until the tool enters the hole in the flywheel. Leave the tool in position.

31 Remove the inspection plug from the top of the pump **(see illustration)**. Position a dial test indicator so that it can read the movement of a probe inserted into the hole. If a magnetic stand is to be used, the absence of ferrous metal in the vicinity poses a problem; a piece of steel plate can be bolted to the engine mounting or valve cover to carry the stand.

32 Insert a probe into the inspection hole so that the tip of the probe rests on the rotor timing piece. Position the dial test indicator so that it reads the movement of the probe.

33 Remove the TDC setting tool. Turn the engine approximately a quarter-turn backwards. Zero the dial test indicator.

34 Turn the engine forwards slowly until the TDC setting tool can be re-inserted. Read the dial test indicator; the reading should correspond to the value engraved on the pump disc (± 0.04 mm).

35 If the reading is not as specified, continue as follows.

36 Disconnect the injector pipes from the pump. Slacken the pump mounting nuts and bolts, and swing the pump away from the engine. Zero the dial test indicator.

37 With the engine still at TDC, slowly swing the pump back towards the engine until the dial test indicator displays the value engraved on the pump disc. In this position, tighten the pump mountings, then remove the TDC setting tool and recheck the timing as just described.

38 When the timing is correct, reconnect the injector pipes, remove the dial test indicator and TDC setting tool and refit the inspection plug.

39 Refit any other disturbed components, remove the plastic bag from the alternator, and lower the vehicle to the ground.

9 Injection pump static timing (Bosch) - checking

Caution: Some of the injection pump settings and access plugs may be sealed by the manufacturers at the factory using locking wire and lead seals. Do not disturb the wire if the vehicle is still within the warranty period otherwise the warranty will be invalidated. Also do not attempt the timing procedure unless accurate instrumentation is available.

Pre October 1987 models

1 Disconnect the battery negative lead.

2 Cover the alternator with a plastic bag as a precaution against spillage of diesel fuel.

3 On Visa models apply the handbrake. On BX models chock the rear wheels and release the handbrake.

4 On manual transmission models jack up the front right-hand corner of the vehicle until the wheel is just clear of the ground. Support the vehicle on an axle stand and engage 4th or 5th gear. This will enable the engine to be turned easily by turning the right-hand wheel. On automatic transmission models use an open ended spanner on the crankshaft pulley bolt.

5 Disconnect the wire and unscrew the heater plug from cylinder No 4 (timing belt end). Note that the engine is timed with No 4 piston at TDC compression (ie No 1 piston at TDC with valves "rocking").

6 Two dial test indicators are now necessary for checking the positions of the No 4 piston and the injection pump. Magnetic type stands will be found helpful or alternatively brackets may be made for fitting to appropriate positions on the engine.

7 Unscrew and remove the blanking plug from the cylinder head next to No 4 injector.

8 Turn the engine forwards until pressure is felt in No 4 cylinder, indicating that No 4 piston is beginning its compression stroke.

9 Position the dial test indicator over the blanking hole and fit the probe.

10 Turn the engine forwards until the maximum lift of piston No 4 is registered on the dial test indicator. Turn the engine slightly to and fro to determine the exact point of maximum lift then zero the indicator.

11 Unscrew the union nuts and disconnect the injector pipes for cylinders 1 and 2 from the injection pump.

12 Unscrew the blanking plug from the end of the injection pump between the injector pipe connections. Be prepared for the loss of some fuel.

13 Insert the probe and connect it to the dial test indicator positioned directly over the hole. The fixture used by Citroën technicians is shown **(see illustration)**.

14 Turn the engine backwards approximately ⅛th of a turn or until the No 4 piston has moved 4.0 mm down the cylinder.

15 Zero the dial test indicator on the injection pump.

16 Turn the engine slowly forwards until the dial test indicator on the injection pump reads

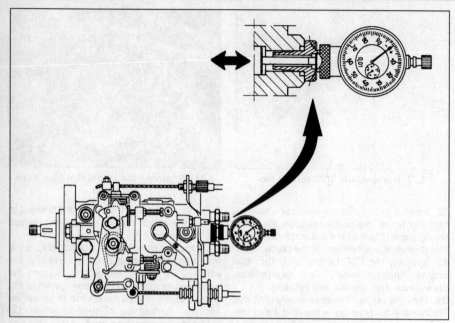

9.13 Checking the timing on the Bosch fuel injection pump

0.30 mm, then check that the upper dial test indicator reads 0.72 ± 0.03 mm before TDC for Visa models, or 0.80 ± 0.03 mm before TDC for BX17 models or 0.57 ± 0.03 mm before TDC for BX19 models. If the timing is incorrect continue as follows.

17 Check the zero setting of the upper dial test indicator by repeating the procedure given in paragraph 10.

18 Turn the engine backwards approximately ⅛th of a turn or until the No 4 piston had moved 4.0 mm down the cylinder. Now turn the engine slowly forwards until the upper dial test indicator reads 0.72 ± 0.03 mm before TDC for Visa models, or 0.80 ± 0.03 mm before TDC for BX17 models, or 0.57 ± 0.03 mm before TDC for BX19 models.

19 Unscrew the union nuts and disconnect the remaining injector pipes from the injection pump. Loosen the injection pump mounting nuts and bolt.

20 Turn the pump body anti-clockwise (from the injector pipe end) and check that the dial test indicator is zeroed. Now turn the pump body slowly clockwise until the dial test indicator reads 0.30 mm.

21 Tighten the mounting nuts and bolts, making sure that there is no movement on the dial test indicator.

22 Recheck the timing as described in paragraphs 14 to 16.

23 Remove the dial test indicators and refit the plugs. Reconnect the injector pipes and tighten the union nuts.

24 Refit the heater plug and connect the wire.

25 Lower the car to the ground and reconnect the battery negative lead. Remove the plastic bag from the alternator.

26 Prime the fuel system as described in Section 23.

October 1987-on models

27 Later Bosch pumps are timed at TDC. Refer to the Specifications for pump identification and timing values. Only one dial test indicator is needed, but it will be necessary to make up a TDC setting tool as just described for the Lucas CAV/Roto-diesel pump.

28 Prepare the engine as described in paragraphs 1 to 4. On Turbo models, disconnect the cold start accelerator.

29 Bring the engine to TDC, No 4 cylinder on compression, and insert the TDC setting tool (refer to Section 8, paragraphs 29 and 30).

30 Fit a dial test indicator to the rear of the pump as described in paragraphs 11 to 13.

31 Remove the TDC setting tool. Turn the engine approximately a quarter-turn backwards. Zero the dial test indicator.

32 Turn the engine forwards slowly until the TDC setting tool can be re-inserted. Read the dial test indicator; the value should correspond to that given in the Specifications.

33 If the reading is not as specified, continue as follows.

34 Disconnect the remaining injector pipes from the pump. Slacken the pump mounting nuts and bolts, and swing the pump away from the engine. Zero the dial test indicator.

35 With the engine still at TDC, slowly swing the pump back towards the engine until the dial test indicator displays the desired value. In this position, tighten the pump mountings, then remove the TDC setting tool and recheck the timing as just described.

36 When the timing is correct, remove the dial test indicator and TDC setting tool. Reconnect the injector pipes.

37 Refit any other disturbed components, remove the plastic bag from the alternator, and lower the vehicle to the ground.

---

10 Fast idle control - removal, refitting and adjustment

Removal

1 Loosen the clamp screw or nut and remove the end fitting from the inner cable **(see illustration)**.

2 Unscrew the locknut and remove the adjustment ferrule and outer cable from the bracket on the injection pump **(see illustration)**.

3 Drain the cooling system as described in Chapter 1.

4 Unscrew the thermostatic sensor from the thermostat housing cover and recover the washer.

Refitting

5 Fit the new thermostatic sensor and washer.

6 Insert the cable and ferrule in the bracket and screw on the locknut finger tight.

7 Fit the end fitting on the inner cable.

Adjustment

8 With the engine cold, push the fast idle lever fully towards the flywheel end of the engine then tighten the clamp screw or nut with the end fitting touching the lever.

9 Adjust the ferrule to ensure that the fast idle lever is touching its stop then tighten the locknuts.

10 Measure the exposed length of the inner cable between the ferrule and end fitting.

10.1 Fast idle inner cable and end fitting (arrowed) on the Bosch injection pump

10.2 Fast idle cable adjustment ferrule on the Roto-diesel injection pump

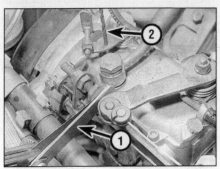

11.3 Anti-stall adjustment on the Roto-diesel injection pump showing feeler blades (1) and twist drill (2)

13.1 Marking the accelerator inner cable 11.0 mm from the end of the outer cable

13.3 Load lever position switch

11 Refill the cooling system as described in Chapter 1, and run the engine to normal operating temperature.
12 With the engine hot, check that the length of the inner cable has increased by at least 6.0 mm indicating that the thermostatic sensor is functioning correctly.
13 Switch off the engine.

11 Injection pump anti-stall (Roto-diesel) - adjustment

Note: This adjustment requires the use of a tachometer - refer to Chapter 1, Section 19, for alternative methods.
1 Run the engine to normal operating temperature then switch it off.
2 Insert a 3.0 mm shim or feeler blade between the accelerator lever and the anti-stall adjustment screw.
3 Turn the stop lever clockwise until it is clear of the hole in the fast idle lever then insert a 3.0 mm dowel rod or twist drill **(see illustration)**.
4 Start the engine and allow it to idle. The engine speed should be 900 ± 100 rpm.
5 If adjustment is necessary loosen the locknut, turn the anti-stall adjustment screw as required, then tighten the locknut.
6 Remove the feeler blade and twist drill and adjust the idling speed as described in Chapter 1.
7 Turn the accelerator lever to increase the engine speed to 3000 rpm then quickly release the lever. If the deceleration is too fast and the engine stalls turn the anti-stall adjustment screw ¼ turn anti-clockwise (viewed from flywheel end of engine). If the deceleration is too slow, resulting in poor engine braking, turn the screw ¼ turn clockwise.
8 Retighten the locknut after making an adjustment then recheck the idling speed as described in Chapter 1.
9 With the engine idling check the operation of the manual stop control by turning the stop lever clockwise. The engine must stop instantly.
10 Switch off the ignition switch.

12 Injection pump anti-stall (Bosch) - adjustment

Note: This adjustment requires the use of a tachometer - refer to Chapter 1, Section 19, for alternative methods.
1 Run the engine to normal operating temperature. Note the exact idling speed then switch off the engine.
2 Insert a 1.0 mm shim or feeler blade between the accelerator lever and the anti-stall adjustment screw.
3 Start the engine and allow it to idle. The engine speed should exceed the normal idling speed by 50 rpm.
4 If adjustment is necessary loosen the locknut and turn the anti-stall adjustment screw as required. Retighten the locknut.
5 Remove the feeler blade and allow the engine to idle.
6 Move the fast idle lever fully towards the flywheel end of the engine and check that the engine speed increases to 950 ± 50 rpm. If necessary loosen the locknut and turn the stop adjusting screw as required, then retighten the locknut.
7 With the engine idling, check the operation of the manual stop control by turning the stop lever. The engine must stop instantly.
8 Switch off the ignition switch.

13 Injection pump load lever position switch (later Bosch models) - adjustment

1 Mark the accelerator inner cable 11.0 mm from the end of the outer cable **(see illustration)**.
2 Move the load lever until the mark on the inner cable coincides with the end of the outer cable, and hold the lever in this position.
3 Loosen the switch mounting screws, then turn the switch until the internal contacts click open **(see illustration)**.
4 Tighten the mounting screws with the switch in this position, then release the lever.
5 Move the lever again, and check that the switch contacts operate when the mark on the

inner cable reaches the end of the outer cable.

14 Maximum engine speed - checking and adjustment

Caution: On Roto-diesel injection pumps the maximum speed setting is sealed by the manufacturers at the factory using locking wire and a lead seal. Do not disturb the wire if the vehicle is still within the warranty period otherwise the warranty will be invalidated. This adjustment requires the use of a tachometer - refer to Chapter 1, Section 19, for alternative methods.

Checking
1 Run the engine to normal operating temperature.
2 Have an assistant fully depress the accelerator pedal and check that the maximum engine speed is as given in the Specifications. Do not keep the engine at maximum speed for more than two or three seconds.

Adjustment
3 If adjustment is necessary stop the engine then loosen the locknut, turn the maximum engine speed adjustment screw as necessary, and retighten the locknut **(see illustration)**.
4 Repeat the procedure in paragraph 2 to check the adjustment.
5 Switch off the ignition switch.

14.3 Maximum engine speed adjustment screw on the Roto-diesel injection pump

15.5 Disconnecting the injector pipes

15.6A Removing an injector

15.6B An injector

15 Fuel injectors - removal and refitting

> ⚠️ **Warning: Exercise extreme caution when working on the fuel injectors. Never expose the hands or any part of the body to injector spray, as the high working pressure can cause the fuel to penetrate the skin, with possibly fatal results. You are strongly advised to have any work that involves testing the injectors under pressure, carried out by a dealer or fuel injection specialist.**

Removal

1 On BX models remove the air duct between the air cleaner and inlet manifold.

2 Clean around the injectors and injector pipe union nuts.

3 Pull the leak off pipes from the injectors **(see illustration)**.

4 Loosen the injector pipe union nuts at the injection pump.

5 Unscrew the union nuts and disconnect the pipes from the injectors **(see illustration)**. If required the injector pipes may be completely removed.

6 Unscrew the injectors and remove them from the cylinder head **(see illustrations)**.

7 Recover the copper washers, fire-seal washers, and sleeves from the cylinder head **(see illustrations)**.

8 If an injector sleeve is tight in the cylinder head, it can be removed using the following procedure. First block the injector sleeve hole with grease, to prevent debris entering the combustion chamber.

9 Cut a thread in the sleeve using a tap, then screw in a stud or bolt, which should have a thread on its entire length.

10 Using a thick washer in contact with the cylinder head, tighten a nut onto the washer, and pull out the sleeve.

Refitting

11 The new injector sleeve may be inserted in the cylinder head by using an old injector as a drift. Do not fit the sealing washer or fire ring while using this method.

12 Obtain new copper washers and fire-seal washers.

13 Take care not to drop the injectors or allow the needles at their tips to become damaged. The injectors are precision-made to fine limits and must not be handled roughly, in particular do not mount them in a bench vice.

14 Begin refitting by inserting the sleeves

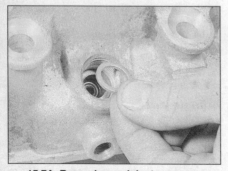

15.7A Removing an injector copper washer . . .

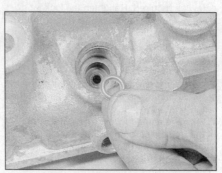

15.7B . . . fire-seal washer . . .

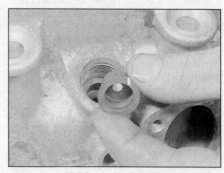

15.7C . . . and sleeve

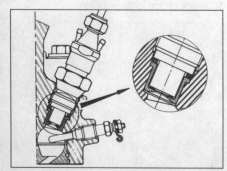

15.15A Cross-section of cylinder head showing location of injector and heater plug
Note fire-seal washer position in inset

15.15B Tightening an injector

15.17 A leak off pipe connected between two injectors

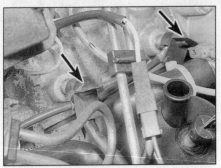

17.3 Plastic clips (arrowed) on heater plug terminals

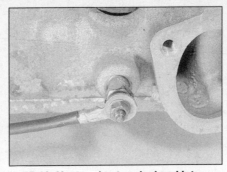

17.4A Heater plug terminal and inter-connecting wire

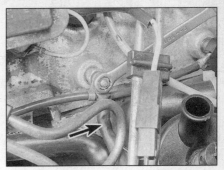

17.4B Removing the heater plug main supply cable (arrowed)

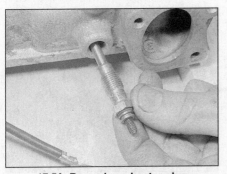

17.5A Removing a heater plug

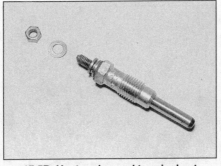

17.5B Heater plug and terminal nut

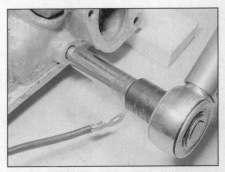

17.6 Tightening a heater plug

followed by the fire-seal washers (convex face uppermost), and copper washers.

15 Insert the injectors and tighten them to the specified torque **(see illustrations)**.

16 Refit the injector pipes and tighten the union nuts to the specified torque.

17 Reconnect the leak off pipes **(see illustration)**.

18 On BX models refit the air duct.

16 Preheater system - description and testing

Description

1 Each swirl chamber has a preheater plug (commonly called a glow plug) screwed into it. The plugs are electrically operated before, during and immediately after starting a cold engine. Preheating is not required on a hot engine.

2 On XUD 9 models, the glow plugs are operated for approximately 7 seconds before starting the engine. A post-heating system keeps the glow plugs operating for 3 minutes after the engine has been started, under the following conditions. The injection pump load lever must be less than 11.0 mm open - a lever position switch switches off the glow plugs when the lever is opened more than this amount. The engine temperature must be lower than 60°C - a thermo-switch located behind the fuel filter housing monitors the temperature. The thermo-switch is identified

by having a mauve plastic ring.

Testing

3 If the system malfunctions, testing is ultimately by substitution of known good units, but some preliminary checks may be made as follows.

4 Disconnect the main supply cable from the No 1 heater plug (counting from the flywheel) on Visa models, or No 2 plug on BX models.

5 Connect a voltmeter between the supply cable and earth making sure that the cable is kept clear of the engine and bodywork. Have an assistant switch on the preheater and check that there is a 12 volt supply for several seconds before the system cuts out. Typically there should be a 7 second supply at an ambient temperature of 20°C (68°F), but this will increase with colder temperatures and decrease with higher temperatures. If there is no supply, the relay or associated wiring is at fault. Switch off the ignition.

6 Connect an ammeter between the battery positive terminal and the heater plug inter-connecting wire. Check that the current draw after 20 seconds is 12 amps per working plug, i.e. 48 amps if all four plugs are working.

7 If one or more heater plugs appear to be not drawing the expected current disconnect the inter-connecting wire and check them individually or use an ohmmeter to check them for continuity and equal resistance.

8 Re-connect the main supply cable after completing the tests.

17 Heater plugs and relay - removal and refitting

Heater plugs

Removal

1 Check that the ignition switch is off.

2 On BX models remove the air duct between the air cleaner and inlet manifold.

3 Prise the plastic clips from the heater plugs **(see illustration)**.

4 Unscrew the nuts from the heater plug terminals. Remove the main supply cable from No 1 plug (counting from the flywheel) on Visa models, or No 2 plug on BX models, then remove the inter-connecting wire from all the plugs **(see illustrations)**.

5 Unscrew the heater plugs and remove them from the cylinder head **(see illustrations)**.

Refitting

6 Refitting is a reversal of removal but tighten the heater plugs to the specified torque **(see illustration)**.

Relay

Removal

7 The relay is located on the left-hand side of the engine compartment near the battery **(see illustrations)**.

8 First disconnect the battery negative lead. Unbolt the relay from the side panel and disconnect the wiring.

4

17.7A Heater plug control relay on Visa models . . .

17.7B . . . and BX models

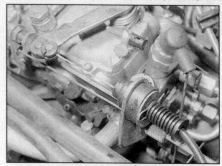

18.1A Accelerator cable on the Roto-diesel injection pump

18.1B Accelerator cable attachment on the Bosch injection pump

18.2 Accelerator cable adjustment ferrule on the Bosch injection pump

19.3 Disconnecting the wiring from the stop solenoid

Refitting

9 Refitting is a reversal of removal.

18 Accelerator cable - removal, refitting and adjustment

Removal

1 Open the accelerator lever on the injection pump and disconnect the inner cable by passing it through the special slot (see illustrations).
2 Disconnect the cable adjustment ferrule and outer cable from the bracket (see illustration).
3 Working inside the vehicle, remove the lower facia panel where necessary then release the inner cable end fitting from the top of the accelerator pedal.
4 Pull the spring shock absorber from the bulkhead and withdraw the accelerator cable from inside the engine compartment.

Refitting

5 Refitting is a reversal of removal, but adjust the cable as follows.

Adjustment

6 Have an assistant fully depress the accelerator pedal then check that the accelerator lever on the injection pump is touching the maximum speed adjustment screw. If not, pull the spring clip from the adjustment ferrule, reposition the ferrule and fit the spring clip in the groove next to the

metal washer. With the accelerator pedal fully released check that the accelerator lever is touching the anti-stall (deceleration) adjustment screw.

19 Stop solenoid - description, removal and refitting

Description

1 The stop solenoid is located on the end of

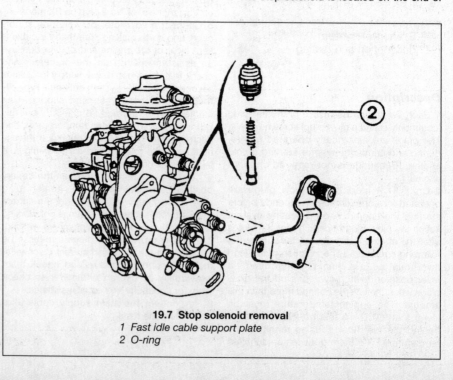

19.7 Stop solenoid removal
1 Fast idle cable support plate
2 O-ring

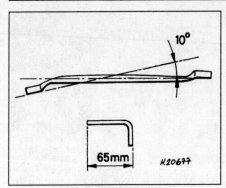

20.1 Tool modifications for turbocharger removal

the injection pump by the injector pipes. Its purpose is to cut the fuel supply when the ignition is switched off. If an open circuit occurs in the supply wiring it will be impossible to start the engine as the fuel will not reach the injectors.

Removal

2 Before removing the stop solenoid, clean the surrounding area, to prevent dust and dirt entering the fuel system.
3 With the ignition switched off unscrew the nut and disconnect the wire **(see illustration)**.
4 Unscrew and remove the stop solenoid and recover the washer.
5 After removing the solenoid, recover the plunger piston and spring from the injection pump.

Refitting

6 With the solenoid removed, operate the priming pump several times, to discharge any debris from the threads in the pump casing.
7 Refitting is a reversal of the removal procedure, but renew the O-ring before refitting the solenoid and tightening it **(see illustration)**.

20 Turbocharger - removal and refitting

Removal

1 Because the manifolds and turbocharger are on the back of the engine, access to the fastenings is difficult. The work will be made easier if two standard tools, a 6 mm Allen key and a 16 mm ring spanner, are modified as shown **(see illustration)**.
2 Disconnect the battery earth lead.
3 Raise and support the vehicle. Remove the exhaust system; recover the two dowels that locate the exhaust downpipe on the turbo outlet flange.
4 Prepare for some oil spillage. Disconnect the turbo oil feed and return pipes from the block. Undo the return pipe union and remove the return pipe completely. Also remove the feed pipe bracket.
5 Unbolt and remove the engine bottom mounting torque link. The engine will move forwards slightly when this is done.
6 Using the modified 16 mm spanner, remove the turbo mounting bolts that are accessible from below.
7 Lower the vehicle. Remove the intercooler and its hoses as described in Section 22.
8 Remove the radiator hose support bracket on the right-hand side of the radiator.
9 Support the engine, either with a hoist from above, or with a jack and wooden blocks from below. Whichever method is used must allow for movement of the engine in subsequent operations.
10 Protect the radiator with a piece of hardboard, or for greater security, remove it altogether.
11 Remove the engine right-hand mounting bracket. Move the engine forwards as far as possible, making sure that it is still securely

supported and that the radiator is not damaged.
12 Remove the air hoses from the turbocharger.
13 Using the modified Allen key, remove the inlet manifold bolts. These may be very tight. The middle bolt hole is in fact slotted, so if wished, the middle bolt may just be slackened.
14 Remove the inlet manifold. The gasket is shared with the exhaust manifold, so it will stay in place for the time being.
15 Disconnect the oil feed pipe from the top of the turbo. Remove the pipe. Note the strainer in the pipe **(see illustrations)**.
16 Slacken the remaining turbo mounting bolt. This fixing bolt is also slotted.
17 Manipulate the turbocharger and lift it out.

Refitting

18 Refit by reversing the removal operations, noting the following points:
 a) *If a new turbocharger is being fitted, change the engine oil and filter. Also renew the strainer in the oil feed pipe.*
 b) *Do not fully tighten the oil feed pipe unions until both ends of the pipe are in place. When tightening the oil return pipe union, position it so that the return hose is not strained.*
 c) *Before starting the engine, prime the turbo lubrication circuit by disconnecting the stop solenoid lead at the fuel pump and cranking the engine on the starter for three ten-second bursts.*
19 After initial start-up, do not race the engine. Inspect the turbo and its lubrication pipes for oil leaks. Stop the engine and check the oil level.
20 A new turbo should be run-in like any other major mechanical component.

4

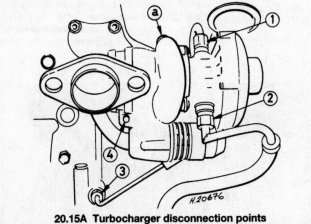

20.15A Turbocharger disconnection points

 a *Turbocharger*
 1 *Oil feed on turbo*
 2 *Oil return on turbo*
 3 *Oil feed on block*
 4 *Turbo mounting bolt*

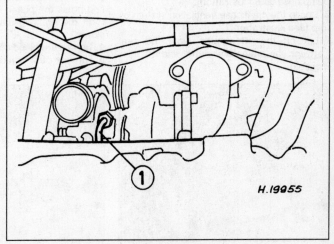

20.15B Turbo oil feed (1) seen from above

21 Turbocharger - examination

1 With the turbocharger removed, inspect the housings for cracks or other visible damage.
2 Spin the turbine or the compressor wheel to verify that the shaft is intact, and to feel for excessive shake or roughness. Some play is normal; in use, the shaft is "floating" on a film of oil. Check that the wheel vanes are undamaged.
3 On the KKK turbo, the wastegate and actuator are integral, and cannot be checked or renewed separately. On the Garrett turbo, the wastegate actuator is a separate unit. Consult a Citroën dealer or other specialist if it is thought that testing or renewal is necessary.
4 If the exhaust or induction passages are oil-contaminated, the turbo shaft oil seals have probably failed (on the induction side, this will also have contaminated the intercooler, which if necessary should be flushed with solvent).
5 No DIY repair of the turbo is possible. A new unit may be available on an exchange basis.

22 Intercooler - removal and refitting

Removal

1 Slacken the intercooler inlet trunking clip (see illustration).
2 Remove the three screws that secure the front edge of the intercooler (see illustration).
3 Remove the three Allen screws that secure the rear edge of the intercooler. These screws are concealed by the intercooler rubber seal (see illustration).
4 Disconnect the intercooler-to-injection pump hose (see illustration).
5 Unclip the crankcase ventilation system oil trap (see illustration).
6 Lift off the intercooler. Note the seal between the intercooler outlet and the inlet manifold.

22.1 Slackening the intercooler inlet trunking clip

Refitting

7 Before refitting, clean the intercooler matrix with a soft brush, or by blowing air through it. Flush the intercooler internally with solvent if contaminated with oil. Make sure that the inlet manifold seal is in good condition, and renew it if necessary.
8 Refit by reversing the removal operations.

23 Fuel injection system - priming

Early models

1 After disconnecting part of the fuel injection system or running out of fuel it is necessary to carry out the priming procedure before starting the engine.
2 Loosen the bleed screw on the fuel filter head two or three turns. On the Roto-diesel filter a plastic drain tube may be fitted to the bleed screw and a small container positioned to catch the fuel.
3 Actuate the plunger until fuel free from air bubbles flows from the bleed screw. On some Roto-diesel filter heads the plunger must first be unscrewed, and with this type the plunger may become detached from the internal piston. If this happens, unscrew the housing and press the piston back onto the plunger. Refit the housing and operate the plunger slowly.
4 Tighten the bleed screw.
5 Turn on the ignition so that the stop

22.2 One of the three screws securing the front of the intercooler. This one secures a hose guide as well

solenoid is energised then activate the plunger until resistance is felt.
6 Where applicable on Roto-diesel filters retighten the plunger.
7 Turn the ignition switch to position "M" and wait for the preheater warning light to go out.
8 Fully depress the accelerator pedal and start the engine. Additional cranking may be necessary to finally bleed the fuel system before the engine starts.

Later models

9 Later models are provided with a rubber hand-operated priming bulb, located on the right-hand side of the engine compartment. When the bulb is squeezed, fuel is forced into the fuel filter housing and then through a double valve. The valve forces fuel initially in the direction of the fuel injection pump, then any excess, along with fuel returned from the injectors, is returned to the fuel tank.
10 To prime the fuel lines, for instance after removing and refitting the injection pump, depress the priming bulb several times to force any trapped air back to the fuel tank.
11 Purging of air from the injection pump itself and the injectors is carried out when the engine is turned by the starter motor. However this process may be accelerated by temporarily slightly loosening each pipe in turn at the injector end until fuel emerges as the engine is being turned. Note that the fuel may spurt out under considerable pressure when doing this - precautions should be taken to prevent personal injury.

22.3 Pulling back the rubber seal to reveal the rear securing screws

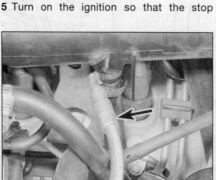

22.4 Disconnecting the hose (arrowed) which runs to the injection pump

22.5 Unclipping the oil trap

24.1 Auxiliary fuel tank - BX Turbo model

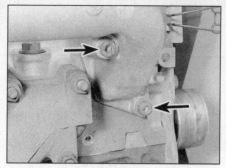

25.3A Inlet manifold bolts (arrowed)

25.3B Removing the inlet manifold (engine removed from car)

25.6 Exhaust manifold resonator and downpipe bolts (arrowed) on a 1.7 engine

25.7A Removing the exhaust manifold on a 1.9 engine

25.7B Exhaust manifold gasket

25.8 Tightening the exhaust manifold nuts

24 Auxiliary fuel tank (BX Turbo, and all models from early 1993) - general

General

An auxiliary fuel tank is fitted to BX Turbo models, and to all models from early 1993. It is located in the rear right-hand corner of the vehicle, immediately below the fuel filler **(see illustration)**.

The auxiliary tank is removed in the same way as the main tank; the fuel must be drained, the hoses and pipes disconnected, and the tank mountings released. Appropriate safety precautions must be observed.

25 Manifolds - removal and refitting

Inlet

Removal

1 Disconnect the battery negative lead.
2 Disconnect and remove the air duct from the inlet manifold and air cleaner. On Visa models unbolt the support bracket.
3 Using a hexagon key, unscrew the bolts and remove the inlet manifold from the cylinder head **(see illustrations)**. There are no gaskets.

Refitting

4 Refitting is a reversal of removal, but tighten the bolts evenly.

Exhaust

Removal

5 Jack up the front of the car and support on axle stands (see *"Jacking and vehicle support"*). Apply the handbrake on Visa models, or chock the rear wheels on BX models.
6 Unscrew and remove the exhaust manifold-to-downpipe bolts, together with the springs and collars **(see illustration)**. Tie the downpipe to one side.
7 Unscrew the nuts and withdraw the exhaust manifold from the studs in the cylinder head. Recover the gaskets **(see illustrations)**.

Refitting

8 Refitting is a reversal of removal, but clean the mating faces and fit new gaskets. Tighten the nuts evenly **(see illustration)**.

4

Notes

Chapter 5
Electrical systems

Contents

Degrees of difficulty

Easy, suitable for novice with little experience | **Fairly easy,** suitable for beginner with some experience | **Fairly difficult,** suitable for competent DIY mechanic 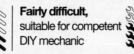 | **Difficult,** suitable for experienced DIY mechanic | **Very difficult,** suitable for expert DIY or professional

Specifications

General
System type .... 12 volt, negative earth, with alternator and pre-engaged starter motor
Battery capacity:
  Visa 42Ah
  BX .... 50Ah or 83Ah

Alternator

	Visa	BX
Make	Bosch, Melco or Paris-Rhone	Melco or Bosch
Output	47 amps	50 amps
Regulated voltage (warm)	13.5 volts	13.8 to 14.5 volts

Starter motor
Make .... Bosch or Mitsubishi/Melco

Fuses (Visa models)

No	Amps	Circuits protected
1	10	RH side and tail lamps, RH number plate lamp, ignition switch lighting
2	16	LH and RH direction indicators, rear screen wash/wipe, electric window relay, instrument lighting, all warning lamps
3	20	Stop-lamps, heated rear screen, electric cooling fan, windscreen wiper and washer
4	16	Cigar lighter, interior lamps, radio, horn, clock, hazard warning
5	10	Rear foglamps
6	10	Reversing lamps
7	20	Front electric windows, central door locking
8	10	LH side and tail lamps, LH number plate lamp, switch illumination

Fuses (BX models), (depending on level of equipment)

No	Amps	Circuits protected
1	10	Reversing lamps, electric cooling fan relay, water temperature control, oil pressure gauge, tachometer, water level warning
2	25	Heater motor, air conditioning, direction indicators, instrument lighting, all warning lamps
3	25	Heated rear screen relay, power window relays, stop-lamps, door warning, front and rear wash/wipe, glovebox lamp, spotlamps, lighting rheostat, clock, ABS warning, sunroof
4	30	Electric cooling fans
5	10	Hazard warning lamps
6	30	Electric rear window winders
7	30	Central door locking, interior lamps, glovebox lamp, cigar lighter, radio, clock
8	25	Heated rear screen, horn
9	30	Electric front window winders
10	5	Rear fog lamps
11	5	RH rear lamp
12	5	LH rear lamp, rear number plate lamp
13	5	LH and RH sidelamps, digital clock, lighting dimmer, illumination for hazard warning switch, heated rear screen, rear fog-lamps and screen wiper, sidelamp indicator
14	10/25	ABS system

Bulbs (watts)

	Visa	BX
Boot lamp	5	5
Direction indicators	21	21
Glovebox lamp	2	2
Headlamps	45/40 (17D) 60/55 (17 RD)	55/60
Interior lamps	7	7
Map reading lamp	7	7
Number plate lamps	5	5
Rear foglamp	21	21
Reversing lamps	21	21
Sidelamps	4	4
Side repeaters	4	4
Stop-lamps	21	21
Tail lamps	5	5

Torque wrench settings

	Nm	lbf ft
Alternator mountings	35	26
Starter motor bolts	34	25

1 Description - general

The electrical system is of 12 volt negative earth type. The main components are a 12 volt battery, an alternator with integral voltage regulator, and a pre-engaged starter motor (with reduction gears on some models). The starter motor incorporates a one-way clutch on its pinion shaft to prevent the engine driving the motor when it starts.

It is important to disconnect the battery leads before charging the battery, removing the alternator, or working on wiring circuits that are permanently live. Additionally the alternator wiring must be disconnected before using electric arc welding equipment.

From late 1986 onwards (1987 model year), all models are equipped with a dim-dip lighting system to comply with UK regulations. The function of the system is to prevent the vehicle being driven with only the sidelights illuminated.

The system uses a relay-controlled resistor circuit. When the sidelights are on, with the ignition also on, the headlights are automatically illuminated at approximately one-sixth their normal dipped beam power.

2 Alternator - removal and refitting

Removal

1 Disconnect the battery negative lead.
2 Disconnect the wiring from the back of the alternator **(see illustration)**.
3 Loosen the pivot bolt and adjustment locknut.
4 Unscrew the adjustment bolt to release the tension then slip the drivebelt from the pulleys.
5 Remove the adjustment locknut, swivel the alternator outwards, and lift it from the engine.

Note that the alternator is slotted to allow removal without removing the pivot bolt.

Refitting

6 Refitting is a reversal of removal. Tension the drivebelt so that there is approximately 6.0 mm deflection under moderate thumb pressure midway between the pulleys.

2.2 Alternator wires (arrowed)

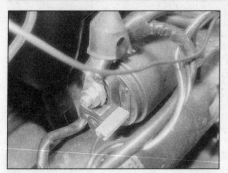

3.3A Starter motor solenoid wiring (Bosch)

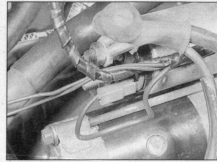

3.3B Starter motor solenoid wiring (Mitsubishi/Melco)

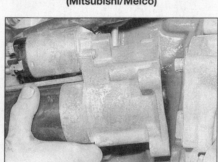

3.5 Removing the starter motor (Mitsubishi/Melco)

5 Stop-lamp switch (Visa models) - removal and refitting

Removal

1 Extract the cross-head screws and withdraw the left-hand side shelf inside the vehicle.
2 Disconnect the wiring from the stop lamp switch **(see illustration)**.
3 Unscrew the locknuts and remove the switch from the bracket.

Refitting

4 Refitting is a reversal of removal, but adjust the switch so that the brake pedal has free movement of 2.5 mm.

6 Turbo over-pressure warning switch - removal and refitting

Removal

1 Unbolt the switch from the battery carrier.
2 Disconnect the hose and the wiring from the switch, and remove it **(see illustration)**.

Refitting

3 Refit by reversing the removal operations.

7 Speedometer cable - general

The procedure is similar to that described for petrol models, but to disconnect the speedometer cable from the transmission pull out the rubber cotter **(see illustration)**. Access may be found easier from beneath the vehicle.

3.4 Removing the starter motor mounting bolts on BX models

3 Starter motor - removal and refitting

Removal

1 Disconnect the battery negative lead.
2 Remove the air cleaner (Chapter 4).
3 Unscrew the nut and disconnect the large cable from the solenoid. Also disconnect the small trigger wire **(see illustrations)**.
4 Using a hexagon key, unscrew the three mounting bolts. On BX models note the location of the hydraulic pipe support bracket **(see illustration)**.
5 Withdraw the starter motor from the transmission **(see illustration)**.

Refitting

6 Refitting is a reversal of removal, but tighten the bolts evenly to the specified torque.

4 Starter motor overhaul - general

If the starter motor is thought to be suspect, it should be removed from the vehicle and taken to an auto-electrician for testing. Most auto-electricians will be able to supply and fit brushes at a reasonable cost. However, check on the cost of repairs before continuing as it may prove more economical to obtain a new or exchange motor.

5

5.2 Stop-lamp switch - Visa models (arrowed)

6.2 Removing the turbo over-pressure warning switch

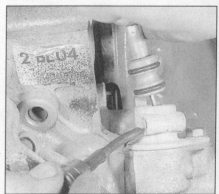

7.1 Disconnecting the speedometer cable from the transmission

8.1 Fusebox location (Visa models)

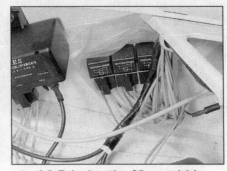

8.2 Relay location (Visa models)

9.1 Washer pump (Visa models)

8 Fuses and relays (Visa models) - general

1 The fuses are located on the bulkhead as on petrol models **(see illustration)**.
2 Relays are located under a polythene cover beside the preheater relay on the left-hand side of the engine compartment **(see illustration)**.

9 Washer pump - removal and refitting

Removal

1 The washer pump is located near the fluid reservoir on the bulkhead **(see illustration)**. First note the location of the two wires then disconnect them from the terminals.

2 Note the location of the inlet and outlet pipes, and disconnect them.
3 Unbolt and remove the pump.

Refitting

4 Refitting is a reversal of removal.

10 Wiring diagrams - general

1 The wiring diagrams appear on the following pages.
2 To assist you in using the diagrams, here is an explanation of the various letters and their use in conjunction with the wiring diagram keys.
a **Large numbers** - identify the various components.
b **Capital letters printed in the middle of a wire** - indicate which harness the wire is located in.
c **Small letters located at the connection points** - indicates the colour of either the wire itself or of the marking on the wire. If the letter has a line drawn above it, this indicates the colour of the wire itself; if there is no line above, the letter indicates the colour of the marking on the wire.
d **Connecting blocks** - the first number and letter(s) inside the box indicates the size and colour of the connecting block. The last number gives the exact location of the relevant wire in that connecting block.
For example:
3 Bl 2 - shows that the wiring connector is blue in colour, and contains three wiring channels; the wire shown in the diagram is located in the second channel of the connector.

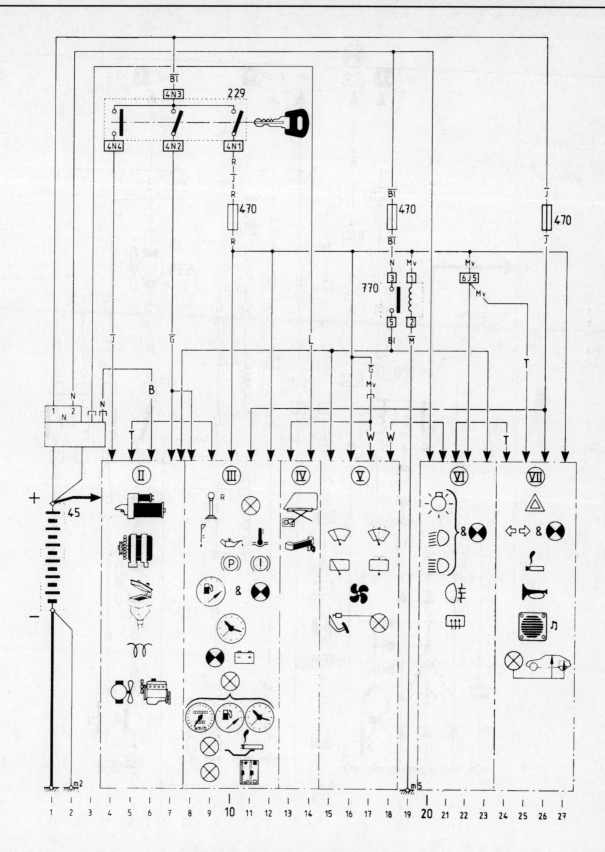

10.3A Wiring diagram for Visa diesel Saloons

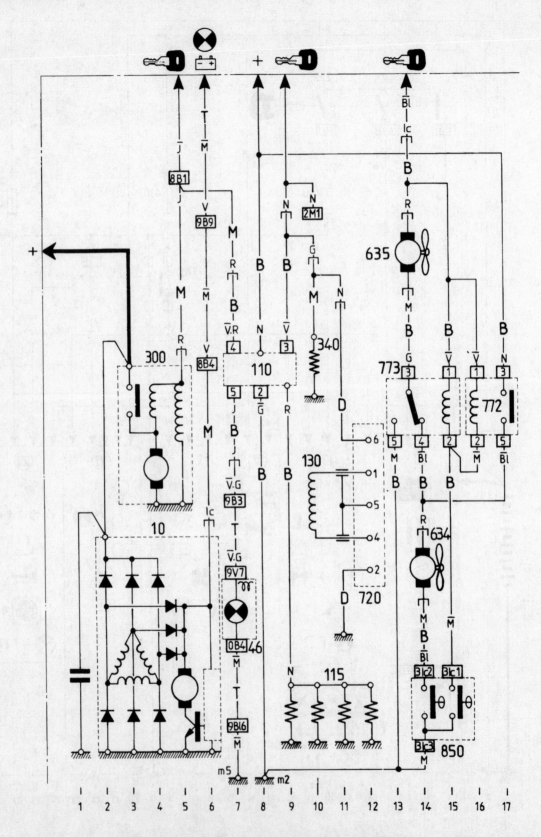

10.3B Wiring diagram for Visa diesel Saloons (continued)

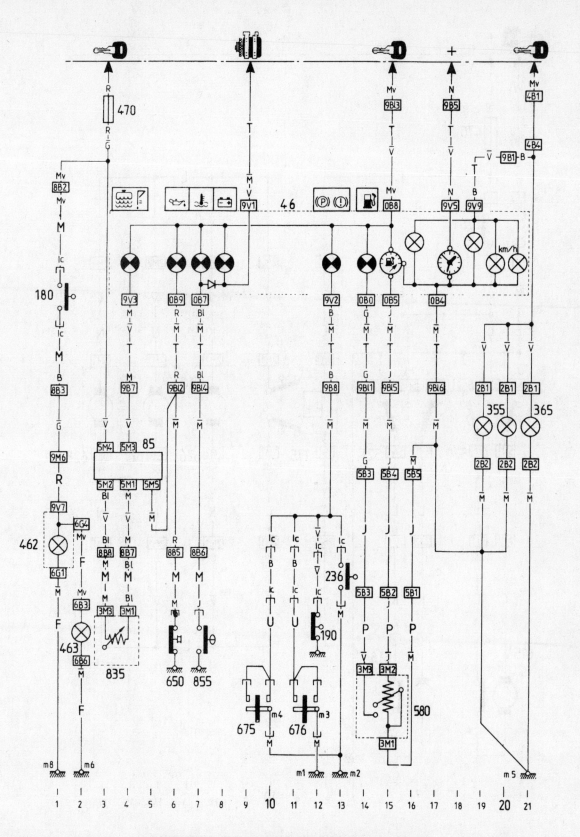

10.3C Wiring diagram for Visa diesel Saloons (continued)

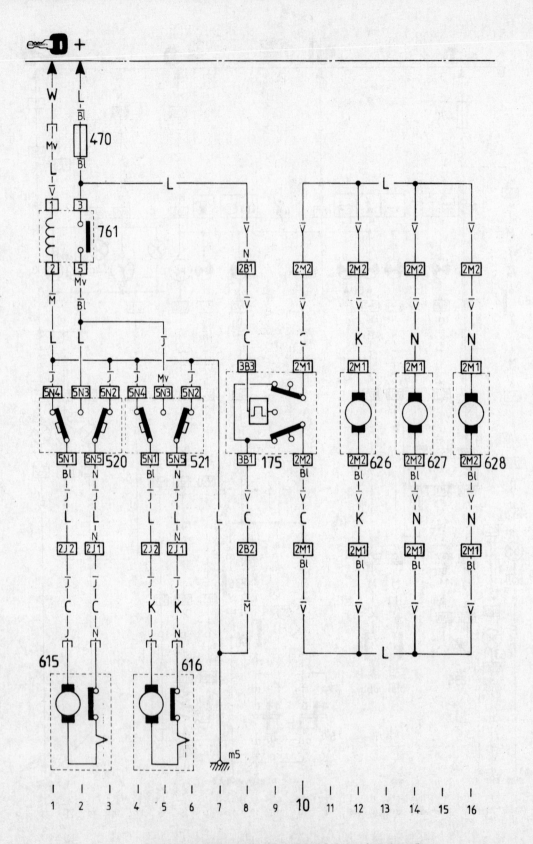

10.3D Wiring diagram for Visa diesel Saloons (continued)

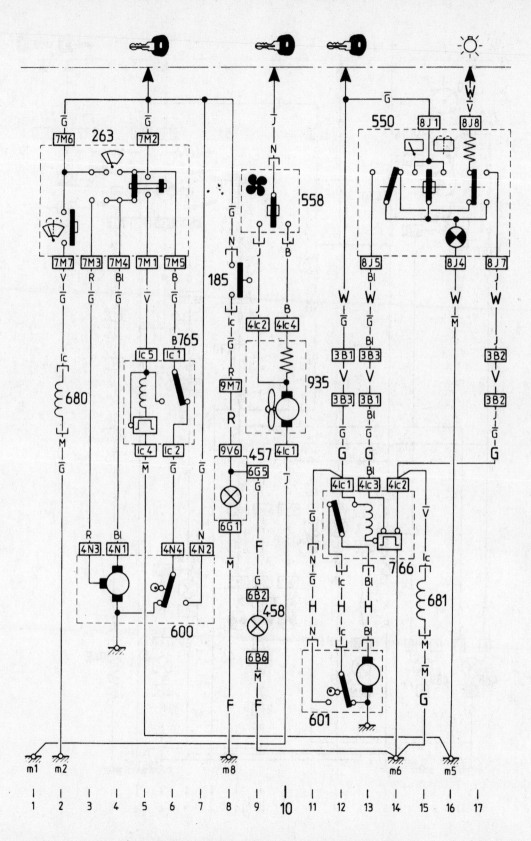

10.3E Wiring diagram for Visa diesel Saloons (continued)

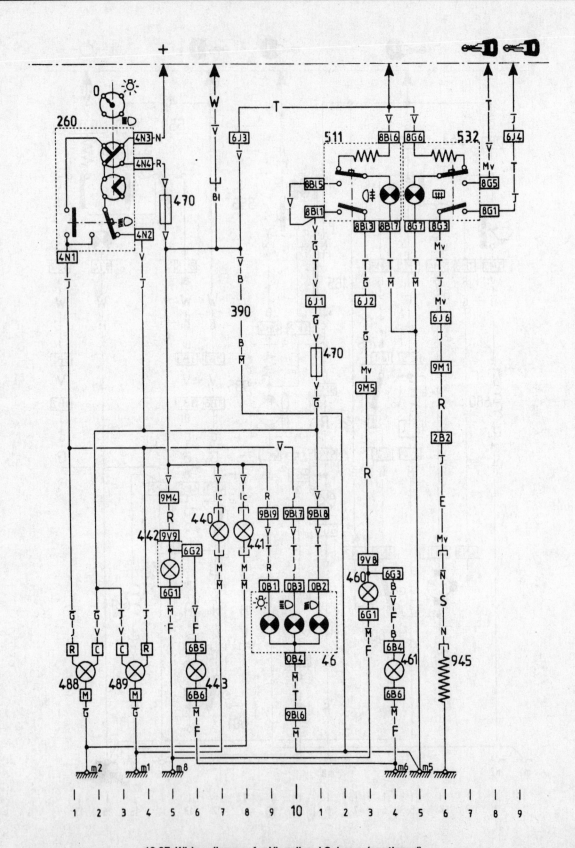

10.3F Wiring diagram for Visa diesel Saloons (continued)

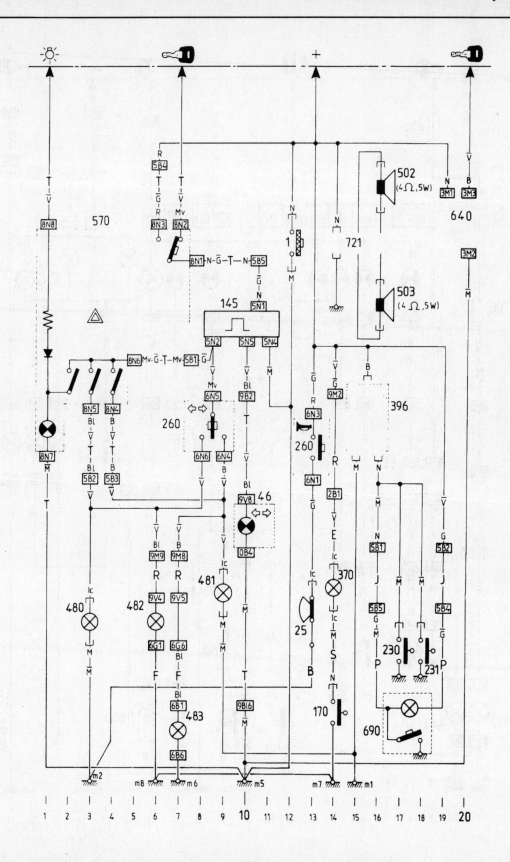

10.3G Wiring diagram for Visa diesel Saloons (continued)

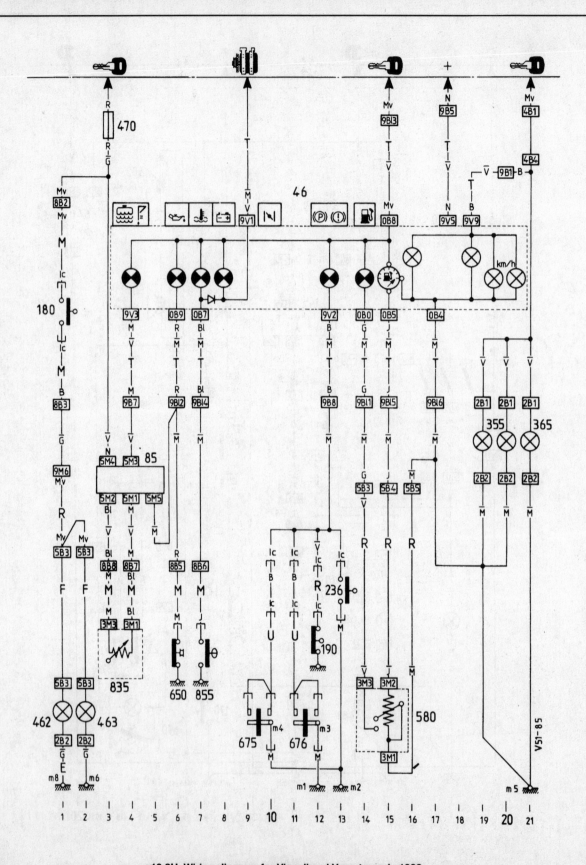

10.3H Wiring diagram for Visa diesel Vans to early 1993

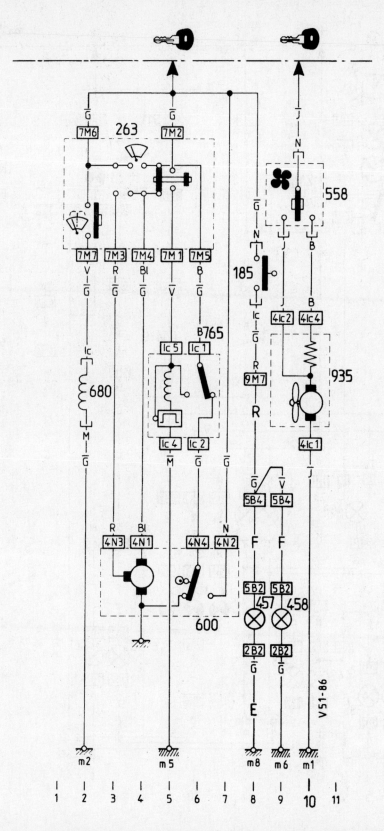

10.3J Wiring diagram for Visa diesel Vans to early 1993 (continued)

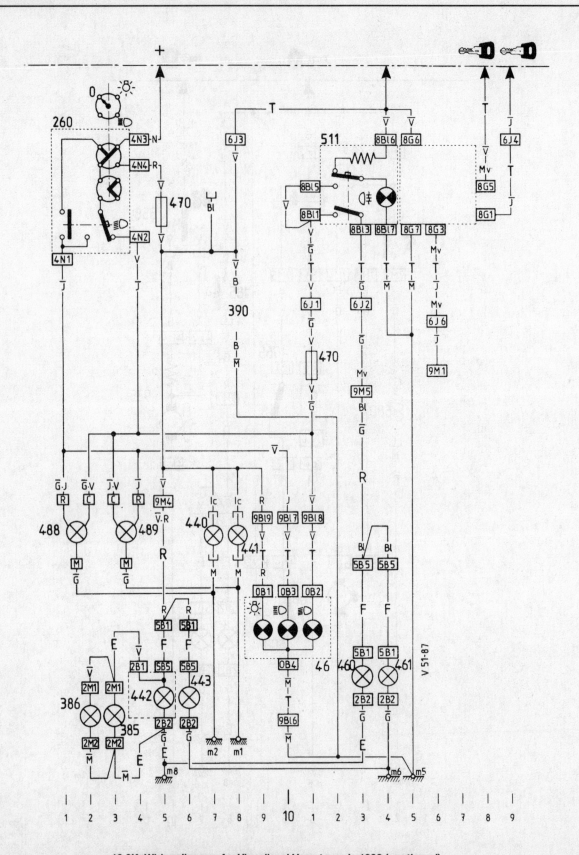

10.3K Wiring diagram for Visa diesel Vans to early 1993 (continued)

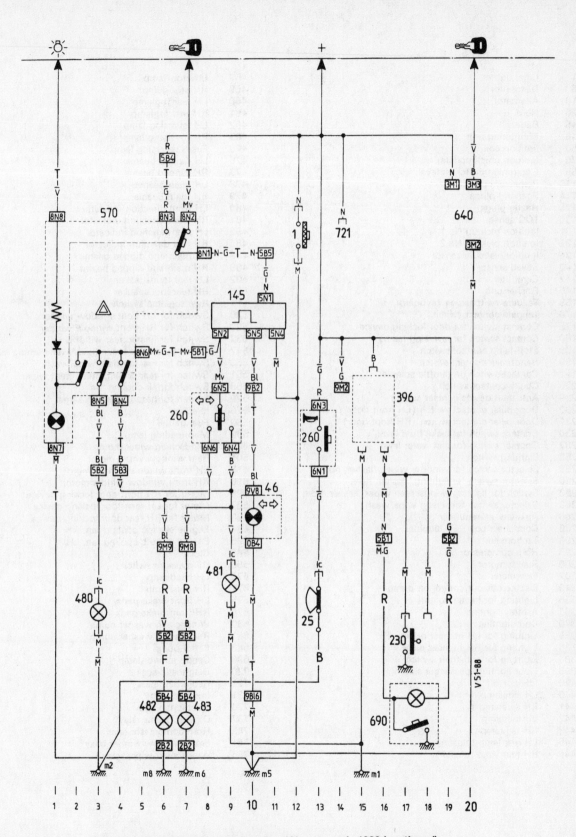

10.3L Wiring diagram for Visa diesel Vans to early 1993 (continued)

1	Cigar lighter	457	LH stop-lamp
5	Distributor	458	RH stop-lamp
10	Alternator	460	LH rear foglamp
25	Horn	461	RH rear foglamp
45	Battery	462	LH reversing lamp
46	Monitoring unit	463	RH reversing lamp
50	Ignition coil	470	Fuses reversing lamp
75	Ignition unit (module)	476	LH dipped beams
85	Electronic unit for oil level	477	RH dipped beams
110	Preheater control unit	478	LH main beams
114	Sparking plugs	479	RH main beams
115	Heater plugs	480	LH front direction indicator
130	TDC sensor	481	RH front direction indicator
131	Ignition pick up No 1	482	LH rear direction indicator
132	Ignition pick up No 2	483	RH rear direction indicator
136	Ignition vacuum sensor	488	LH main and dipped beams
140	Speed sensor	489	RH main and dipped beams
142	Computer	502	LH rear loudspeaker
145	Flasher unit	503	RH rear loudspeaker
158	Tailgate switches on keyboard	511	Rear foglamp switch
170	Tailgate contact switch	520	Switch for LH front window winder
175	Contact switch for door locking device	521	Switch for RH front window winder
180	Contact switch for reversing lamps	532	Switch for heated rear window
185	Stop-lamp contact switch	547	Check button for brake fluid level warning lamp
190	Handbrake contact switch	550	Switch for rear window wipe/wash
192	Contact switch on throttle spindle	551	Switch for rear screen intermittent wiper
225	Choke contact switch	558	Switch for air cooling fan
229	Anti-theft device contact switch	570	Switch for hazard warning signal
230	Door pillar contact switch (LH front door)	576	Injectors
231	Door pillar contact switch (RH front door)	580	Fuel gauge
236	Contact switch for brake fluid level	590	Map reading lamp
237	Contact switch for min water level	600	Windscreen wiper motor
258	Lighting switch	601	Rear window wiper motor
259	Selector switch for window wiper, flasher, horn	615	LH front window winder motor
260	Selector switch for lighting, flasher, horn	616	RH front window winder motor
262	Switch for lighting, windscreen wiper, flasher, horn	626	Motor for RH front door locking device
263	Selector switch for screen wipe/wash	627	Motor for LH rear door locking device
280	Auxiliary-air regulator	628	Motor for RH rear door locking device
285	Condenser coil "+" terminal	634	Engine electric cooling fan, RH
290	Tachometer	635	Engine electric cooling fan, LH
295	Horn compressor	640	Clock
300	Starter motor	650	Oil pressure switch
302	Flowmeter	670	LH headlamp
340	Electric cut-out control on pump	671	RH headlamp
355	Lighting for heater control	675	LH front brake pads
365	Ashtray lighting	676	RH front brake pads
370	Boot lighting	680	Windscreen washer pump
385	Lighting for LH number plate	681	Rear screen washer pump
386	Lighting for RH number plate	683	Petrol pump
390	Lighting for anti-theft switch	690	Centre interior lamp
396	Floor lighting, passenger side	720	Diagnostic socket
420	Idle cut-off	721	Radio terminals
440	LH sidelamp	731	Injection relay
441	RH sidelamp	733	Electric fan relay
442	LH tail lamp	737	Dipped beams relay
443	RH tail lamp	743	Horn compressor relay
445	LH rear lamp (cluster)	761	Front window winder relay
446	RH rear lamp (cluster)	765	Windscreen wiper relay

10.3M Key to wiring diagrams for Visa models to early 1993

766	Rear screen wiper relay		840	Water temperature sensor
770	Relays for accesories		841	Water temperature sensor (injection)
772	Relay for electric fan 2nd speed		842	Oil pressure sensor
773	Relay reversing the electric fan speeds		843	Oil temperature sensor
788	Electric fan 2nd speed resistance		850	Electric fan thermal switch on coolant circuit
795	Rheostat for illumination		855	Water temperature switch
810	LH side repeater		935	Air conditioning cooling fan
811	RH side repeater		945	Heated rear window
835	Probe for oil level		958	Preheating warning lamp

Not all items fitted to all models

Harness code

A	Front (no mark on feed and function diagrams)		M	Engine
B	Electric fan		N	Rear door
C	LH front door		P	Interior lamp, gauge
D	Diagnostic		R	Rear
E	Boot lighting		S	Tailgate, LH
F	From LH rear lamp to RH rear lamp		T	Instrument panel
G	Rear screen washer time-delay		U	Brake wear
H	Tailgate, RH		V	Rear window wiper
J	Gauge		W	Rear window wiper switch
K	Passenger's door		Y	Injection
L	Window winder locking device		Z	Ignition

Colour code

B	White		Mv	Mauve
BL	Blue		N	Black
G	Grey		Or	Orange
Ic	Transparent		R	Red
J	Yellow		V	Green
M	Brown			

10.3N Key to wiring diagrams for Visa models to early 1993 (continued)

5

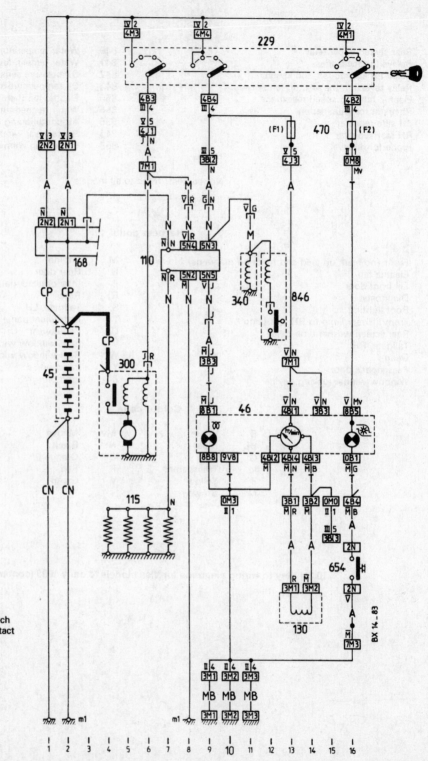

45	Battery
46	Instrument panel
110	Pre-heater control
115	Pre-heater plugs
130	TDC sensor
168	Battery connector
229	'Ignition' switch
300	Starter motor
340	Fuel pump stop solenoid
470	Fuses
654	Over-pressure warning switch
846	Electromagnetic timing contact

Harness code

A	Front harness
CN	Battery negative
CP	Battery positive
M	Engine harness
MB	Junction box earth
N	Pre-heater harness
T	Instrument panel harness

10.30 Wiring diagram - BX Turbo models
For colour code see key to main wiring diagrams

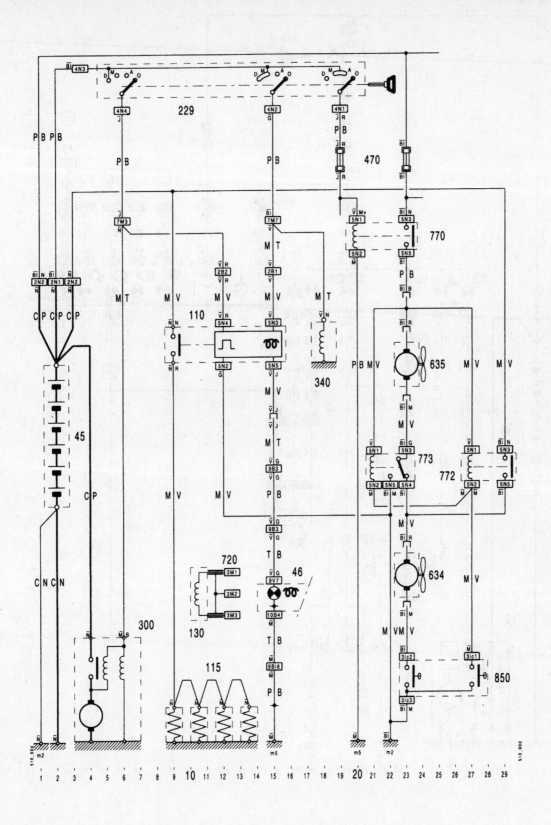

10.3P Wiring diagram for C15/Champ Van from early 1993
Starting, pre-heating and cooling

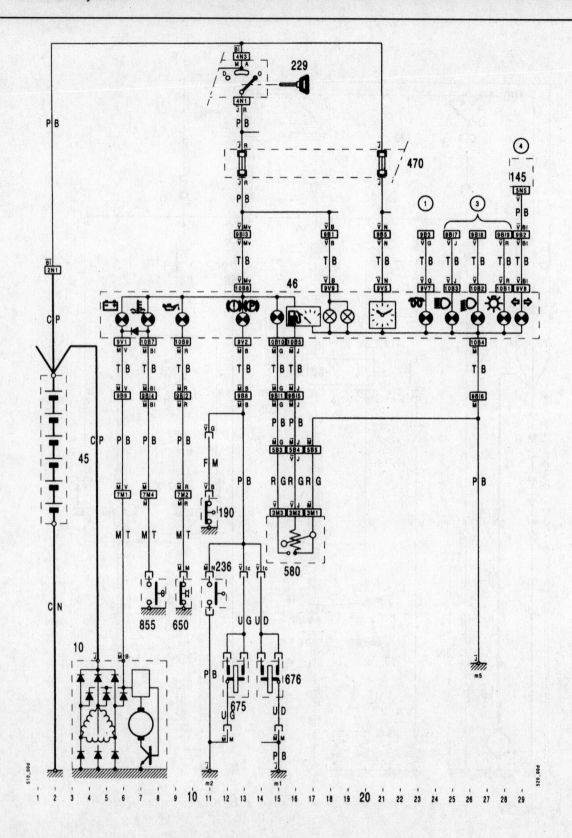

10.3Q Wiring diagram for C15/Champ Van from early 1993
Instrument panel

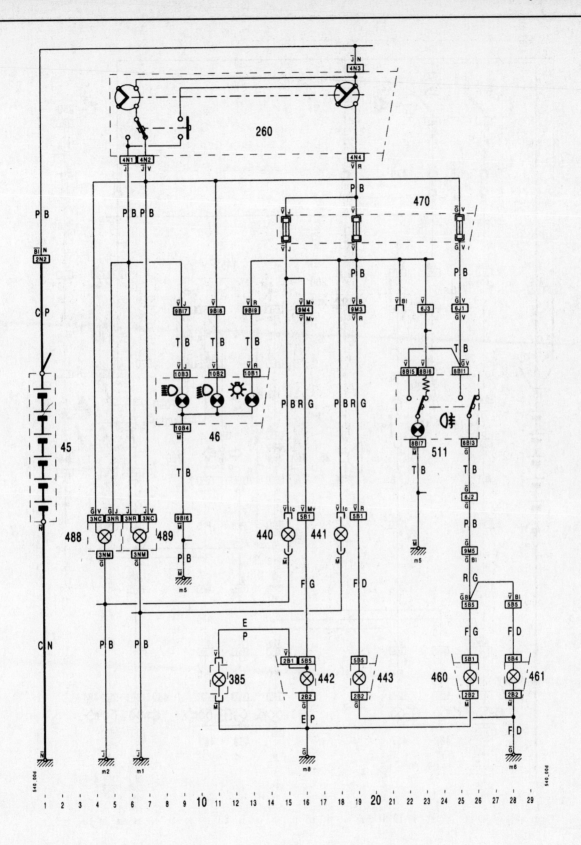

10.3R Wiring diagram for C15/Champ Van from early 1993
Lighting

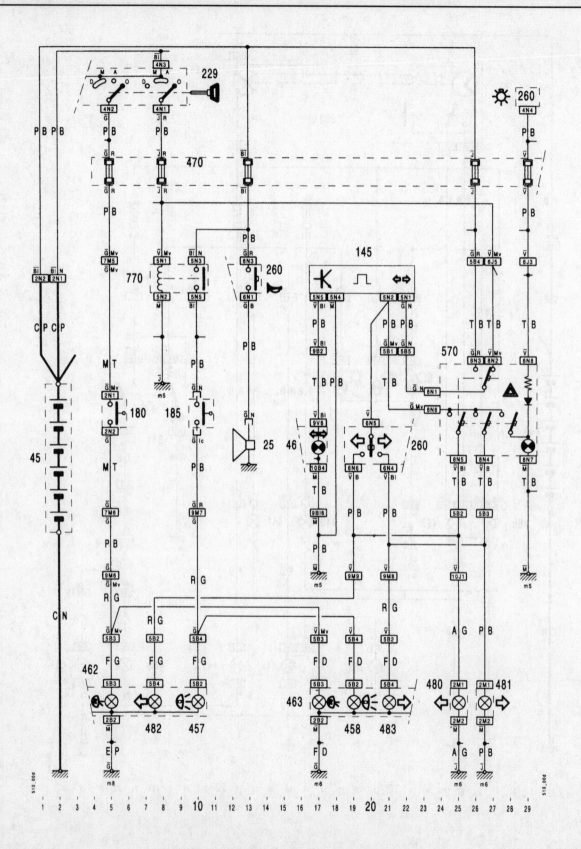

10.3S Wiring diagram for C15/Champ Van from early 1993
Signalling

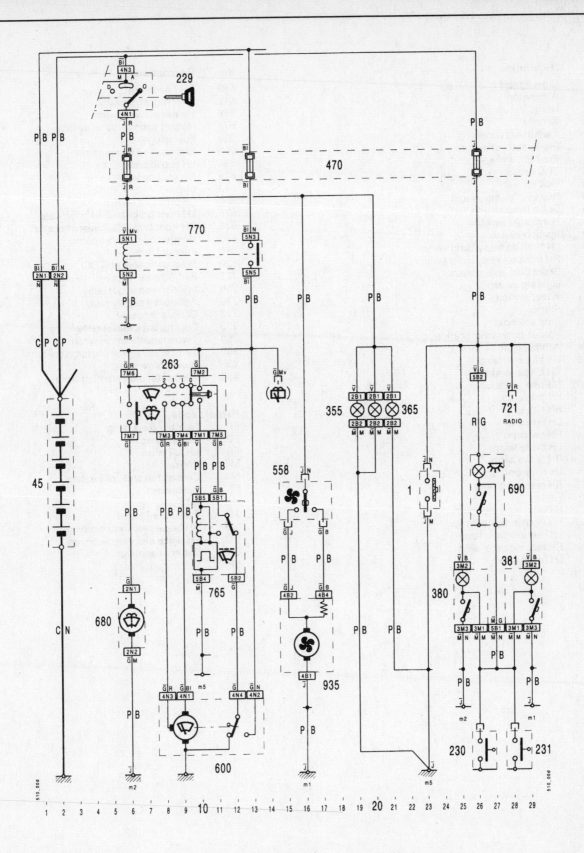

10.3T Wiring diagram for C15/Champ Van from early 1993
Wipers, heating and interior equipment

No	Description	No	Description
1	Cigar lighter	489	RH headlamp
10	Alternator	511	Rear foglamp switch
25	Horn	558	Heater blower switch
45	Battery	570	Hazard warning lamp switch
46	Instrument panel	580	Fuel gauge
110	Pre-heater control unit	600	Windscreen wiper motor
115	Pre-heater plugs	634	LH cooling fan
130	TDC sensor	635	RH cooling fan
145	Flasher unit	640	Clock
180	Reversing lamp switch	650	Oil pressure switch
185	Brake lamp switch	675	LH front brake pad wear indicator
190	Handbrake switch	676	RH front brake pad wear indicator
229	Ignition switch	680	Windscreen washer pump
230	LH front courtesy lamp switch	690	Interior lamp
231	RH front courtesy lamp switch	720	Diagnostic socket (TDC)
236	Brake fluid level switch	721	Radio power supply
260	Lighting switch	765	Windscreen wiper relay
262	Wiper switch	770	Accessory supply relay
300	Starter	772	Cooling fan relay
340	Stop solenoid	773	Cooling fan inverter relay
355	Heater control illumination	850	Two-stage thermo-switch
365	Ashtray illumination	855	Temperature warning lamp switch
380	LH sill panel lamp	935	Heater blower fan
381	RH sill panel lamp	958	Pre-heater plug warning lamp
385	Number plate lamp		
440	LH sidelamp		
441	RH sidelamp	**Harness code**	
442	LH tail lamp	EP	Number plate lamp
443	RH tail lamp	FD	RH tail lamp
457	LH brake lamp	FG	LH tail lamp
458	RH brake lamp	MT	Engine
462	LH reversing lamp	MV	Cooling fan and pre-heating
463	RH reversing lamp	PB	Dashboard
470	Fuses	RG	LH rear
480	LH front indicator lamp	TB	Instrument panel
481	RH front indicator lamp	UD	RH brake pad wear warning
482	LH rear indicator lamp	UG	LH brake pad wear warning
483	RH rear indicator lamp	CN	Battery negative
488	LH headlamp	CP	Battery positive

10.3U Key to 10.3P to 10.3T
Not all items are fitted to all models

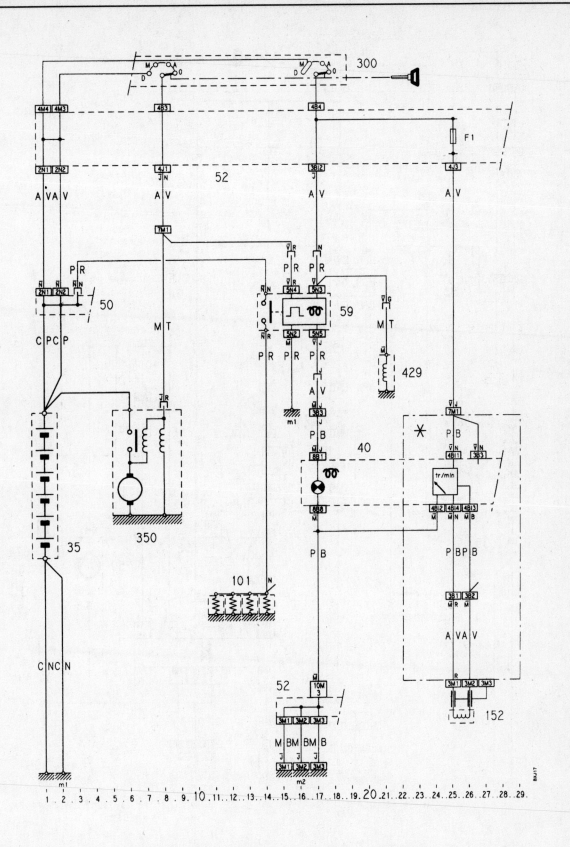

10.3V Wiring diagram for BX models with XUD7 or XUD9 engines

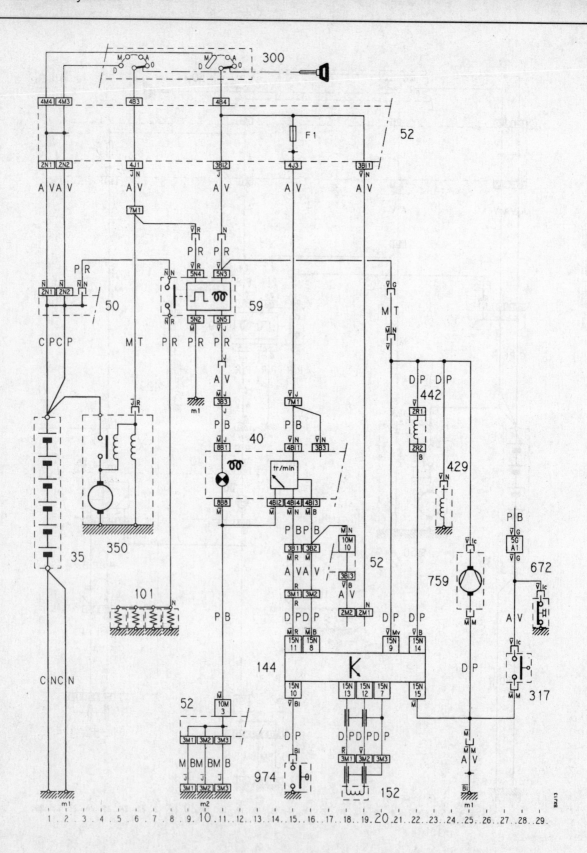

10.3W Wiring diagram for BX models with XUD9 or XUD9A engines (not UK models)

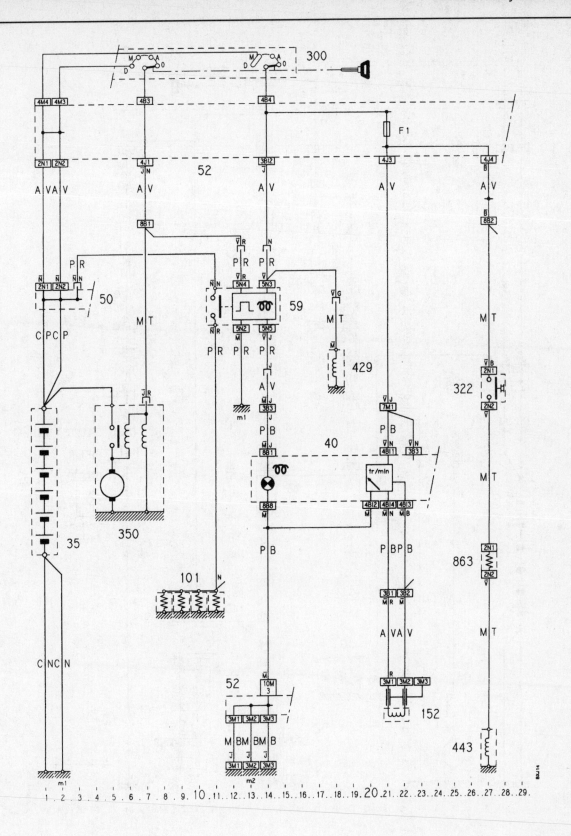

10.3X Wiring diagram for BX Turbo with XUD7TE/Y engine (not UK models)

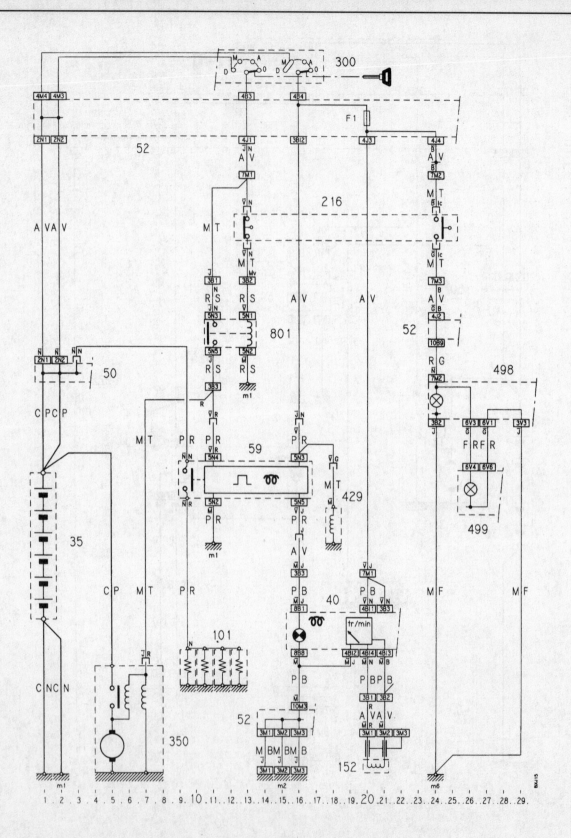

10.3Y Wiring diagram for BX models with automatic transmission

No	Description
10	Distributor
35	Battery
40	Instrument panel
50	Supply box
52	Junction box
59	Pre-heating control unit
101	Pre-heater plugs
144	Exhaust gas recirculation ECU*
152	Flywheel sensor
216	Automatic gearbox switch
255	Air conditioning compressor
300	'Ignition' switch
317	Hydraulic level switch
322	Enrichment switch
350	Starter motor
429	Stop solenoid
442	Canister-purge solenoid*
443	Advance correction solenoid
498	LH reversing lamp
499	RH reversing lamp

No	Description
672	Hydraulic pressure switch
759	Exhaust gas recirculation pump*
783	Diagnostic socket
801	Automatic gearbox relay
863	Atmospheric pressure switch resistance
974	Coolant thermo-switch*
*	Not UK models

Harness code

AA	'Ignition'
AV	Front
CN	Battery negative
CP	Battery positive
DP	Anti-pollution (not UK)
FR	Rear lamps
MB	Junction box earth
MF	Lighting earth
MT	Engine
PB	Dashboard
PR	Pre-heating
RG	Left rear
RS	Starter inhibitor relay (automatic transmission)

5

10.3Z Key to 10.3X to 10.3Y
Not all items are fitted to all models

Notes

Chapter 6
Clutch, transmission and driveshafts

Contents

Degrees of difficulty

| **Easy,** suitable for novice with little experience | **Fairly easy,** suitable for beginner with some experience | **Fairly difficult,** suitable for competent DIY mechanic | **Difficult,** suitable for experienced DIY mechanic | **Very difficult,** suitable for expert DIY or professional |

Specifications

Clutch

Type	Single dry plate with diaphragm spring. Cable operated
Friction plate diameter	
Except BX Turbo	200 mm
BX Turbo	215 mm
Lining thickness	7.7 ± 0.3 mm
Release bearing type	Sealed ball
Pedal free play	Not applicable
Pedal travel:	
Visa	120.0 mm minimum
BX	130.0 to 150.0 mm

Manual transmission

Type	Four or five forward speeds and one reverse, synchromesh on all forward gears

Designation and type:
Pre 1989 models:

Visa Van	BE1 (BM61) 5-speed
Visa 17D and 17RD	BE1 (BM60) 4-speed or BE1 (BL04) 5-speed
BX 17D	BE1 (BL03) 5-speed
BX 19D and 19RD	BE1 (BL04) 5-speed or BE1 (BL62) 5-speed
1989 - on models:	
4-speed	BE 3/4
5-speed	BE 3/5

Ratios (overall):

	BM60	BM61	BL03	BL04	BL62
1st	3.31:1	3.31:1	3.31:1	3.31:1	3.31:1
2nd	1.88:1	1.88:1	1.88:1	1.88:1	1.88:1
3rd	1.15:1	1.15:1	1.28:1	1.28:1	1.28:1
4th	0.80:1	0.80:1	0.97:1	0.97:1	0.97:1
5th	-	-	0.76:1	0.76:1	0.76:1
Reverse	3.33:1	3.33:1	3.33:1	3.33:1	3.33:1
Final drive	3.59:1	3.81:1	4.19:1	3.94:1	4.06:1

Oil type/specification	Gear oil, viscosity SAE 75W/80W
Oil capacity (depending on model)	2.0 ± 0.2 litres

6

Automatic transmission

Type		Four forwards and one reverse gear	
Designation		ZF 4 H P14	
Ratios (overall):		**Up to 1988**	**From 1988**
1st		0.564	0.606
2nd		0.321	0.344
3rd		0.234	0.251
4th		0.174	0.186
Reverse		0.663	0.711
Final drive ratio		51/59	49/51
Oil type/specification		Dexron II type ATF	
Oil capacity (drain and refill)		2.5 litres	

Driveshafts

Type		Solid shaft with inner tri-axe joints and outer six-ball constant velocity joints
Grease capacity:		
Inner (tri-axe) joint		150 grams
Outer (CV) joint		100 grams

Torque wrench settings

	Nm	lbf ft
Driveshaft nut	250	185
Engine-to-transmission bolts	40	30
Left-hand engine mounting nut	35	26
Left-hand engine mounting stud to transmission	35	26
Right-hand driveshaft intermediate bearing retaining bolts	10	7

1 Description - general

Clutch components are virtually identical to those used in petrol-engined models. However, on models with BE3 transmissions, instead of the clutch release fork pivoting on a ball stud, a pivot shaft is used (see illustration). Refer to the main manuals for replacement details.

A BE1 type manual transmission is fitted. On Visa models the procedures for the five-speed version are described in the Visa main manual. The differences applicable to the four-speed transmission are described in this Chapter. For BX models the procedures are identical to those for the BL type transmission given in the BX Main Manual.

The BE3 transmissions progressively replaced the BE1 transmissions from the beginning of 1989, the main difference being in the gearshift components. The driver will notice that reverse gear is now in the same plane as 2nd and 4th gears - opposite 5th gear, when applicable - and the lifting collar below the gear knob for selecting reverse gear is now obsolete.

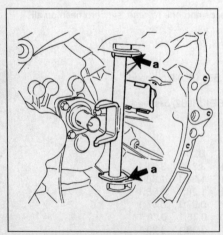

1.1 Clutch release pivot shaft - BE3 transmission

a Bearings

2 Manual transmission - removal and refitting

Removal

1 Jack up the front of the vehicle and support on axle stands (see "*Jacking and vehicle support*"). Also jack up the rear of the vehicle and support on axle stands so that the vehicle is level.
2 Remove the air cleaner (Chapter 4).
3 Remove the battery and its tray.
4 Unscrew the drain plug(s) and drain the transmission oil into a container. On completion refit and tighten the plug(s).
5 Unbolt the earth cable from the transmission.
6 Unbolt the high pressure pump on BX models from the transmission, leaving the lines attached. Remove the vacuum pump completely on Visa models (Chapter 7).
7 Unbolt the cable guide where fitted.
8 Disconnect the clutch cable and position it to one side. Recover the pushrod and, if fitted, the balance weight and the return spring (see illustrations).
9 Disconnect the gearchange control rods (and cable if fitted).
10 Pull out the rubber cotter and disconnect the speedometer cable. Position it to one side.
11 Remove the left-hand front roadwheel.
12 Unbolt the inner shield from the wheel arch (where fitted).
13 Disconnect the wiring from the reversing lamp switch.
14 Disconnect the front track control arms from the stub axle carriers and, on BX models, unscrew the nut and separate the left-hand link rod from the anti-roll bar.
15 Have an assistant pull the left-hand strut outwards while the left-hand driveshaft is levered from the differential side gear. Hold the strut outwards with a block of wood.
16 On BX models manufactured before July 1984 the left-hand differential side gear must be supported using a dowel, preferably wooden. If this precaution is not taken, the side gears may become misaligned when the right-hand driveshaft is removed.
17 Loosen the two nuts retaining the right-hand driveshaft intermediate bearing in the bracket bolted to the rear of the cylinder block and turn the bolt heads through 90° to release the bearing.
18 Have an assistant pull the right-hand wheel outwards while the right-hand driveshaft is removed from the differential side gear. Hold the wheel and strut out with a block of wood.
19 Position a piece of thin board over the radiator to protect it from possible damage.
20 Remove the starter motor.
21 On BX models unbolt the hydraulic

2.8A Clutch cable and lever return spring

2.8B Removing the balance weight from the clutch cable

2.8C Feeding the clutch cable through the bracket

pressure regulator from the transmission leaving the pressure lines attached.

22 Unbolt and remove the transmission-to-engine lower cover.

23 Support the engine under the sump with a trolley jack and block of wood.

24 Unscrew the nut from the left-hand engine mounting and remove the rubber mounting.

25 On Visa models unbolt the support bracket.

26 Unscrew the left-hand mounting stud from the transmission.

27 Lower the engine two or three inches, or on BX models until it touches the crossmember.

28 Unscrew and remove the four engine-to-transmission bolts.

29 Lift the transmission directly from the engine keeping it horizontal until clear of the clutch, then lower it to the ground.

Refitting

30 Refitting is a reversal of removal, but before lifting the transmission onto the engine, temporarily hold the clutch release arm in position using wire as shown **(see illustration)**. Remove the wire after fitting the mounting bolts. Make sure that the two dowels are in place on the mating face of the transmission. When fitting the left-hand mounting stud apply locking fluid to its threads before tightening to the specified torque. Tension the hydraulic pump or vacuum pump drivebelt, referring to Chapter 1 of this manual for Visa models or the main BX model manual. Refill the transmission with oil as described in Chapter 1.

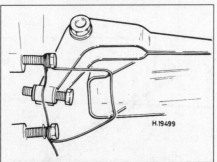

2.30 Using two bolts and wire to hold the clutch release arm while refitting the transmission

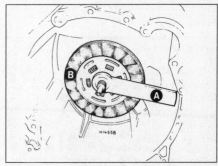

3.2 Tool for locking the transmission input shaft

Lever (A) welded to old clutch disc (driven plate) (B)

---

3 Manual transmission - dismantling and reassembly

Dismantling

1 The four-speed and five-speed manual transmissions differ only in respect of the 5th gear and its associated components.

2 To remove the components the input and output shafts must be locked before unscrewing the end nuts. The best way to do this is to engage a gear then immobilise the input shaft using an old clutch disc to which a metal bar has been welded **(see illustration)**. It is unwise to attempt to grip the input shaft splines with any other tool as damage may be caused.

3 With the input and output shaft nuts slackened continue as described for the five-speed transmission.

Reassembly

4 When reassembling the transmission use the same method described in paragraph 2 to tighten the shaft nuts. Remember to stake the nuts after tightening them.

---

4 Driveshaft rubber bellows - removal and refitting

Removal

1 With the driveshaft removed (refer to the relevant manual for petrol-engined models for

6

4.1 Plastic straps on the outer rubber bellows

4.2 Removing the rubber bellows from the outer joint housing

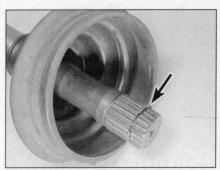

4.3 Driveshaft outer joint retaining circlip (arrowed)

4.4A Removing the outer rubber bellows from the driveshaft

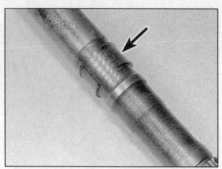

4.4B Plastic seating (arrowed) for the outer rubber bellows

4.6 Removing the inner rubber bellows

4.7 Separating the driveshaft and rollers from the inner joint housing

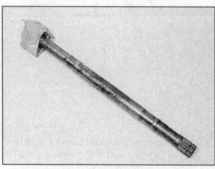

4.8 Left-hand driveshaft with rollers retained with adhesive tape

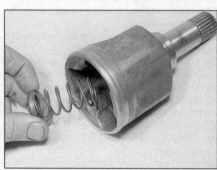

4.9 Removing the pressure pad and spring from the inner joint housing

4.11 Injecting grease into the inner joint housing

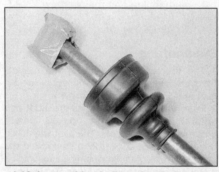

4.12 Inner rubber bellows located on the driveshaft

4.15A Tighten the metal clip. . .

4.15B . . . and bend it back under the buckle

removal procedure) loosen the clips on the outer rubber bellows. If plastic straps are fitted cut them free with snips **(see illustration)**.

2 Prise the bellows large diameter from the outer joint housing **(see illustration)**, then tap the centre hub outwards using a soft metal drift to release it from the retaining circlip. Slide the outer joint complete from the driveshaft splines.

3 Extract the circlip from the groove in the driveshaft **(see illustration)**.

4 Prise off the rubber bellows. If necessary remove the plastic seating from the recess in the driveshaft **(see illustrations)**.

5 Loosen the clips on the inner rubber

bellows. If plastic straps are fitted cut them free.

6 Prise the bellows large diameter from the inner joint housing and slide the rubber bellows off the outer end of the driveshaft **(see illustration)**.

7 Mark the driveshaft and inner joint housing in relation to each other then separate them, keeping the rollers engaged with their respective spigots **(see illustration)**.

8 Clean away the grease then retain the rollers using adhesive tape **(see illustration)**.

9 Remove the pressure pad and spring from inside the inner joint housing **(see illustration)**.

Refitting

10 Clean away the grease then begin reassembly by inserting the pressure pad and spring into the inner joint housing with the housing mounted upright in a soft-jawed vice.

11 Inject half the required amount of grease into the inner joint housing **(see illustration)**.

12 Locate the new inner rubber bellows halfway along the driveshaft **(see illustration)**.

13 Remove the adhesive tape and insert the driveshaft into the housing.

14 Inject the remaining amount of grease in the joint.

15 Keeping the driveshaft pressed against the internal spring, refit the rubber bellows and tighten the clips. Metal type clips can be tightened using two pliers, by holding the buckle and pulling the clip through. Cut off the excess and bend the clip back under the buckle **(see illustrations)**.

16 Fit the plastic seating in the driveshaft recess and refit the new rubber bellows small diameter on it.

17 Refit the circlip in the driveshaft groove.

18 Inject the required amount of grease in the outer joint then insert the driveshaft, engage the splines, and press in until the circlip snaps into the groove.

19 Ease the rubber bellows onto the outer joint, and fit the two clips, tightening them as previously described.

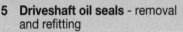

5 Driveshaft oil seals - removal and refitting

Removal

1 Jack up the front of the vehicle and support on axle stands (see "*Jacking and vehicle support*"). Apply the handbrake on Visa models or chock the rear wheels on BX models.

2 Unscrew the drain plug(s) and drain the transmission oil into a container. On completion refit and tighten the plug(s).

3 Disconnect the front track control arms from the stub axle carriers **(see illustration)**, and, on BX models, unscrew the nuts and separate the link rods from the anti-roll bar.

4 Have an assistant pull the left-hand wheel outwards while the left-hand driveshaft is levered from the differential side gear. Hold the strut outwards with a block of wood.

5 On BX models manufactured before July 1984 the left-hand differential side gear must be supported using a dowel, preferably wooden. If this precaution is not taken, the side gears may become misaligned when the right-hand driveshaft is removed.

6 Loosen the two nuts retaining the right-hand driveshaft intermediate bearing in the bracket bolted to the rear of the cylinder block and turn the bolt heads through 90° to release the bearing.

7 Have an assistant pull the right-hand wheel

5.3 Disconnecting a front track control arm (BX model)

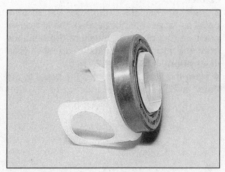

5.11A The right-hand driveshaft oil seal is supplied with a protector

5.12 Refitting the right-hand driveshaft

5.8 Levering a driveshaft and oil seal from the transmission

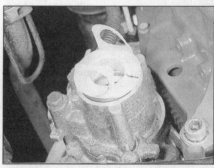

5.11B Right-hand driveshaft oil seal installed ready for driveshaft refitting

5.14 Right-hand driveshaft rubber dust seal

outwards while the right-hand driveshaft is removed from the differential side gear. Hold the strut out with a block of wood.

8 Using a screwdriver lever the oil seals from the transmission **(see illustration)**.

Refitting

9 Clean the oil seal seatings in the transmission.

10 Press the new left-hand oil seal squarely into the transmission until flush using a block of wood.

11 The new right-hand oil seal is supplied with a protector to be used when fitting the driveshaft. First remove the protector and

press the oil seal squarely into the transmission until flush using a block of wood. Refit the protector having applied a little grease to the seal lips **(see illustrations)**.

12 Insert the right-hand driveshaft while guiding the intermediate bearing in the bracket **(see illustration)**.

13 Pull out the protector and discard it. The protector is split so that it will pass over the driveshaft.

14 Slide the rubber dust seal next to the oil seal **(see illustration)**.

15 Refit and tighten the intermediate bearing bolts.

6

5.16 Refitting the left-hand driveshaft

16 Apply a little grease to the left-hand oil seal lips then insert the left-hand driveshaft (see illustration).
17 Reconnect the front track control arms to the stub axle carriers and, on BX models, reconnect the anti-roll bar links.
18 Lower the vehicle to the ground and refill the transmission with oil as described in Chapter 1.

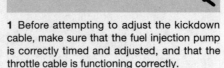

6 Kickdown cable (automatic transmission) - adjustment

1 Before attempting to adjust the kickdown cable, make sure that the fuel injection pump is correctly timed and adjusted, and that the throttle cable is functioning correctly.
2 Check that, with the throttle pedal released, the kickdown inner cable at the pump is free of tension without being slack. There should be a clearance of 0.5 to 1.0 mm between the lug on the cable and the tip of the adjuster. Slacken the adjuster locknuts, and turn the adjuster if necessary until the setting is correct.
3 Have an assistant depress the throttle pedal as far as, but not beyond, the kickdown point. In this position, measure the distance from the lug to the adjuster tip "X" (see illustration). It should be 39 mm.
4 Have the assistant depress the pedal to the floor, and re-measure the lug-to-adjuster

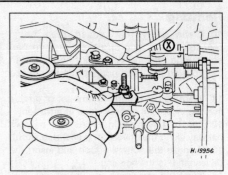

6.3 Kickdown cable adjustment
For X see text

distance. Now it should be 47 mm.
5 If either of the last two values were incorrect, reposition the kickdown cable end within the limits of the adjustment slot on the pump lever.

Chapter 7
Braking and hydraulic systems

Contents

Degrees of difficulty

Easy, suitable for novice with little experience	**Fairly easy,** suitable for beginner with some experience	**Fairly difficult,** suitable for competent DIY mechanic	**Difficult,** suitable for experienced DIY mechanic	**Very difficult,** suitable for expert DIY or professional

Specifications

General

System type . . . . Discs front, drums rear on Visa models. Discs all round on BX models. Cable-operated handbrake on rear wheels for Visa models and front wheels for BX models.

Front brakes (Visa models)

Disc diameter	247.0 mm
Minimum disc thickness	8.0 mm
Maximum disc run-out	0.07 mm
Maximum variation of disc thickness	0.02 mm
Minimum disc pad lining thickness	2.0 mm

Rear brakes (Visa models)

Maximum drum internal diameter:
Saloon	181.0 mm
Van	229.6 mm

Brake limiter adjustment (Van models):
Cable clamp-to-lever contact faces clearance	4.0 to 5.0 mm

Torque wrench settings (Visa models)

	Nm	lbf ft
Brake vacuum pump (direct-driven from camshaft)	25	18
Cross-tube brackets	14	10
Master cylinder	8	6
Rear hub nut (Saloon models)	190	140
Servo unit	8	6

7

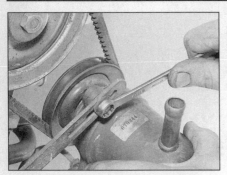

1.2A HP pump adjusting bolt on BX models

1.2B HP pump pivot bolt on BX models

1.2C HP pump mounting bracket on BX models

1 Description - general

1 In Visa models the braking system is similar to that for petrol engine models, but there is insufficient vacuum for a vacuum servo unit. A vacuum pump, driven from the camshaft, is therefore used. The vacuum servo unit and master cylinder are located on the left-hand side of the bulkhead. A cross-tube mounted inside the passenger compartment links the brake pedal to the vacuum servo unit.

2 On BX models the hydraulic braking system is virtually identical to that on petrol-engined models. The high pressure pump is belt-driven from a pulley attached to the end of the camshaft. The pump mounting bracket is bolted to the top of the transmission as also is the adjusting link **(see illustrations)**.

3 Apart from the different location of the high pressure pump, the hydraulic system components and procedures are as described in the main BX manual.

2 Master cylinder (Visa models) - general

1 The master cylinder is located on the servo unit on the left-hand side of the bulkhead **(see illustrations)**.

2 Removal and refitting procedures can be found in the main manual, but before starting work remove the air cleaner and battery.

3 Servo unit (Visa models) - general

1 The servo unit is located on the left-hand side of the bulkhead.

2 Removal and refitting procedures are given in the main manual, but access to the mounting nuts is gained by extracting the cross-head screws and removing the left-hand side shelf **(see illustrations)**.

4 Pedal cross-tube (Visa models) - removal and refitting

Removal

1 Disconnect the battery negative lead.

2 Extract the cross-head screws and remove the right-hand side shelf **(see illustrations)**. Similarly remove the left-hand side shelf.

3 Remove the steering column as described for petrol-engined models.

4 Disconnect the accelerator cable from the pedal.

5 Disconnect the clutch cable from the pedal.

6 Remove the clevis pin and disconnect the servo unit pushrod from the cross-tube.

7 Disconnect the wiring from the stop-lamp switch.

8 Unscrew the nuts and detach the left and right-hand brackets from the bulkhead.

9 Extract the spring clips and disconnect the link from the brake pedal and cross-tube.

10 Withdraw the brackets from each end of the cross-tube, then withdraw the cross-tube from the vehicle.

Refitting

11 Refitting is a reversal of removal, but adjust the clutch and accelerator cables.

5 Brake vacuum pump (Visa models) - removal and refitting

Note: *This section describes the procedure for models with belt driven vacuum pumps. Refer to Section 7, for camshaft driven types.*

Removal

1 Remove the air cleaner and ducting.

2 Disconnect the inlet and outlet hoses.

3 Loosen the pivot and adjustment link bolts and nuts, swivel the vacuum pump upwards and slip the drivebelt from the pulleys.

4 Unscrew the bolts and remove the vacuum pump from the mounting bracket and adjustment link.

Refitting

5 Refitting is a reversal of removal, but swivel the pump downwards until the drivebelt tension is as given in the Specifications before tightening the pivot and adjustment link bolts and nuts. With the vehicle on level ground, unscrew the filler/level plug and check that

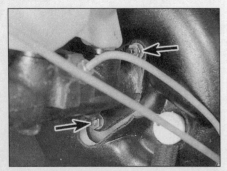

2.1 Master cylinder mounting nuts (arrowed) on Visa models

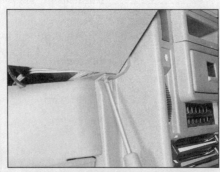

3.2A Extract the shelf cross-head screws . . .

3.2B . . . for access to the servo unit mounting nuts (arrowed)

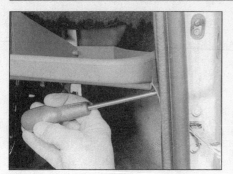

4.2A Removing the right-hand shelf side . . .

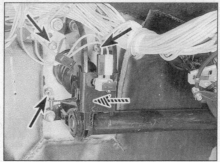

4.2B . . . and centre screws

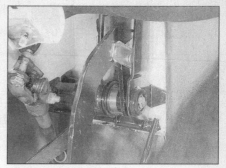

4.2C Brake pedal and cross-tube with shelf removed

the oil level is up to the bottom of the hole. If not, top-up with the correct grade of oil then refit and tighten the plug.

6 Brake vacuum pump (C15 Van) - general

General

1 For the period from December 1989 to January 1991, C15 Vans were fitted with a vane-type brake vacuum pump, driven directly from the rear of the camshaft. This modification resulted in a modified cylinder head, incorporating mounting bolt holes for the pump, and an oil channel that passes oil from the engine lubrication system to the pump. The end of the (shorter) camshaft also incorporates a slot for engagement with the pump drive dog.

2 On models between January 1991 and early 1993, the original (longer) camshaft is fitted, with the original belt-driven vacuum pump driven from a pulley on the end of the camshaft.

3 From early 1993, the XUD 7 engine featured an improved (second generation) direct-driven vane-type brake vacuum pump, and the engine was modified as described in paragraph 1.

7 Brake vacuum pump (C15 Van) - removal and refitting

Note: *This section describes the procedure for models with vacuum pumps that are driven directly from the camshaft. Refer to Section 5, for belt driven types.*

Removal

1 Loosen the clip and disconnect the vacuum hose from the vacuum pump **(see illustration)**.

2 Unscrew the mounting bolts and remove the brake vacuum pump from the end of the cylinder head **(see illustrations)**.

3 Extract the two O-rings from the grooves in the pump **(see illustrations)**.

4 Using a small screwdriver, extract the filter from the oil lubrication channel in the vacuum pump.

Refitting

5 Before refitting the pump, clean the O-ring grooves, and also clean the mating surfaces of the pump and cylinder head. Clean the filter, or if necessary renew it.

6 Locate the filter in the oil lubrication channel.

7 Fit new O-rings in the grooves on the pump, and lightly oil them.

8 Locate the pump on the end of the cylinder head, making sure that the dog engages correctly with the end of the camshaft. To avoid the O-rings being displaced, align the slot in the end of the camshaft with the dog on the vacuum pump before refitting the pump.

9 Insert the mounting bolts, and tighten them to the specified torque.

10 Connect the vacuum hose and tighten the clip

11 Start the engine, and check that the brake

7.2A Unscrew the mounting bolts . . .

7.3A Removing the large O-ring . . .

pedal operates correctly, with assistance from the vacuum pump. Check around the pump for signs of oil leakage.

7.1 Disconnecting the vacuum hose from the vacuum pump

7.2B . . . and remove the vacuum pump

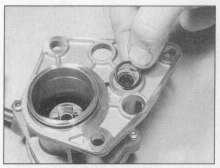

7.3B . . . and small O-ring from the grooves in the pump

7

Notes

Chapter 8
Suspension and steering

Contents

Degrees of difficulty

Easy, suitable for novice with little experience	Fairly easy, suitable for beginner with some experience	Fairly difficult, suitable for competent DIY mechanic	Difficult, suitable for experienced DIY mechanic	Very difficult, suitable for expert DIY or professional

Specifications

Front suspension

Type:

	Visa	BX
Visa models	Independent, MacPherson strut and coil spring, with anti-roll bar. Front subframe carries track control arms, steering gear and anti-roll bar	
BX models	Independent, with upper and lower arms, hydropneumatic cylinders	

Wheel alignment:

	Visa	BX
Camber	0°16' ± 30'	0° ±30'
Castor		
Pre August 1985 models	1°20' ± 30'	2° ± 35'
August 1985 on models	1°33' ± 30'	2° ± 35'
Steering axis inclination	9°16' ± 40'	12°
Toe setting:		
Pre August 1985	2.0 ± 1 mm (toe-out)	0 to 3.0 mm (toe-out)
August 1985	0 to 2.0 mm (toe-in)	0 to 3.0 mm (toe-out)

Rear suspension

Type:

Visa models .... Independent, trailing arms and hydraulic dampers with coil springs
BX models .... Independent, trailing arms, hydropneumatic cylinders

Wheel alignment:

	Visa	BX
Camber	1°30'	0°09' ± 20'
Toe setting	1.0 to 4.0 mm (toe-in)	0 to 5.0 mm (toe-in)

Steering

Type .... Rack and pinion with safety column

Turning circle (between kerbs):

Visa .... 10.06 m
BX:
  Manual steering .... 10.17 m
  Power steering .... 10.37 m

Wheels

Type .... Pressed steel

Size:
Visa .... 4.50 B 13 FH 4.35 or 4.30
BX .... 5.00 B 14 FH 4.25

Tyres

Size:
Visa .... 145 SR 13 or 155 SR 13
BX .... 165/70 R 14

Torque wrench settings (Visa models)

	Nm	lbf ft
Anti-roll bar to track control arm	75	55
Anti-roll bar mounting	35	26
Anti-roll guide bar to anti-roll bar	30	22
Anti-roll guide bar to subframe	25	18
Steering gear mounting	35	26
Steering shaft to pinion	15	11
Track control arm pivot bolt	35	26
Track rod end nut	35	26

2.2 Front track control arm inner pivot bolt (arrowed) on Visa models

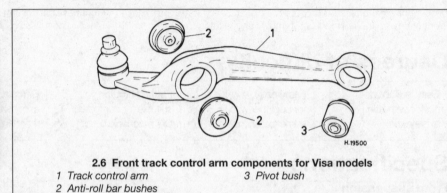

2.6 Front track control arm components for Visa models
1 *Track control arm*   3 *Pivot bush*
2 *Anti-roll bar bushes*

1 Description - general

On Visa models the front subframe differs from that fitted to petrol engine models in that it carries the track control arm inner pivots, the steering gear and the anti-roll bar that is mounted from the rear. In all other respects the components and work procedures are similar to those described for the GTi model in the main Visa manual.

The suspension and steering components fitted to BX models are identical to those on petrol engine models.

2 Front track control arm (Visa models) - removal, overhaul and refitting

Removal

1 Jack up the front of the vehicle and support on axle stands (see *"Jacking and vehicle support"*). Apply the handbrake and remove the roadwheel.
2 Unscrew the nut from the inner pivot bolt **(see illustration)**.
3 Have an assistant hold the suspension strut pressed inwards then remove the bolt and release the strut. Note that the bolt head faces to the rear.
4 Unscrew the clamp bolt securing the lower balljoint to the hub carrier, then drive a wedge into the slot and release the lower suspension arm. Remove the balljoint protector where fitted.

5 Unscrew the nut from the end of the anti-roll bar, remove the washer, and withdraw the track control arm.

Overhaul

6 The rubber bushes may be renewed if necessary. Lever or drive out the anti-roll bar bushes. Ideally, the pivot bush should be pressed out using a bench press or flypress. However, it is possible to remove and insert the bush using a long bolt, nut and washers and a metal tube **(see illustration)**.

Refitting

7 Refitting is a reversal of removal, but tighten the bolts to the specified torque with the weight of the vehicle on the front suspension. On completion check and if necessary adjust the steering angles and front wheel alignment.

3 Front anti-roll bar (Visa models) - removal and refitting

Removal

1 Jack up the front of the vehicle and support on axle stands (see *"Jacking and vehicle support"*). Apply the handbrake and remove both roadwheels.
2 Remove one track control arm, referring to Section 2.
3 Unscrew the nut securing the remaining end of the anti-roll bar to the other track control arm and recover the washer.
4 Unbolt the guide bar from the subframe.
5 Unscrew the mounting clamp bolts **(see illustration)** and withdraw the anti-roll bar over the subframe. If necessary disconnect the gearchange rods to provide additional working room.

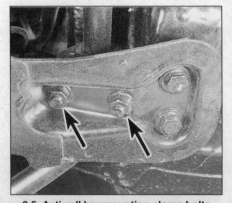

3.5 Anti-roll bar mounting clamp bolts (arrowed) on Visa models

3.7A Guide bar adjustment clamp for the anti-roll bar on Visa models

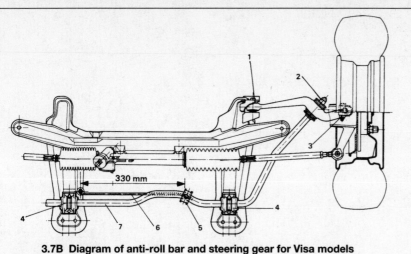

3.7B **Diagram of anti-roll bar and steering gear for Visa models**

1 Track control arm inner pivot bolt
2 Anti-roll bar front mounting nut
3 Lower balljoint pinch-bolt
4 Rear mounting clamps
5 Guide bar adjustment clamp
6 Guide bar
7 Anti-roll bar

4.4 **Steering gear mounting bolt (arrowed) on Visa models**

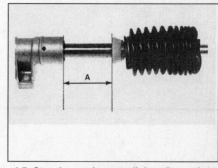

4.5 **Steering rack centralising dimension for Visa models**
A = 72.5 mm (2.85 in)

Refitting

6 Examine the rubber bearings for damage and deterioration, and renew them if necessary.

7 Refitting is a reversal of removal, but delay fully tightening the clamp bolts until the full weight of the vehicle is on the suspension. The guide bar bolt **(see illustration)** should also remain loosened until after the bearing clamp bolts have been tightened and its length should be suitably adjusted **(see illustration)**.

4 Steering gear (Visa models) - removal and refitting

Removal

1 Jack up the front of the vehicle and support on axle stands (see "*Jacking and vehicle support*"). Apply the handbrake. Remove the front roadwheels.

2 Unscrew the nuts from the track rod end balljoint studs and, with a balljoint splitter, disconnect the balljoints from the steering arms.

3 Unscrew and remove the pinch-bolt securing the bottom of the steering shaft to the steering gear pinion splines.

4 Unscrew the mounting bolts **(see illustration)**, and withdraw the steering gear sideways from the subframe.

Refitting

5 Begin refitting by centralising the rack. To do this, disconnect the rubber bellows and set the rack to the dimension shown **(see illustration)**.

6 With the steering wheel in the straight-ahead position, refit the steering gear and connect the steering shaft to the pinion splines.

7 Refit and tighten the mounting bolts to the specified torque.

8 Insert the steering shaft pinch-bolt and tighten it.

9 Reconnect the rubber bellows to the steering gear.

10 Reconnect the track rod ends to the steering arms and tighten the nuts.

11 Refit the front roadwheels and lower the vehicle to the ground. On completion check and if necessary adjust the front wheel alignment.

8

Notes

Dimensions and weights

Note: *All figures and dimensions are approximate and may vary according to model. Refer to manufacturer's data for exact figures.*

Dimensions

Overall length:

Visa Saloon	3.725 m
C15/Champ Van	3.995 m
BX Saloon	4.237 m
BX Estate	4.399 m

Overall width:

Visa Saloon	1.526 m
C15/Champ Van	1.636 m
BX	1.682 m

Overall height:

Visa Saloon	1:410 m
C15/Champ Van	1.801 m
BX Saloon	1.360 m
BX Estate	1.431 m

Wheelbase:

Visa Saloon/Van	2.420 m
BX	2.660 m

Weights

Kerb weight:

Visa Saloon	890 kg
C15/Champ Van	850 kg
BX Saloon (non-Turbo)	990 kg
BX Saloon (Turbo)	1025 kg
BX Estate (non-Turbo)	1037 kg
BX Estate (Turbo)	1077 kg

Maximum trailer weight:

Visa Saloon/Van	750 kg
BX	1100 kg

Maximum roof rack load:

Visa Saloon/Van	60 kg
BX Saloon	75 kg
BX Estate	100 kg

Gross train weight:

Visa Saloon/Van	2050 kg
BX Saloon	2600 kg
BX Estate	2700 kg

Conversion factors

Length (distance)

Inches (in)	x 25.4	=	Millimetres (mm)	x 0.0394	= Inches (in)
Feet (ft)	x 0.305	=	Metres (m)	x 3.281	= Feet (ft)
Miles	x 1.609	=	Kilometres (km)	x 0.621	= Miles

Volume (capacity)

Cubic inches (cu in; in³)	x 16.387	=	Cubic centimetres (cc; cm³)	x 0.061	= Cubic inches (cu in; in³)
Imperial pints (Imp pt)	x 0.568	=	Litres (l)	x 1.76	= Imperial pints (Imp pt)
Imperial quarts (Imp qt)	x 1.137	=	Litres (l)	x 0.88	= Imperial quarts (Imp qt)
Imperial quarts (Imp qt)	x 1.201	=	US quarts (US qt)	x 0.833	= Imperial quarts (Imp qt)
US quarts (US qt)	x 0.946	=	Litres (l)	x 1.057	= US quarts (US qt)
Imperial gallons (Imp gal)	x 4.546	=	Litres (l)	x 0.22	= Imperial gallons (Imp gal)
Imperial gallons (Imp gal)	x 1.201	=	US gallons (US gal)	x 0.833	= Imperial gallons (Imp gal)
US gallons (US gal)	x 3.785	=	Litres (l)	x 0.264	= US gallons (US gal)

Mass (weight)

Ounces (oz)	x 28.35	=	Grams (g)	x 0.035	= Ounces (oz)
Pounds (lb)	x 0.454	=	Kilograms (kg)	x 2.205	= Pounds (lb)

Force

Ounces-force (ozf; oz)	x 0.278	=	Newtons (N)	x 3.6	= Ounces-force (ozf; oz)
Pounds-force (lbf; lb)	x 4.448	=	Newtons (N)	x 0.225	= Pounds-force (lbf; lb)
Newtons (N)	x 0.1	=	Kilograms-force (kgf; kg)	x 9.81	= Newtons (N)

Pressure

Pounds-force per square inch (psi; lbf/in²; lb/in²)	x 0.070	=	Kilograms-force per square centimetre (kgf/cm²; kg/cm²)	x 14.223	= Pounds-force per square inch (psi; lbf/in²; lb/in²)
Pounds-force per square inch (psi; lbf/in²; lb/in²)	x 0.068	=	Atmospheres (atm)	x 14.696	= Pounds-force per square inch (psi; lbf/in²; lb/in²)
Pounds-force per square inch (psi; lbf/in²; lb/in²)	x 0.069	=	Bars	x 14.5	= Pounds-force per square inch (psi; lbf/in²; lb/in²)
Pounds-force per square inch (psi; lbf/in²; lb/in²)	x 6.895	=	Kilopascals (kPa)	x 0.145	= Pounds-force per square inch (psi; lbf/in²; lb/in²)
Kilopascals (kPa)	x 0.01	=	Kilograms-force per square centimetre (kgf/cm²; kg/cm²)	x 98.1	= Kilopascals (kPa)
Millibar (mbar)	x 100	=	Pascals (Pa)	x 0.01	= Millibar (mbar)
Millibar (mbar)	x 0.0145	=	Pounds-force per square inch (psi; lbf/in²; lb/in²)	x 68.947	= Millibar (mbar)
Millibar (mbar)	x 0.75	=	Millimetres of mercury (mmHg)	x 1.333	= Millibar (mbar)
Millibar (mbar)	x 0.401	=	Inches of water (inH₂O)	x 2.491	= Millibar (mbar)
Millimetres of mercury (mmHg)	x 0.535	=	Inches of water (inH₂O)	x 1.868	= Millimetres of mercury (mmHg)
Inches of water (inH₂O)	x 0.036	=	Pounds-force per square inch (psi; lbf/in²; lb/in²)	x 27.68	= Inches of water (inH₂O)

Torque (moment of force)

Pounds-force inches (lbf in; lb in)	x 1.152	=	Kilograms-force centimetre (kgf cm; kg cm)	x 0.868	= Pounds-force inches (lbf in; lb in)
Pounds-force inches (lbf in; lb in)	x 0.113	=	Newton metres (Nm)	x 8.85	= Pounds-force inches (lbf in; lb in)
Pounds-force inches (lbf in; lb in)	x 0.083	=	Pounds-force feet (lbf ft; lb ft)	x 12	= Pounds-force inches (lbf in; lb in)
Pounds-force feet (lbf ft; lb ft)	x 0.138	=	Kilograms-force metres (kgf m; kg m)	x 7.233	= Pounds-force feet (lbf ft; lb ft)
Pounds-force feet (lbf ft; lb ft)	x 1.356	=	Newton metres (Nm)	x 0.738	= Pounds-force feet (lbf ft; lb ft)
Newton metres (Nm)	x 0.102	=	Kilograms-force metres (kgf m; kg m)	x 9.804	= Newton metres (Nm)

Power

Horsepower (hp)	x 745.7	=	Watts (W)	x 0.0013	= Horsepower (hp)

Velocity (speed)

Miles per hour (miles/hr; mph)	x 1.609	=	Kilometres per hour (km/hr; kph)	x 0.621	= Miles per hour (miles/hr; mph)

Fuel consumption*

Miles per gallon (mpg)	x 0.354	=	Kilometres per litre (km/l)	x 2.825	= Miles per gallon (mpg)

Temperature

Degrees Fahrenheit = (°C x 1.8) + 32   Degrees Celsius (Degrees Centigrade; °C) = (°F - 32) x 0.56

It is common practice to convert from miles per gallon (mpg) to litres/100 kilometres (l/100km), where mpg x l/100 km = 282

Spare parts are available from many sources, including maker's appointed garages, accessory shops and motor factors. To be sure of obtaining the correct parts, it will sometimes be necessary to quote the vehicle identification number. If possible, it can also be useful to take the old part along for positive identification. Items such as starter motors and alternators may be available through a service exchange scheme - any parts returned should always be clean.

Our advice regarding spare part sources is as follows.

Officially appointed dealers

This is the best source of parts that are peculiar to your car, that are otherwise not generally available. It is also the only place at which you should buy parts if your vehicle is still under warranty.

Accessory shops

These are often very good places to buy materials and components needed for the maintenance of your car (e.g. oil filters, drivebelts, oils and greases, etc.). They also sell general accessories, usually have convenient opening hours, charge lower prices and can often be found not far from home.

Motor factors

Good factors will stock all the more important components that wear out relatively quickly (e.g. clutch components, pistons, valves, exhaust systems, brake cylinders/pipes/hoses/seals/shoes and pads, etc.). Motor factors will often provide new or reconditioned components on a part exchange basis - this can save a considerable amount of money.

Vehicle identification

Modifications are a continuing and unpublished process in vehicle manufacture, quite apart from major model changes. Spare parts manuals and lists are compiled upon a numerical basis, the individual vehicle numbers being essential to correct identification of the component required.

When ordering spare parts, always give as much information as possible. Quote the car model, year of manufacture and vehicle identification and/or engine numbers as appropriate (see illustrations).

The *chassis or identification number* is stamped on the makers plate that is located on the right front wheel arch in the engine compartment. On some models a *chassis number* is also stamped onto a plate located on the front panel.

The *vehicle type* can be found stamped into the drip rail next to the right front wing.

The *engine serial number is* stamped in the centre and at the front of the engine.

The *transmission number* is stamped on the transmission casing.

Some later models also have a *replacement parts identification number* on the right hand front wheel arch.

Individual components, such as the starter motor, alternator, injection pump, etc., also have identification numbers stamped on the components themselves.

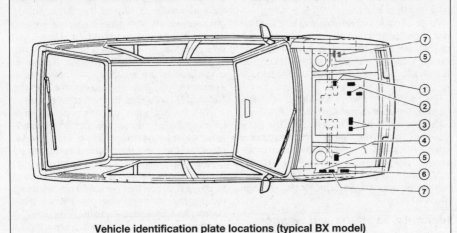

Vehicle identification plate locations (typical BX model)

1 *Transmission number*
2 *Engine number*
3 *Manufacturers plate*
4 *Replacement parts number*
5 *Chassis number*
6 *Paint number*
7 *Model year*

Location of vehicle identification plate (Visa models)

Vehicle identification plate
1 *Vehicle identification number*
2 *Gross vehicle weight*
3 *Gross train weight*
4 *Maximum weight on front axle*
5 *Maximum weight on rear axle*

General repair procedures

Whenever servicing, repair or overhaul work is carried out on the car or its components, observe the following procedures and instructions. This will assist in carrying out the operation efficiently and to a professional standard of workmanship.

Joint mating faces and gaskets

When separating components at their mating faces, never insert screwdrivers or similar implements into the joint between the faces in order to prise them apart. This can cause severe damage which results in oil leaks, coolant leaks, etc upon reassembly. Separation is usually achieved by tapping along the joint with a soft-faced hammer in order to break the seal. However, note that this method may not be suitable where dowels are used for component location.

Where a gasket is used between the mating faces of two components, a new one must be fitted on reassembly; fit it dry unless otherwise stated in the repair procedure. Make sure that the mating faces are clean and dry, with all traces of old gasket removed. When cleaning a joint face, use a tool which is unlikely to score or damage the face, and remove any burrs or nicks with an oilstone or fine file.

Make sure that tapped holes are cleaned with a pipe cleaner, and keep them free of jointing compound, if this is being used, unless specifically instructed otherwise.

Ensure that all orifices, channels or pipes are clear, and blow through them, preferably using compressed air.

Oil seals

Oil seals can be removed by levering them out with a wide flat-bladed screwdriver or similar implement. Alternatively, a number of self-tapping screws may be screwed into the seal, and these used as a purchase for pliers or some similar device in order to pull the seal free.

Whenever an oil seal is removed from its working location, either individually or as part of an assembly, it should be renewed.

The very fine sealing lip of the seal is easily damaged, and will not seal if the surface it contacts is not completely clean and free from scratches, nicks or grooves. If the original sealing surface of the component cannot be restored, and the manufacturer has not made provision for slight relocation of the seal relative to the sealing surface, the component should be renewed.

Protect the lips of the seal from any surface which may damage them in the course of fitting. Use tape or a conical sleeve where possible. Lubricate the seal lips with oil before fitting and, on dual-lipped seals, fill the space between the lips with grease.

Unless otherwise stated, oil seals must be fitted with their sealing lips toward the lubricant to be sealed.

Use a tubular drift or block of wood of the appropriate size to install the seal and, if the seal housing is shouldered, drive the seal down to the shoulder. If the seal housing is unshouldered, the seal should be fitted with its face flush with the housing top face (unless otherwise instructed).

Screw threads and fastenings

Seized nuts, bolts and screws are quite a common occurrence where corrosion has set in, and the use of penetrating oil or releasing fluid will often overcome this problem if the offending item is soaked for a while before attempting to release it. The use of an impact driver may also provide a means of releasing such stubborn fastening devices, when used in conjunction with the appropriate screwdriver bit or socket. If none of these methods works, it may be necessary to resort to the careful application of heat, or the use of a hacksaw or nut splitter device.

Studs are usually removed by locking two nuts together on the threaded part, and then using a spanner on the lower nut to unscrew the stud. Studs or bolts which have broken off below the surface of the component in which they are mounted can sometimes be removed using a stud extractor. Always ensure that a blind tapped hole is completely free from oil, grease, water or other fluid before installing the bolt or stud. Failure to do this could cause the housing to crack due to the hydraulic action of the bolt or stud as it is screwed in.

When tightening a castellated nut to accept a split pin, tighten the nut to the specified torque, where applicable, and then tighten further to the next split pin hole. Never slacken the nut to align the split pin hole, unless stated in the repair procedure.

When checking or retightening a nut or bolt to a specified torque setting, slacken the nut or bolt by a quarter of a turn, and then retighten to the specified setting. However, this should not be attempted where angular tightening has been used.

For some screw fastenings, notably cylinder head bolts or nuts, torque wrench settings are no longer specified for the latter stages of tightening, "angle-tightening" being called up instead. Typically, a fairly low torque wrench setting will be applied to the bolts/nuts in the correct sequence, followed by one or more stages of tightening through specified angles.

Locknuts, locktabs and washers

Any fastening which will rotate against a component or housing during tightening should always have a washer between it and the relevant component or housing.

Spring or split washers should always be renewed when they are used to lock a critical component such as a big-end bearing retaining bolt or nut. Locktabs which are folded over to retain a nut or bolt should always be renewed.

Self-locking nuts can be re-used in non-critical areas, providing resistance can be felt when the locking portion passes over the bolt or stud thread. However, it should be noted that self-locking stiffnuts tend to lose their effectiveness after long periods of use, and should then be renewed as a matter of course.

Split pins must always be replaced with new ones of the correct size for the hole.

When thread-locking compound is found on the threads of a fastener which is to be re-used, it should be cleaned off with a wire brush and solvent, and fresh compound applied on reassembly.

Special tools

Some repair procedures in this manual entail the use of special tools such as a press, two or three-legged pullers, spring compressors, etc. Wherever possible, suitable readily-available alternatives to the manufacturer's special tools are described, and are shown in use. In some instances, where no alternative is possible, it has been necessary to resort to the use of a manufacturer's tool, and this has been done for reasons of safety as well as the efficient completion of the repair operation. Unless you are highly-skilled and have a thorough understanding of the procedures described, never attempt to bypass the use of any special tool when the procedure described specifies its use. Not only is there a very great risk of personal injury, but expensive damage could be caused to the components involved.

Environmental considerations

When disposing of used engine oil, brake fluid, antifreeze, etc, give due consideration to any detrimental environmental effects. Do not, for instance, pour any of the above liquids down drains into the general sewage system, or onto the ground to soak away. Many local council refuse tips provide a facility for waste oil disposal, as do some garages. If none of these facilities are available, consult your local Environmental Health Department, or the National Rivers Authority, for further advice.

With the universal tightening-up of legislation regarding the emission of environmentally-harmful substances from motor vehicles, most vehicles have tamperproof devices fitted to the main adjustment points of the fuel system. These devices are primarily designed to prevent unqualified persons from adjusting the fuel/air mixture, with the chance of a consequent increase in toxic emissions. If such devices are found during servicing or overhaul, they should, wherever possible, be renewed or refitted in accordance with the manufacturer's requirements or current legislation.

OIL CARE
FOLLOW THE CODE

OIL BANK LINE
0800 66 33 66

Note: It is antisocial and illegal to dump oil down the drain. To find the location of your local oil recycling bank, call this number free.

The jack supplied with the vehicle tool kit should only be used for changing roadwheels **(see illustrations)**. The jack and wheel brace are located either in the engine compartment or in the luggage compartment, depending on the model. When carrying out any other kind of work, raise the vehicle using a hydraulic jack, and always supplement the jack with axle stands positioned under the vehicle jacking points.

When jacking up the vehicle with a trolley jack, position the jack head under one of the relevant jacking points. **Do not** jack the vehicle under the sump or any of the steering or suspension components. Supplement the jack using axle stands. The jacking points are shown in the accompanying illustrations. **Never** *work under, around, or near a raised vehicle, unless it is adequately supported in at least two places.*

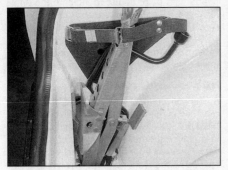

Jack and wheel brace on Visa Saloon models

Front jacking point (Visa model shown)

A *Jack location hole*
B *Reinforced panel*

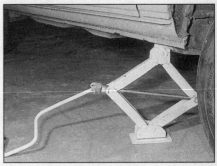

Jacking the rear of the vehicle (Visa model shown)

Contents

1 Normal workshop tools

1 The decision as to what range of tools is necessary will depend on the work to be done, the range of vehicles which it is expected to encounter, and not least the financial resources available. The tools in the following list, with additions as necessary from the various categories of diesel-specific tools described later, should be sufficient for carrying out most routine maintenance and repair operations.

> Combination spanners (see below)
> Socket spanners (see below)
> Ratchet, extension piece and universal joint (for use with sockets)
> Torque wrench
> Angle tightening indicator (see below)
> Adjustable spanner
> Set of sump drain plug keys
> Strap or chain wrench (for fuel and oil filters)
> Oil drain tray
> Feeler gauges
> Combination pliers
> Long-nosed pliers
> Self-locking pliers (Mole wrench)
> Screwdrivers (large and small, flat blade and cross blade)
> Set of Allen keys
> Set of splined and Torx keys and sockets (see below)
> Ball pein hammer
> Soft-faced hammer
> Puller (universal type, with interchangeable jaws)
> Cold chisel
> Scriber
> Scraper
> Centre punch
> Hacksaw
> File
> Steel rule/straight-edge
> Axle stands and/or ramps
> Trolley jack
> Inspection light
> Inspection mirror
> Telescopic magnet/pick-up tool

Socket and spanner size

2 A good range of open-ended, ring and socket spanners will be required. Most modern vehicles use metric size fastenings throughout.

3 Split ring spanners (also known as flare nut spanners) are particularly useful for dealing with fuel pipe unions, on which a conventional ring or socket cannot be used because the pipe is in the way. The most common sizes are 17 mm and 19 mm on metric systems.

4 Sockets are available in various drive sizes. The half inch square drive size is most widely used and accepts most torque wrenches. Smaller drive sizes (⅜ or ¼ in) are useful for working in confined spaces, while for large high-torque fastenings (driveshaft or hub nuts, crankshaft pulley bolts) ¾ inch drive is most satisfactory.

5 The humble box spanner should not be overlooked. Box spanners are cheap and will sometimes serve as a substitute for a deep socket, though they cannot be used with a torque wrench and are easily deformed.

Angle tightening

6 For fastenings such as cylinder head bolts, many manufacturers now specify tightening in terms of angular rotation rather than an absolute torque. After an initial 'snug' torque wrench setting, subsequent tightening stages are specified as angles through which each bolt must be turned. Variations in tightening torque which could be caused by the presence or absence of dirt, oil etc. on the bolt threads thus have no effect. A further benefit is that there is no need for a high-range torque wrench.

7 The owner-mechanic who expects to use this method of tightening only once or twice in the life of the vehicle may be content to make up a cardboard template, or mark the bolt heads with paint spots, to indicate the angle required. Greater speed and accuracy will result from using one of the many angle tightening indicators commercially available. Most of them are intended for use with ½ in drive sockets or keys (**see illustration**).

Splined bolt heads

8 The conventional hexagon head bolt is being replaced in many areas by the splined or 'Torx' head bolt. This type of bolt has multiple splines in place of the hexagon. A set of splined or Torx keys will be needed to deal with female splined heads. Torx bolts with male heads also exist, and for these Torx sockets will be needed. Both keys and sockets are available to accept ½ in square drives.

2 Diesel-specific tools

Basic tune-up and service

1 Besides the normal range of spanners, screwdrivers and so on, the following tools and equipment will be needed for basic tune-up and service operations :

> Deep socket for removing and tightening screw-in injectors
> Optical or pulse-sensitive tachometer
> Electrical multi-meter, or dedicated glow plug tester
> Compression or leakdown tester
> Vacuum pump and/or gauge

Injector socket

2 The size most commonly required is 27mm. The socket needs to be deep in order not to foul the injector body. On some engines it also needs to be thin-walled. Suitable sockets are sold by Dieseltune, Sykes-Pickavant and

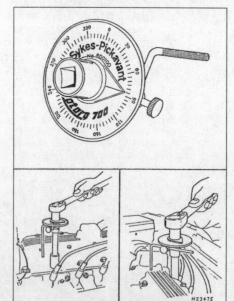

1.7 Sykes-Pickavant 800700 angle tightening gear

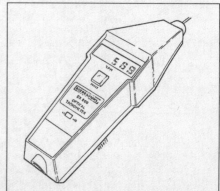

2.5 Dieseltune DX 800 optical tachometer

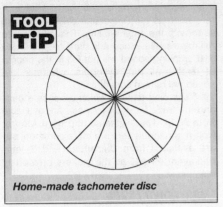

Home-made tachometer disc

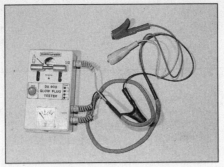

2.14 Dieseltune DX 900 glow plug tester

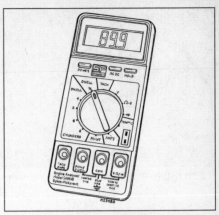

2.15 Sykes-Pickavant 300510 engine analyser/multi-meter

Snap-On, among others.

Tachometer

3 The type of tachometer which senses ignition system HT pulses via an inductive pick-up cannot be used on diesel engines, unless a device such as the Sykes-Pickavant timing light adapter is available.

4 If an engine is fitted with a TDC sensor and a diagnostic socket, an electronic tachometer which reads the signals from the TDC sensor can be used.

5 Not all engines have TDC sensors. On those which do not, the use of an optical or pulse-sensitive tachometer is necessary (see illustration).

6 The optical tachometer registers the passage of a paint mark or (more usually) a strip of reflective foil placed on the crankshaft pulley. It is not so convenient to use as the electronic or pulse-sensitive types, since it has to be held so that it can 'see' the pulley, but it has the advantage that it can be used on any engine, petrol or diesel, with or without a diagnostic socket.

7 The pulse-sensitive tachometer uses a transducer similar to that needed for a timing light. The transducer converts hydraulic or mechanical impulses in an injector pipe into electrical signals, which are displayed on the tachometer as engine speed.

8 Some dynamic timing equipment for diesel engines incorporates a means of displaying engine speed. If this equipment is available, a separate tachometer will not be required.

9 Both optical and pulse-sensitive tachometers are sold by A. M. Test Systems and Kent-Moore. Optical tachometers are sold by (inter alia) Dieseltune, and pulse-sensitive by Souriau and Bosch.

DIY alternative tachometer

10 The owner-mechanic who only wishes to check the idle speed of one engine occasionally may well feel that the purchase of a special tachometer is not justified. Assuming that mains electric light is available, the use of a stroboscopic disc is a cheap alternative. The principle will be familiar to anyone who has used such a disc to check the speed of a record-player turntable.

11 A disc must be constructed of stiff paper or card to fit onto the crankshaft pulley (or camshaft pulley, if appropriate - but remember that this rotates at half speed). The disc should be white or light-coloured, and divided using a protractor into regular segments with heavy black lines (see Tool Tip). The number of segments required will depend on the desired idle speed and the frequency of the alternating current supply. For the 50 Hz supply used in the UK and most of Europe the figures are as follows:

Speed (rpm)	No of segments	Angle per segment
706	17	21° 11'
750	16	22° 30'
800	15	24°
857	14	25° 43'
923	13	27° 42'

12 Attach the disc to the crankshaft pulley and position the car so that the disc can be viewed using only artificial light. A fluorescent tube is best. Failing this a low-wattage incandescent bulb will give better results than a high-wattage one. Run the engine at idle and observe the disc.

 Warning : Do not run the engine in a confined space without some means of extracting the exhaust fumes.

13 If the engine speed corresponds to the calculated disc speed, the disc segments will appear to be stationary. If the speed is different, the segments will appear to drift in the direction of engine rotation (too fast) or against it (too slow). The segments will also appear to be stationary at multiples or sub-multiples of the calculated speed - twice or half the speed, and so on - so some common sense must be used.

Electrical multi-meter or glow plug tester

14 It is possible to test glow plugs and their control circuitry with a multi-meter, or even (to a limited extent) with a 12 volt test lamp. A purpose-made glow plug tester will do the job faster and is much easier to use, but on the other hand it will not do anything else (see illustration).

15 If it is decided to purchase a multi-meter, make sure that it has a high current range - ideally 0 to 100 amps - for checking glow plug

current draw. Some meters require an external shunt to be fitted for this. An inductive clamp connection is preferred for high current measurement since it can be used without breaking into the circuit. Other ranges required are dc voltage (0 to 20 or 30 volts is suitable for most applications) and resistance. Some meters have a continuity buzzer in addition to a resistance scale ; the buzzer is particularly useful when working single-handed (see illustration).

16 Glow plug testers are available from makers such as Beru, Dieseltune and Kent-Moore. Some incorporate a 'hot test chamber' in which the heating of individual plugs can be observed.

Compression tester

17 A tester specifically intended for diesel engines must be used (see illustration). The push-in connectors used with some petrol engine compression testers cannot be used for diesel engines because of the higher pressures involved. Instead, the diesel engine compression tester screws into an injector or glow plug hole, using one of the adapters supplied with the tester.

18 Most compression testers are used while

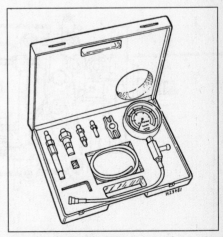

2.17 Dieseltune DX 511 compression tester

2.20 Sykes-Pickavant 013800 leak-down tester

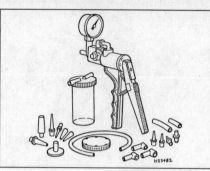

2.22 Dieseltune DX 760 'Mityvac' test kit

3.4 Dial test indicator and stand being used to check swirl chamber protrusion

3.6a DTI and locally-made bellcrank adapter for timing a Bosch VE pump

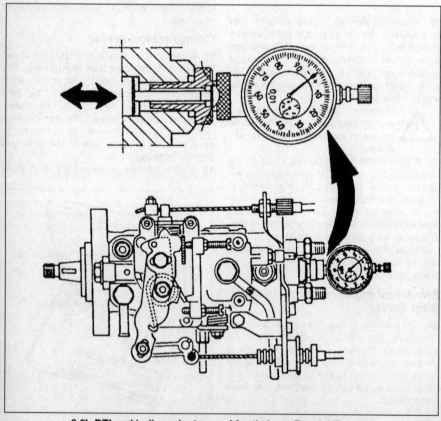

3.6b DTI and in-line adapter used for timing a Bosch VE pump

cranking the engine on the starter motor. A few, such as the Dieseltune DX 511, can be used with the engine idling. This gives more reliable results, since it is hard to guarantee that cranking speed will not fall in the course of testing all four cylinders, whereas idle speed will remain constant.

19 Recording testers, which produce a pen-and-ink trace for each cylinder, are available from A. M. Test Systems and Kent-Moore. Non-recording testers are more common and are available from Dieseltune and Sykes-Pickavant as well as the makers previously mentioned.

Leak-down tester

20 The leak-down tester measures the rate at which air pressure is lost from each cylinder, and can also be used to pinpoint the source of pressure loss (valves, head gasket or bores). It depends on the availability of a supply of compressed air, typically at 5 to 10 bar (73 to 145 lbf/in²). The same tester (with different adapters) can be used on both petrol and diesel engines **(see illustration)**.

21 In use, the tester is connected to an air line and to an adapter screwed into the injector or glow plug hole, with the piston concerned at TDC on the compression stroke. Leak-down testers are offered by Dieseltune, Sykes-Pickavant and others.

Vacuum pump and/or gauge

22 A vacuum gauge, with suitable adapters, is useful for locating blockages or air leaks in the supply side of the fuel system. A simple gauge is used with the engine running to create vacuum in the supply lines. A hand-held vacuum pump with its own gauge can be used without running the engine, and is also useful for bleeding the fuel system when a hand priming pump is not fitted **(see illustration)**.

3   Injection pump timing tools

1 If work is undertaken which disturbs the position of the fuel injection pump, certain tools will be needed to check the injection timing on reassembly. This also applies if the pump drive is disturbed - including renewal of the timing belt on some models. Checking of the timing is also a necessary part of fault diagnosis when investigating complaints such as power loss, knock and smoke.

Static timing tools

2 Static timing is still the most widely-used method of setting diesel injection pumps. It is time-consuming and sometimes messy. Precision measuring instruments are often needed for dealing with distributor pumps. Good results depend on the skill and patience of the operator.

3 The owner-mechanic who will only be

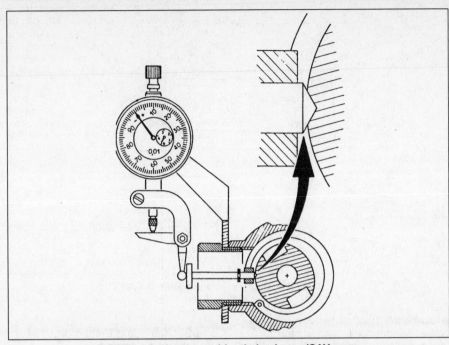

3.7 DTI and adapter used for timing Lucas/CAV pump

3.14 Clamping a timing light transducer onto an injector pipe

dealing with one engine should refer to the appropriate text to find out what tools will be required. The diesel tune-up specialist will typically need the following :

Dial test indicator (DTI) with magnetic stand
DTI adapters and probes for Bosch or CAV distributor pumps
Timing gear pins or pegs (when applicable)
Crankshaft or flywheel locking pins (when applicable)

Dial test indicator and magnetic stand

4 This is a useful workshop tool for many operations besides timing. It is the most accurate means of checking the protrusion or recession of swirl chambers, pistons and liners when renewing cylinder head gaskets. If major overhauls are undertaken it can also be used for measuring values such as crankshaft endfloat **(see illustration)**.

5 Two DTIs may be needed for setting the timing on some engines - one to measure the pump plunger or rotor movement and one to measure engine piston position.

DTI adapters

6 Adapters and probes for fitting the DTI to the distributor pump are of various patterns, due partly to the need to be able to use them in conditions of poor access on the vehicle **(see illustrations)**. This means that the same adapter cannot necessarily be used on the same type of pump and engine if the under-bonnet layout is different. On the bench it is often possible to use simpler equipment.

7 A spring-loaded probe is used on some CAV/RotoDiesel pumps to find the timing groove in the pump rotor **(see illustration)**.

Timing gear pins or pegs

8 Pins or pegs are used on some engines to lock the pump and/or the camshaft in a particular position. They are generally specific to a particular engine or manufacturer. It is sometimes possible to use suitably sized dowel rods, drill shanks or bolts instead.

Crankshaft or flywheel locking pins

9 These are used for locking the crankshaft at TDC (or at the injection point on some models).

10 The crankshaft locking pin is inserted through a hole in the side of the crankcase after removal of a plug, and enters a slot in a crankshaft counterweight or web. The flywheel pin passes through a hole in the flywheel end of the crankcase and enters a hole in the flywheel. Again, suitably sized rods or bolts can sometimes be used instead.

Dynamic timing tools

11 Dynamic timing on diesel engines has not yet become widespread, due no doubt in part to the relatively expensive equipment required. Additionally, not all vehicle manufacturers provide dynamic timing values. In principle it makes possible much faster and more accurate checking of the injection timing, just as on petrol engines. It can also be used to verify the operation of cold start advance systems.

12 Most dynamic timing equipment depends on converting mechanical or hydraulic impulses in the injection system into electrical signals. An alternative approach is adopted by one or two manufacturers who use an optical-to-electrical conversion, with a sensor which screws into a glow plug hole and 'sees' the

light of combustion. The electrical signals are used to trigger a timing light, or as part of the information fed into a diagnostic analyser.

13 Not all diesel engines have ready-made timing marks. If the engine has a TDC sensor (or provision for fitting one) and the timing equipment can read the sensor output, this is not a problem. Some engines have neither timing marks nor TDC sensors. In such cases there is no choice but to establish TDC accurately and make marks on the flywheel or crankshaft pulley.

Timing lights

14 The simplest dynamic timing equipment uses a transducer to convert the pressure pulse in the injector pipe into an electrical signal which triggers a timing light. Such transducers are of two types - in-line and clamp-on **(see illustration)**.

15 The in-line transducer is connected into No 1 injector pipe using adapters to suit the fuel pipe unions. The electrical connection from the transducer goes to the timing light, which will also require a 12 volt or mains supply to energise its tube.

16 The clamp-on transducer is used in a similar way but instead of actually tapping into the injector pipe it clamps onto it. The transducer must be of the right size for the pipe concerned and any dirt, rust or protective coating on the pipe must be removed.

17 The position of the clamp-on transducer on the pipe is important. The injection pulse takes a finite amount of time to travel from one end of the pipe to the other. If the transducer is in the wrong place, a false result will be obtained. Place the transducer as directed by the equipment or engine manufacturer.

18 The timing light itself may be an existing inductive type light normally used on petrol engines, if the transducer output is suitable. Other types of transducer can only be used with their own timing light.

Diagnostic analysers

19 Diagnostic engine analysers (Crypton, AVL, Souriau etc.) will display timing and speed information with the aid of diesel adapters or interface units. These will normally be specific to the equipment concerned; consult the manufacturers for details.

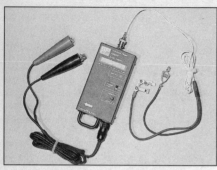

3.22a Sykes-Pickavant 300540 diesel timing light adapter

20 The output from the Sykes-Pickavant diesel adapter can be used to drive the inductive HT pick-up on a diagnostic analyser.

Injection testers

21 Injection testers are halfway between simple timing light/tachometer combinations and full-blown diagnostic analysers. They interpret the transducer output to provide a 'start-of-injection' signal, enabling comparison to be made between all the injectors on an engine, so that defective injectors can be identified.

22 The diesel adapter sold by Sykes-Pickavant for use with a conventional inductive timing light has an injection testing facility **(see illustration)**. More sophisticated equipment, such as the AVL Diesel Injection Tester 873 **(see illustration)**, accepts an input from the engine's TDC sensor (if fitted) as well, giving a digital read-out of injection timing without the need for a stroboscope.

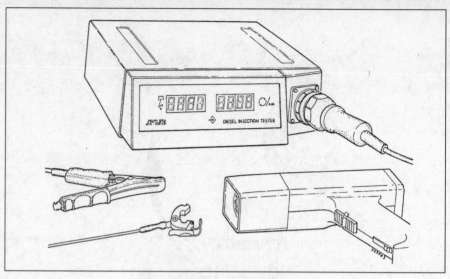

3.22b AVL Diesel Injection Tester 873

4 Injector testing equipment

⚠️ **Warning : Never expose the hands, face or any other part of the body to injector spray. The high working pressure can penetrate the skin, with potentially fatal results. When possible use injector test oil rather than fuel for testing. Take precautions to avoid inhaling the vaporised fuel or injector test fluid. Remember that even diesel fuel is inflammable when vaporised.**

1 Some kind of injector tester will be needed if it is wished to identify defective injectors, or to test them after cleaning or prolonged storage. Various makes and models are available, but the essential components of all of them are a high pressure hand-operated pump and a pressure gauge.

2 For safety reasons, injector test or calibration fluid should be used for bench testing rather than diesel fuel or paraffin. Use the fluid specified by the maker of the test equipment if possible.

3 One of the simplest testers currently available is Dieseltune's DX 710 **(see illustrations)**. This has the advantage that (access permitting) it can be used to test opening pressure and back leakage without removing the injectors from the engine. Its small reservoir makes it of limited use for bench testing, but good results can be obtained with practice.

4 Another method of testing injectors on the engine is to connect a pressure gauge into the line between the injection pump and the injector. This test can also detect faults caused by the injection pump high pressure piston or delivery valve.

5 The workshop which tests or calibrates injectors regularly will need a bench-mounted tester. These testers have a lever-operated pump, and a larger fluid reservoir than the hand-held tester. The best models also incorporate a transparent chamber for safe viewing of the injector spray pattern and perhaps a test fluid recirculation system **(see illustration)**.

6 Some means of extracting the vapour produced when testing, such as a hood connected to the workshop's fume extraction system, is desirable. Although injector test fluid is relatively non-toxic, its vapour is not particularly pleasant to inhale.

5 Injection pump testing and calibration equipment

The equipment needed for testing and calibration of injection pumps is beyond the scope of this book. Any such work should be entrusted to the pump manufacturer's agent - though the opportunity is taken to say yet again that the injection pump is often blamed for faults when in fact the trouble lies elsewhere.

6 Smoke testing equipment

1 Smoke emission testing is part of the MOT test for cars and light commercial vehicles.

2 Smoke testing equipment falls into two categories - indirect and direct reading. With the indirect systems, a sample of exhaust gas is passed over a filter paper and the change in opacity of the paper is measured using a separate machine. With the direct systems, an optically sensitive probe measures the opacity

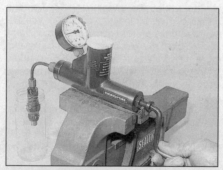

4.3a Dieseltune DX 710 tester in use on the bench. . .

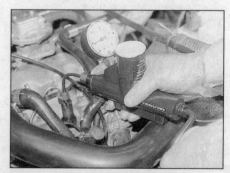

4.3b . . . and on the engine

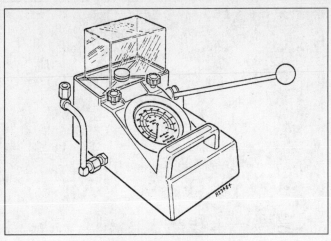

4.5 Dieseltune 111 injector tester

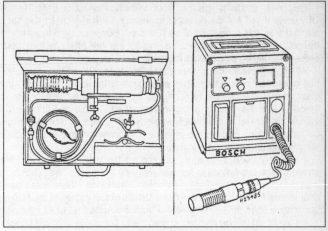

6.3a Bosch smoke sampling kit (left) and measuring unit

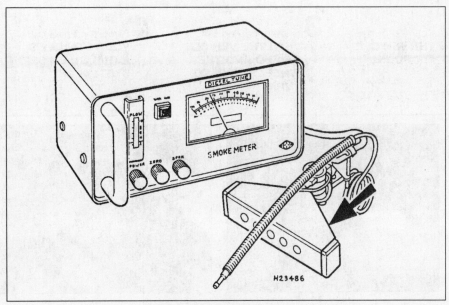

6.3b Dieseltune Smokemeter

of the exhaust gas and an immediate read-out is available.

3 The smoke sampling kit from Bosch is an example of the indirect reading system and is used in conjunction with a photoelectric measuring unit. Dieseltune's Smokemeter is an example of the direct reading machine **(see illustrations)**.

4 As far as the DIY mechanic is concerned, the purchase of smoke testing equipment is unlikely to be an economic proposition. If accurate smoke testing is necessary, take the vehicle to an MOT testing station or a Diesel injection specialist.

MOT Test Checks

This is a guide to getting your vehicle through the MOT test. Obviously it will not be possible to examine the vehicle to the same standard as the professional MOT tester. However, working through the following checks will enable you to identify any problem areas before submitting the vehicle for the test.

Where a testable component is in borderline condition, the tester has discretion in deciding whether to pass or fail it. The basis of such discretion is whether the tester would be happy for a close relative or friend to use the vehicle with the component in that condition. If the vehicle presented is clean and evidently well cared for, the tester may be more inclined to pass a borderline component than if the vehicle is scruffy and apparently neglected.

It has only been possible to summarise the test requirements here, based on the regulations in force at the time of printing. Test standards are becoming increasingly stringent, although there are some exemptions for older vehicles. For full details obtain a copy of the Haynes publication Pass the MOT! (available from stockists of Haynes manuals).

An assistant will be needed to help carry out some of these checks.

The checks have been sub-divided into four categories, as follows:

1 Checks carried out **FROM THE DRIVER'S SEAT**

2 Checks carried out **WITH THE VEHICLE ON THE GROUND**

3 Checks carried out **WITH THE VEHICLE RAISED AND THE WHEELS FREE TO TURN**

4 Checks carried out on **YOUR VEHICLE'S EXHAUST EMISSION SYSTEM**

1 Checks carried out **FROM THE DRIVER'S SEAT**

Handbrake

☐ Test the operation of the handbrake. Excessive travel (too many clicks) indicates incorrect brake or cable adjustment.

☐ Check that the handbrake cannot be released by tapping the lever sideways. Check the security of the lever mountings.

Footbrake

☐ Depress the brake pedal and check that it does not creep down to the floor, indicating a master cylinder fault. Release the pedal, wait a few seconds, then depress it again. If the pedal travels nearly to the floor before firm resistance is felt, brake adjustment or repair is necessary. If the pedal feels spongy, there is air in the hydraulic system which must be removed by bleeding.

☐ Check that the brake pedal is secure and in good condition. Check also for signs of fluid leaks on the pedal, floor or carpets, which would indicate failed seals in the brake master cylinder.

☐ Check the servo unit (when applicable) by operating the brake pedal several times, then keeping the pedal depressed and starting the engine. As the engine starts, the pedal will move down slightly. If not, the vacuum hose or the servo itself may be faulty.

Steering wheel and column

☐ Examine the steering wheel for fractures or looseness of the hub, spokes or rim.

☐ Move the steering wheel from side to side and then up and down. Check that the steering wheel is not loose on the column, indicating wear or a loose retaining nut. Continue moving the steering wheel as before, but also turn it slightly from left to right.

☐ Check that the steering wheel is not loose on the column, and that there is no abnormal

movement of the steering wheel, indicating wear in the column support bearings or couplings.

Windscreen and mirrors

☐ The windscreen must be free of cracks or other significant damage within the driver's field of view. (Small stone chips are acceptable.) Rear view mirrors must be secure, intact, and capable of being adjusted.

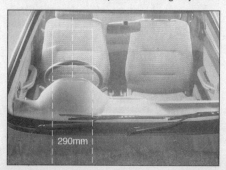

290mm

Seat belts and seats

Note: *The following checks are applicable to all seat belts, front and rear.*

☐ Examine the webbing of all the belts (including rear belts if fitted) for cuts, serious fraying or deterioration. Fasten and unfasten each belt to check the buckles. If applicable, check the retracting mechanism. Check the security of all seat belt mountings accessible from inside the vehicle.

☐ The front seats themselves must be securely attached and the backrests must lock in the upright position.

Doors

☐ Both front doors must be able to be opened and closed from outside and inside, and must latch securely when closed.

2 Checks carried out WITH THE VEHICLE ON THE GROUND

Vehicle identification

☐ Number plates must be in good condition, secure and legible, with letters and numbers correctly spaced – spacing at (A) should be twice that at (B).

☐ The VIN plate and/or homologation plate must be legible.

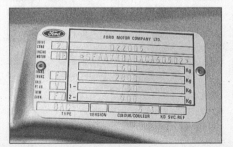

Electrical equipment

☐ Switch on the ignition and check the operation of the horn.

☐ Check the windscreen washers and wipers, examining the wiper blades; renew damaged or perished blades. Also check the operation of the stop-lights.

☐ Check the operation of the sidelights and number plate lights. The lenses and reflectors must be secure, clean and undamaged.

☐ Check the operation and alignment of the headlights. The headlight reflectors must not be tarnished and the lenses must be undamaged.

☐ Switch on the ignition and check the operation of the direction indicators (including the instrument panel tell-tale) and the hazard warning lights. Operation of the sidelights and stop-lights must not affect the indicators - if it does, the cause is usually a bad earth at the rear light cluster.

☐ Check the operation of the rear foglight(s), including the warning light on the instrument panel or in the switch.

Footbrake

☐ Examine the master cylinder, brake pipes and servo unit for leaks, loose mountings, corrosion or other damage.

☐ The fluid reservoir must be secure and the fluid level must be between the upper (**A**) and lower (**B**) markings.

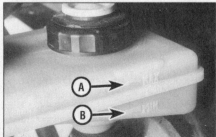

☐ Inspect both front brake flexible hoses for cracks or deterioration of the rubber. Turn the steering from lock to lock, and ensure that the hoses do not contact the wheel, tyre, or any part of the steering or suspension mechanism. With the brake pedal firmly depressed, check the hoses for bulges or leaks under pressure.

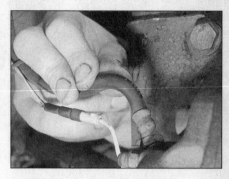

Steering and suspension

☐ Have your assistant turn the steering wheel from side to side slightly, up to the point where the steering gear just begins to transmit this movement to the roadwheels. Check for excessive free play between the steering wheel and the steering gear, indicating wear or insecurity of the steering column joints, the column-to-steering gear coupling, or the steering gear itself.

☐ Have your assistant turn the steering wheel more vigorously in each direction, so that the roadwheels just begin to turn. As this is done, examine all the steering joints, linkages, fittings and attachments. Renew any component that shows signs of wear or damage. On vehicles with power steering, check the security and condition of the steering pump, drivebelt and hoses.

☐ Check that the vehicle is standing level, and at approximately the correct ride height.

Shock absorbers

☐ Depress each corner of the vehicle in turn, then release it. The vehicle should rise and then settle in its normal position. If the vehicle continues to rise and fall, the shock absorber is defective. A shock absorber which has seized will also cause the vehicle to fail.

Exhaust system

☐ Start the engine. With your assistant holding a rag over the tailpipe, check the entire system for leaks. Repair or renew leaking sections.

3 Checks carried out **WITH THE VEHICLE RAISED AND THE WHEELS FREE TO TURN**

Jack up the front and rear of the vehicle, and securely support it on axle stands. Position the stands clear of the suspension assemblies. Ensure that the wheels are clear of the ground and that the steering can be turned from lock to lock.

Steering mechanism

☐ Have your assistant turn the steering from lock to lock. Check that the steering turns smoothly, and that no part of the steering mechanism, including a wheel or tyre, fouls any brake hose or pipe or any part of the body structure.

☐ Examine the steering rack rubber gaiters for damage or insecurity of the retaining clips. If power steering is fitted, check for signs of damage or leakage of the fluid hoses, pipes or connections. Also check for excessive stiffness or binding of the steering, a missing split pin or locking device, or severe corrosion of the body structure within 30 cm of any steering component attachment point.

Front and rear suspension and wheel bearings

☐ Starting at the front right-hand side, grasp the roadwheel at the 3 o'clock and 9 o'clock positions and shake it vigorously. Check for free play or insecurity at the wheel bearings, suspension balljoints, or suspension mountings, pivots and attachments.

☐ Now grasp the wheel at the 12 o'clock and 6 o'clock positions and repeat the previous inspection. Spin the wheel, and check for roughness or tightness of the front wheel bearing.

☐ If excess free play is suspected at a component pivot point, this can be confirmed by using a large screwdriver or similar tool and levering between the mounting and the component attachment. This will confirm whether the wear is in the pivot bush, its retaining bolt, or in the mounting itself (the bolt holes can often become elongated).

☐ Carry out all the above checks at the other front wheel, and then at both rear wheels.

Springs and shock absorbers

☐ Examine the suspension struts (when applicable) for serious fluid leakage, corrosion, or damage to the casing. Also check the security of the mounting points.

☐ If coil springs are fitted, check that the spring ends locate in their seats, and that the spring is not corroded, cracked or broken.

☐ If leaf springs are fitted, check that all leaves are intact, that the axle is securely attached to each spring, and that there is no deterioration of the spring eye mountings, bushes, and shackles.

☐ The same general checks apply to vehicles fitted with other suspension types, such as torsion bars, hydraulic displacer units, etc. Ensure that all mountings and attachments are secure, that there are no signs of excessive wear, corrosion or damage, and (on hydraulic types) that there are no fluid leaks or damaged pipes.

☐ Inspect the shock absorbers for signs of serious fluid leakage. Check for wear of the mounting bushes or attachments, or damage to the body of the unit.

Driveshafts (fwd vehicles only)

☐ Rotate each front wheel in turn and inspect the constant velocity joint gaiters for splits or damage. Also check that each driveshaft is straight and undamaged.

Braking system

☐ If possible without dismantling, check brake pad wear and disc condition. Ensure that the friction lining material has not worn excessively, (A) and that the discs are not fractured, pitted, scored or badly worn (B).

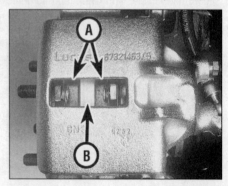

☐ Examine all the rigid brake pipes underneath the vehicle, and the flexible hose(s) at the rear. Look for corrosion, chafing or insecurity of the pipes, and for signs of bulging under pressure, chafing, splits or deterioration of the flexible hoses.

☐ Look for signs of fluid leaks at the brake calipers or on the brake backplates. Repair or renew leaking components.

☐ Slowly spin each wheel, while your assistant depresses and releases the footbrake. Ensure that each brake is operating and does not bind when the pedal is released.

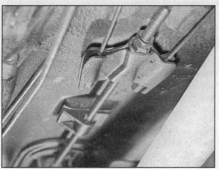

☐ Examine the handbrake mechanism, checking for frayed or broken cables, excessive corrosion, or wear or insecurity of the linkage. Check that the mechanism works on each relevant wheel, and releases fully, without binding.

☐ It is not possible to test brake efficiency without special equipment, but a road test can be carried out later to check that the vehicle pulls up in a straight line.

Fuel and exhaust systems

☐ Inspect the fuel tank (including the filler cap), fuel pipes, hoses and unions. All components must be secure and free from leaks.

☐ Examine the exhaust system over its entire length, checking for any damaged, broken or missing mountings, security of the retaining clamps and rust or corrosion.

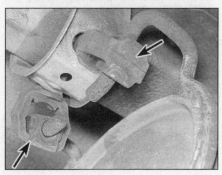

Wheels and tyres

☐ Examine the sidewalls and tread area of each tyre in turn. Check for cuts, tears, lumps, bulges, separation of the tread, and exposure of the ply or cord due to wear or damage. Check that the tyre bead is correctly seated on the wheel rim, that the valve is sound and

properly seated, and that the wheel is not distorted or damaged.

☐ Check that the tyres are of the correct size for the vehicle, that they are of the same size and type on each axle, and that the pressures are correct.

☐ Check the tyre tread depth. The legal minimum at the time of writing is 1.6 mm over at least three-quarters of the tread width. Abnormal tread wear may indicate incorrect front wheel alignment.

Body corrosion

☐ Check the condition of the entire vehicle structure for signs of corrosion in load-bearing areas. (These include chassis box sections, side sills, cross-members, pillars, and all suspension, steering, braking system and seat belt mountings and anchorages.) Any corrosion which has seriously reduced the thickness of a load-bearing area is likely to cause the vehicle to fail. In this case professional repairs are likely to be needed.

☐ Damage or corrosion which causes sharp or otherwise dangerous edges to be exposed will also cause the vehicle to fail.

4 Checks carried out on
YOUR VEHICLE'S EXHAUST EMISSION SYSTEM

Petrol models

☐ Have the engine at normal operating temperature, and make sure that it is in good tune (ignition system in good order, air filter element clean, etc).

☐ Before any measurements are carried out, raise the engine speed to around 2500 rpm, and hold it at this speed for 20 seconds. Allow the engine speed to return to idle, and watch for smoke emissions from the exhaust tailpipe. If the idle speed is obviously much too high, or if dense blue or clearly-visible black smoke comes from the tailpipe for more than 5 seconds, the vehicle will fail. As a rule of thumb, blue smoke signifies oil being burnt (engine wear) while black smoke signifies unburnt fuel (dirty air cleaner element, or other carburettor or fuel system fault).

☐ An exhaust gas analyser capable of measuring carbon monoxide (CO) and hydrocarbons (HC) is now needed. If such an instrument cannot be hired or borrowed, a local garage may agree to perform the check for a small fee.

CO emissions (mixture)

☐ At the time of writing, the maximum CO level at idle is 3.5% for vehicles first used after August 1986 and 4.5% for older vehicles. From January 1996 a much tighter limit (around 0.5%) applies to catalyst-equipped vehicles first used from August 1992. If the CO level cannot be reduced far enough to pass the test (and the fuel and ignition systems are otherwise in good condition) then the carburettor is badly worn, or there is some problem in the fuel injection system or catalytic converter (as applicable).

HC emissions

☐ With the CO emissions within limits, HC emissions must be no more than 1200 ppm (parts per million). If the vehicle fails this test at idle, it can be re-tested at around 2000 rpm; if the HC level is then 1200 ppm or less, this counts as a pass.

☐ Excessive HC emissions can be caused by oil being burnt, but they are more likely to be due to unburnt fuel.

Diesel models

☐ The only emission test applicable to Diesel engines is the measuring of exhaust smoke density. The test involves accelerating the engine several times to its maximum unloaded speed.

Note: *It is of the utmost importance that the engine timing belt is in good condition before the test is carried out.*

☐ Excessive smoke can be caused by a dirty air cleaner element. Otherwise, professional advice may be needed to find the cause.

Contents

1 Introduction

The majority of starting problems on small diesel engines are electrical in origin. The mechanic who is familiar with petrol engines but less so with diesel may be inclined to view the diesel's injectors and pump in the same light as the spark plugs and distributor, but this is generally a mistake.

When investigating complaints of difficult starting for someone else, make sure that the correct starting procedure is understood and is being followed. Some drivers are unaware of the significance of the preheating warning light - many modern engines are sufficiently forgiving for this not to matter in mild weather, but with the onset of winter problems begin.

As a rule of thumb, if the engine is difficult to start but runs well when it has finally got going, the problem is electrical (battery, starter motor or preheating system). If poor performance is combined with difficult starting, the problem is likely to be in the fuel system. The low pressure (supply) side of the fuel system should be checked before suspecting the injectors and injection pump.

HAYNES HINT *Normally the pump is the last item to suspect, since unless it has been tampered with there is no reason for it to be at fault.*

The following table lists various possible causes of faults. Further discussion of some faults will be found in the Sections indicated.

2 Fault diagnosis - symptoms and reasons

Engine turns but will not start (cold)

☐ Incorrect use of preheating system
☐ Preheating system fault
☐ Fuel waxing (in very cold weather) (Section 5)
☐ Overfuelling or cold start advance mechanism defective

Engine turns but will not start (hot or cold)

☐ Low cranking speed (see below)
☐ Poor compression (Section 3)
☐ No fuel in tank
☐ Air in fuel system (Section 4)
☐ Fuel feed restriction (Section 5)
☐ Fuel contaminated
☐ Stop solenoid defective (Section 17)
☐ Major mechanical failure
☐ Injection pump internal fault

Low cranking speed

☐ Inadequate battery capacity
☐ Incorrect grade of oil (*Lubricants, fluids and capacities*)
☐ High resistance in starter motor circuit
☐ Starter motor internal fault

Engine is difficult to start

☐ Incorrect starting procedure
☐ Battery or starter motor fault (Chapters 2 and 5)
☐ Preheating system fault
☐ Air in fuel system (Section 4)
☐ Fuel feed restriction (Section 5)
☐ Poor compression (Section 3)
☐ Valve clearances incorrect
☐ Valves sticking
☐ Blockage in exhaust system
☐ Valve timing incorrect
☐ Injector(s) faulty
☐ Injection pump timing incorrect
☐ Injection pump internal fault

Engine starts but stops again

☐ Fuel very low in tank
☐ Air in fuel system (Section 4)
☐ Idle adjustment incorrect
☐ Fuel feed restriction (Section 5)
☐ Fuel return restriction
☐ Air cleaner dirty
☐ Blockage in induction system
☐ Blockage in exhaust system
☐ Injector(s) faulty

Engine will not stop when switched off

☐ Stop solenoid defective (Section 17)

Misfiring/rough idle

☐ Air cleaner dirty
☐ Blockage in induction system
☐ Air in fuel system (Section 4)
☐ Fuel feed restriction (Section 5)
☐ Valve clearances incorrect
☐ Valve(s) sticking
☐ Valve spring(s) weak or broken
☐ Poor compression (Section 3)
☐ Overheating (Section 15)
☐ Injector pipe(s) wrongly connected or wrong type
☐ Valve timing incorrect
☐ Injector(s) faulty or wrong type
☐ Injection pump timing incorrect
☐ Injection pump faulty or wrong type

Lack of power (Section 6)

☐ Accelerator linkage not moving through full travel (cable slack or pedal obstructed)
☐ Injection pump control linkages sticking or maladjusted
☐ Air cleaner dirty
☐ Blockage in induction system
☐ Air in fuel system (Section 4)
☐ Fuel feed restriction (Section 5)
☐ Valve timing incorrect
☐ Injection pump timing incorrect
☐ Blockage in exhaust system
☐ Turbo boost pressure inadequate, when applicable (Section 7)
☐ Valve clearances incorrect
☐ Poor compression (Section 3)
☐ Injector(s) faulty or wrong type
☐ Injection pump faulty

Fuel consumption excessive (Section 8)

☐ External leakage
☐ Fuel passing into sump (Section 9)
☐ Air cleaner dirty
☐ Blockage in induction system
☐ Valve clearances incorrect
☐ Valve(s) sticking
☐ Valve spring(s) weak
☐ Poor compression (Section 3)
☐ Valve timing incorrect
☐ Injection pump timing incorrect
☐ Injector(s) faulty or wrong type
☐ Injection pump faulty

Engine knocks (Section 10)

☐ Air in fuel system (Section 4)
☐ Fuel grade incorrect or quality poor
☐ Injector(s) faulty or wrong type (Section 10)
☐ Valve spring(s) weak or broken
☐ Valve(s) sticking
☐ Valve clearances incorrect
☐ Valve timing incorrect
☐ Injection pump timing incorrect
☐ Piston protrusion excessive/head gasket thickness inadequate (after repair)

☐ Valve recess incorrect (after repair)
☐ Piston rings broken or worn
☐ Pistons and/or bores worn
☐ Crankshaft bearings worn or damaged
☐ Small-end bearings worn
☐ Camshaft worn

Black smoke in exhaust (Section 11)

☐ Air cleaner dirty
☐ Blockage in induction system
☐ Valve clearances incorrect
☐ Poor compression (Section 3)
☐ Turbo boost pressure inadequate, when applicable (Section 7)
☐ Blockage in exhaust system
☐ Valve timing incorrect
☐ Injector(s) faulty or wrong type
☐ Injection pump timing incorrect
☐ Injection pump faulty

Blue or white smoke in exhaust (Section 11)

☐ Engine oil incorrect grade or poor quality (*Lubricants, fluids and capacities*)
☐ Glow plug(s) defective, or controller faulty (smoke at start-up only)
☐ Air cleaner dirty(Chapter 2)
☐ Blockage in induction system
☐ Valve timing incorrect
☐ Injection pump timing incorrect
☐ Injector(s) defective, or heat shields damaged or missing
☐ Engine running too cool
☐ Oil entering via valve stems (Section 12)
☐ Poor compression (Section 3)
☐ Head gasket blown
☐ Piston rings broken or worn
☐ Pistons and/or bores worn

Oil consumption excessive (Section 13)

☐ External leakage (standing or running)
☐ New engine not yet run-in
☐ Engine oil incorrect grade or poor quality (*Lubricants, fluids and capacities*)
☐ Oil level too high
☐ Crankcase ventilation system obstructed
☐ Oil leaking from oil feed pipe into fuel feed pipe
☐ Oil leakage from ancillary component (vacuum pump etc.)
☐ Oil leaking into coolant
☐ Oil leaking into injection pump
☐ Air cleaner dirty
☐ Blockage in induction system
☐ Cylinder bores glazed (Section 14)
☐ Piston rings broken or worn
☐ Pistons and/or bores worn
☐ Valve stems or guides worn
☐ Valve stem oil seals worn

Overheating (Section 15)

☐ Coolant leakage
☐ Engine oil level too high
☐ Electric cooling fan malfunctioning
☐ Coolant pump defective
☐ Radiator clogged externally

☐ Radiator clogged internally
☐ Coolant hoses blocked or collapsed
☐ Coolant reservoir pressure cap defective or incorrect
☐ Coolant thermostat defective or incorrect
☐ Thermostat missing
☐ Air cleaner dirty
☐ Blockage in induction system
☐ Blockage in exhaust system
☐ Head gasket blown
☐ Cylinder head cracked or warped
☐ Valve timing incorrect
☐ Injection pump timing incorrect (over-advanced)
☐ Injector(s) faulty or wrong type
☐ Injection pump faulty
☐ Imminent seizure (piston pick-up)

Crankcase pressure excessive (oil being blown out)

☐ Blockage in crankcase ventilation system
☐ Leakage in vacuum pump
☐ Piston rings broken or sticking
☐ Pistons or bores worn
☐ Head gasket blown

Erratic running

☐ Operating temperature incorrect
☐ Accelerator linkage maladjusted or sticking
☐ Air cleaner dirty
☐ Blockage in induction system
☐ Air in fuel system (Section 4)
☐ Injector pipe(s) wrongly connected or wrong type
☐ Fuel feed restriction (Section 5)
☐ Fuel return restriction
☐ Valve clearances incorrect
☐ Valve(s) sticking
☐ Valve spring(s) broken or weak
☐ Valve timing incorrect
☐ Poor compression (Section 3)
☐ Injector(s) faulty or wrong type
☐ Injection pump mountings loose
☐ Injection pump timing incorrect
☐ Injection pump faulty

Vibration

☐ Accelerator linkage sticking
☐ Engine mountings loose or worn
☐ Cooling fan damaged or loose
☐ Crankshaft pulley/damper damaged or loose
☐ Injector pipe(s) wrongly connected or wrong type
☐ Valve(s) sticking
☐ Flywheel or (when applicable) flywheel housing loose
☐ Poor (uneven) compression (Section 3)

Low oil pressure

☐ Oil level low
☐ Oil grade or quality incorrect (*Lubricants, fluids and capacities*)
☐ Oil filter clogged
☐ Overheating (Section 15)
☐ Oil contaminated (Section 16)
☐ Gauge or warning light sender inaccurate
☐ Oil pump pick-up strainer clogged

☐ Oil pump suction pipe loose or cracked
☐ Oil pressure relief valve defective or stuck open
☐ Oil pump worn
☐ Crankshaft bearings worn

High oil pressure

☐ Oil grade or quality incorrect (*Lubricants, fluids and capacities*)
☐ Gauge inaccurate
☐ Oil pressure relief valve stuck shut

Injector pipe(s) break or split repeatedly

☐ Missing or wrongly located clamps
☐ Wrong type or length of pipe
☐ Faulty injector
☐ Faulty delivery valve

3 Poor compression

1 Poor compression may give rise to a number of faults, including difficult starting, loss of power, misfiring or uneven running and smoke in the exhaust.

2 Before looking for mechanical reasons for compression loss, check that the problem is not on the induction side. A dirty air cleaner or some other blockage in the induction system can restrict air inlet to the point where compression suffers.

3 Mechanical reasons for low compression include :

a) *Incorrect valve clearances*
b) *Sticking valves*
c) *Weak or broken valve springs*
d) *Incorrect valve timing*
e) *Worn or burnt valve heads and seats*
f) *Worn valve stems and guides*
g) *Head gasket blown*
h) *Piston rings broken or sticking*
j) *Pistons or bores worn*
k) *Head gasket thickness incorrect (after rebuild)*

4 Compression loss on one cylinder alone can be due to a defective or badly seated glow plug, or a leaking injector sealing washer. Some engines also have a cylinder head plug for the insertion of a dial test indicator probe when determining TDC and this should not be overlooked.

5 Compression loss on two adjacent cylinders is almost certainly due to the head gasket blowing between them. Sometimes the fault will be corrected by renewing the gasket but a blown gasket can also be an indication that the cylinder head itself is warped. Always check the head mating face for distortion when renewing the gasket. On wet liner engines also check liner protrusion.

Compression test

6 A compression tester specifically intended for diesel engines must be used, because of the higher pressures involved - see Chapter 3.

3.14a Leakdown test adapter being fitted to a glow plug hole

3.14b Whistle fitted to adapter to find TDC

3.15 Leakdown tester in use

The tester is connected to an adapter which screws into the glow plug or injector hole. Normally sealing washers must be used on both sides of the adapter.

7 Unless specific instructions to the contrary are supplied with the tester, observe the following points :

a) *The battery must be in a good state of charge, the air cleaner element must be clean and the engine should be at normal operating temperature*

b) *All the injectors or glow plugs should be removed before starting the test. If removing the injectors, also remove their heat shields (when fitted), otherwise they may be blown out*

c) *The stop control lever on the injection pump must be operated, or the stop solenoid disconnected, to prevent the engine from running or fuel from being discharged*

8 There is no need to hold the accelerator pedal down during the test because the diesel engine air inlet is not throttled. There are rare exceptions to this case, when a throttle valve is used to produce vacuum for servo or governor operation.

9 The actual compression pressures measured are not so important as the balance between cylinders. Typical values at cranking speed are:

Good condition - 25 to 30 bar (363 to 435 lbf/in²)

Minimum - 18 bar (261 lbf/in²)

Maximum difference between cylinders - 5 bar (73 lbf/in²)

10 The cause of poor compression is less easy to establish on a diesel engine than on a petrol one. The effect of introducing oil into the cylinders (wet testing) is not conclusive, because there is a risk that the oil will sit in the bowl in the piston crown (direct injection engines) or in the swirl chamber (indirect) instead of passing to the rings.

Leakdown test

11 A leakdown test measures the rate at which compressed air fed into the cylinder is lost. It is an alternative to a compression test and in many ways it is better, since it provides easy identification of where pressure loss is occurring (piston rings, valves or head gasket). However, it does require a source of compressed air.

12 Before beginning the test, remove the cooling system pressure cap. This is necessary because if there is a leak into the cooling system, the introduction of compressed air may damage the radiator. Similarly, it is advisable to remove the dipstick or the oil filler cap to prevent excessive crankcase pressurisation.

13 Connect the tester to a compressed air line and adjust the reading to 100% as instructed by the manufacturer.

14 Remove the glow plugs or injectors and screw the appropriate adapter into a glow plug or injector hole. Fit the whistle to the adapter and turn the crankshaft. When the whistle begins to sound, the piston in question is rising on compression. When the whistle stops, TDC has been reached **(see illustrations)**.

15 Engage a gear and apply the handbrake to stop the engine turning. Remove the whistle and connect the tester to the adapter. Note the tester reading, which indicates the rate at which the air escapes. Repeat the test on the other cylinders **(see illustration)**.

16 The tester reading is in the form of a percentage, where 100% is perfect. Readings of 80% or better are to be expected from an engine in good condition. The actual reading is less important than the balance between cylinders, which should be within 5%.

17 The areas from which escaping air emerges show where a fault lies, as follows:

Air escaping from	Probable cause
Oil filler cap or dipstick tube	*Worn piston rings or cylinder bores*
Exhaust pipe	*Worn or burnt exhaust valve*
Air cleaner/inlet manifold	*Worn or burnt inlet valve*
Cooling system	*Blown head gasket or cracked cylinder head*

18 Bear in mind that if the head gasket is blown between two adjacent cylinders, air escaping from the cylinder under test may emerge via an open valve in the cylinder adjacent.

4   Air in fuel system

The diesel engine will not run at all, or at best will run erratically, if there is air in the fuel lines. If the fuel tank has been allowed to run dry, or after operations in which the fuel supply lines have been opened, the fuel system must be bled before the engine will run. Methods of bleeding are given in Chapter 4.

Air will also enter the fuel lines through any leaking joint or seal, since the supply side is under negative pressure all the time that the engine is running.

5   Fuel feed restricted

1 Restriction in the fuel feed from the tank to the pump may be caused by any of the following faults :

a) *Fuel filter blocked*

b) *Tank vent blocked*

c) *Feed pipe blocked or collapsed*

d) *Fuel waxing (in very cold weather)*

Fuel waxing

2 In the case of fuel waxing, the wax normally builds up first in the filter. If the filter can be warmed this will often allow the engine to run. *Caution : Do not use a naked flame for this.* Only in exceptionally severe weather will waxing prevent winter grade fuel from being pumped out of the tank.

Microbiological contamination

3 Under certain conditions it is possible for micro-organisms to colonise the fuel tank and supply lines. These micro-organisms produce a black sludge or slime which can block the filter and cause corrosion of metal parts. The problem normally shows up first as an unexpected blockage of the filter.

4 If such contamination is found, drain the fuel tank and discard the drained fuel. Flush the tank and fuel lines with clean fuel and renew the fuel filter - in bad cases steam clean the tank as well. If there is evidence that the contamination has passed the fuel filter, have the injection pump cleaned by a specialist.

5 Further trouble may be avoided by only using fuel from reputable outlets with a high turnover. Proprietary additives are also available to inhibit the growth of micro-organisms in storage tanks or in the vehicle fuel tank.

6 Lack of power

Complaints of lack of power are not always justified. If necessary, perform a road or dynamometer test to verify the condition. Even if power is definitely down, the complaint is not necessarily due to an engine or injection system fault.

Before commencing detailed investigation, check that the accelerator linkage is moving through its full travel. Also make sure that an apparent power loss is not caused by items such as binding brakes, under-inflated tyres, overloading of the vehicle, or some particular feature of operation.

7 Turbo boost pressure inadequate

If boost pressure is low, power will be down and too much fuel may be delivered at high engine speeds (depending on the method of pump control). Possible reasons for low boost pressure include :

a) Air cleaner dirty
b) Leaks in induction system
c) Blockage in exhaust system
d) Turbo control fault (wastegate or actuator)
e) Turbo mechanical fault

8 Fuel consumption excessive

Complaints of excessive fuel consumption, as with lack of power, may not mean that a fault exists. If the complaint is justified and there are no obvious fuel leaks, check the same external factors as for lack of power before turning to the engine and injection system.

9 Fuel in sump

If fuel oil is found to be diluting the oil in the sump, this can only have arrived by passing down the cylinder bores. Assuming that the problem is not one of excessive fuel delivery, piston and bore wear is indicated.

Fuel contamination of the oil can be detected by smell, and in bad cases by an obvious reduction in viscosity.

10 Knocking caused by injector fault

1 A faulty injector which is causing knocking noises can be identified as follows.

2 Clean around the injector fuel pipe unions. Run the engine at a fast idle so that the knock can be heard. Using for preference a split ring spanner, slacken and retighten each injector union in turn.

Warning: Protect yourself against contact with diesel fuel by covering each union with a piece of rag to absorb the fuel which will spray out.

3 When the union supplying the defective injector is slackened, the knock will disappear. Stop the engine and remove the injector for inspection.

11 Excessive exhaust smoke

1 Check first that the smoke is still excessive when the engine has reached normal operating temperature. A cold engine may produce some blue or white smoke until it has warmed up; this is not necessarily a fault.

Black smoke

2 This is produced by incomplete combustion of the fuel in such a way that carbon particles (soot) are formed. Incomplete combustion shows that there is a lack of oxygen, either because too much fuel is being delivered or because not enough air is being drawn into the cylinders. A dirty air cleaner is an obvious cause of air starvation; incorrect valve clearances should also be considered. Combustion may also be incomplete because the injection timing is incorrect (too far retarded) or because the injector spray pattern is poor.

Blue smoke

3 This is produced either by incomplete combustion of the fuel or by burning lubricating oil. This type of incomplete combustion may be caused by incorrect injection timing (too far advanced), by defective injectors or by damaged or missing injector heat shields.

4 All engines burn a certain amount of oil, especially when cold, but if enough is being burnt to cause excessive exhaust smoke this suggests that there is a significant degree of wear or some other problem.

White smoke

5 Not to be confused with steam, this is produced by unburnt or partially burnt fuel appearing in the exhaust gases. Some white smoke is normal during and immediately after start-up, especially in cold conditions. Excessive amounts of white smoke can be caused by a preheating system fault, by incorrect injection pump timing, or by too much fuel being delivered by the injection pump (overfuelling device malfunctioning). The use of poor quality fuel with a low cetane number, and thus a long ignition delay, can also increase emissions of white smoke.

6 Accurate measurement of exhaust smoke requires the use of a smoke meter. This is not a DIY job, but any garage which carries out diesel MoT tests will have such a meter.

12 Oil entering engine via valve stems

Excessive oil consumption due to oil passing down the valve stems can have three causes :

a) Valve stem wear
b) Valve guide wear
c) Valve stem oil seal wear

In the first two cases the cylinder head must be removed and dismantled so that the valves and guides can be inspected and measured for wear.

13 Oil consumption excessive

When investigating complaints of excessive oil consumption, make sure that the correct level checking procedure is being followed. If insufficient time is allowed for the oil to drain down after stopping the engine, or if the level is checked while the vehicle is standing on a slope, a false low reading may result. The unnecessary topping-up which follows may of itself cause increased oil consumption as a result of the level being too high.

17.3 Stop solenoid wire secured by nut (arrowed)

17.5a Removing the stop solenoid plunger from the pump

17.5b Stop solenoid components

14 Cylinder bore glazing

Engines which spend long periods idling can suffer from glazing of the cylinder bores, leading to high oil consumption even though no significant wear has taken place. The same effect can be produced by incorrect running-in procedures, or by the use of the incorrect grade of oil during running-in. The remedy is to remove the pistons, deglaze the bores with a hone or 'glaze buster' tool and to fit new piston rings.

15 Overheating

Any modern engine will certainly suffer serious damage if overheating is allowed to occur. The importance of regular and conscientious cooling system maintenance cannot be overstressed. Always use a good quality antifreeze and renew it regularly. When refilling the cooling system, follow the specified procedures carefully in order to eliminate any airlocks.

If overheating does occur, do not continue to drive. Stop at once and do not proceed until the problem is fixed.

16 Oil contamination

1 Oil contamination falls into three categories - dirt, sludge and dilution.

Dirt

2 Dirt or soot builds up in the oil in normal operation. It is not a problem if regular oil and filter changes are carried out. If it gets to the stage where it is causing low oil pressure, change the oil and filter immediately.

Sludge

3 This occurs when inferior grades of oil are used, or when regular oil changing has been neglected. It is more likely to occur on engines which rarely reach operating temperature. If sludge is found when draining, a flushing oil may be used if the engine manufacturer allows it. *Caution : Some engine manufacturers forbid the use of flushing oil, because it cannot all be drained afterwards. If in doubt, consult a dealer or specialist.* The engine should then be refilled with fresh oil of the correct grade and a new oil filter be fitted.

Dilution

4 This is of two kinds - fuel and coolant. In either case if the dilution is bad enough the engine oil level will appear to rise with use.
5 Coolant dilution of the oil is indicated by the 'mayonnaise' appearance of the oil and water mixture. Sometimes oil will also appear in the coolant. Possible reasons are :
  a) Blown head gasket
  b) Cracked or porous cylinder head or block
  c) Cylinder liner seal failure (on wet liner engines)
  d) Leaking oil-to-coolant oil cooler (when fitted)
6 With either type of dilution, the cause must be dealt with and the oil and filter changed.

17 Engine stop (fuel cut-off) solenoid - emergency repair

1 The solenoid valve cuts off the supply of fuel to the high pressure side of the injection pump when the ignition is switched off. If the solenoid fails electrically or mechanically so that its plunger is in the shut position, the engine will not run. One possible reason for such a failure is that the ignition has been switched off while engine speed is still high. In such a case the plunger will be sucked onto its seat with considerable force, and perhaps jam.
2 Should the valve fail on the road and a spare not be immediately available, the following procedure will serve to get the engine running again. *Caution : It is important that no dirt is allowed to enter the injection pump via the solenoid hole.*
3 With the ignition off, disconnect the wire from the solenoid. Thoroughly clean around the solenoid where it screws into the pump (see illustration).
4 Unscrew the solenoid and remove it. If a hand priming pump is fitted, operate the pump a few times while lifting out the solenoid to wash away any particles of dirt. Do not lose the sealing washer.
5 Remove the plunger from the solenoid (or from the recess in the pump, if it is stuck inside) (see illustrations). Refit the solenoid body, making sure the sealing washer is in place, again operating the priming pump at the same time to flush away dirt.
6 Tape up the end of the solenoid wire so that it cannot touch bare metal.
7 The engine will now start and run as usual, but it will not stop when the ignition is switched off. It will be necessary to use the manual stop lever (if fitted) on the injection pump, or to stall the engine in gear.
8 Fit a new solenoid and sealing washer at the earliest opportunity.

A

ABS (Anti-lock brake system) A system, usually electronically controlled, that senses incipient wheel lockup during braking and relieves hydraulic pressure at wheels that are about to skid.

Air bag An inflatable bag hidden in the steering wheel (driver's side) or the dash or glovebox (passenger side). In a head-on collision, the bags inflate, preventing the driver and front passenger from being thrown forward into the steering wheel or windscreen.

Air cleaner A metal or plastic housing, containing a filter element, which removes dust and dirt from the air being drawn into the engine.

Air filter element The actual filter in an air cleaner system, usually manufactured from pleated paper and requiring renewal at regular intervals.

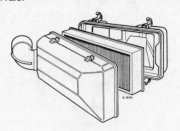

Air filter

Allen key A hexagonal wrench which fits into a recessed hexagonal hole.

Alligator clip A long-nosed spring-loaded metal clip with meshing teeth. Used to make temporary electrical connections.

Alternator A component in the electrical system which converts mechanical energy from a drivebelt into electrical energy to charge the battery and to operate the starting system, ignition system and electrical accessories.

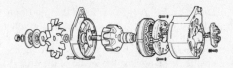

Alternator (exploded view)

Ampere (amp) A unit of measurement for the flow of electric current. One amp is the amount of current produced by one volt acting through a resistance of one ohm.

Anaerobic sealer A substance used to prevent bolts and screws from loosening. Anaerobic means that it does not require oxygen for activation. The Loctite brand is widely used.

Antifreeze A substance (usually ethylene glycol) mixed with water, and added to a vehicle's cooling system, to prevent freezing of the coolant in winter. Antifreeze also contains chemicals to inhibit corrosion and the formation of rust and other deposits that would tend to clog the radiator and coolant passages and reduce cooling efficiency.

Anti-seize compound A coating that reduces the risk of seizing on fasteners that are subjected to high temperatures, such as exhaust manifold bolts and nuts.

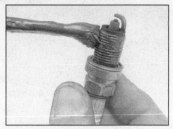

Anti-seize compound

Asbestos A natural fibrous mineral with great heat resistance, commonly used in the composition of brake friction materials. Asbestos is a health hazard and the dust created by brake systems should never be inhaled or ingested.

Axle A shaft on which a wheel revolves, or which revolves with a wheel. Also, a solid beam that connects the two wheels at one end of the vehicle. An axle which also transmits power to the wheels is known as a live axle.

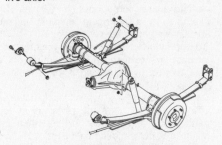

Axle assembly

Axleshaft A single rotating shaft, on either side of the differential, which delivers power from the final drive assembly to the drive wheels. Also called a driveshaft or a halfshaft.

B

Ball bearing An anti-friction bearing consisting of a hardened inner and outer race with hardened steel balls between two races.

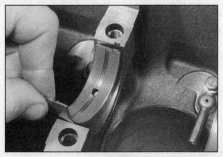

Bearing

Bearing The curved surface on a shaft or in a bore, or the part assembled into either, that permits relative motion between them with minimum wear and friction.

Big-end bearing The bearing in the end of the connecting rod that's attached to the crankshaft.

Bleed nipple A valve on a brake wheel cylinder, caliper or other hydraulic component that is opened to purge the hydraulic system of air. Also called a bleed screw.

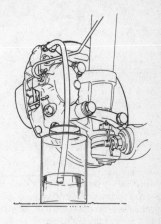

Brake bleeding

Brake bleeding Procedure for removing air from lines of a hydraulic brake system.

Brake disc The component of a disc brake that rotates with the wheels.

Brake drum The component of a drum brake that rotates with the wheels.

Brake linings The friction material which contacts the brake disc or drum to retard the vehicle's speed. The linings are bonded or riveted to the brake pads or shoes.

Brake pads The replaceable friction pads that pinch the brake disc when the brakes are applied. Brake pads consist of a friction material bonded or riveted to a rigid backing plate.

Brake shoe The crescent-shaped carrier to which the brake linings are mounted and which forces the lining against the rotating drum during braking.

Braking systems For more information on braking systems, consult the *Haynes Automotive Brake Manual*.

Breaker bar A long socket wrench handle providing greater leverage.

Bulkhead The insulated partition between the engine and the passenger compartment.

C

Caliper The non-rotating part of a disc-brake assembly that straddles the disc and carries the brake pads. The caliper also contains the hydraulic components that cause the pads to pinch the disc when the brakes are applied. A caliper is also a measuring tool that can be set to measure inside or outside dimensions of an object.

Glossary of technical terms

Camshaft A rotating shaft on which a series of cam lobes operate the valve mechanisms. The camshaft may be driven by gears, by sprockets and chain or by sprockets and a belt.

Canister A container in an evaporative emission control system; contains activated charcoal granules to trap vapours from the fuel system.

Canister

Carburettor A device which mixes fuel with air in the proper proportions to provide a desired power output from a spark ignition internal combustion engine.

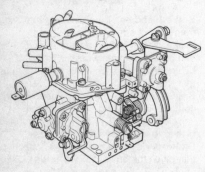

Carburettor

Castellated Resembling the parapets along the top of a castle wall. For example, a castellated balljoint stud nut.

Castellated nut

Castor In wheel alignment, the backward or forward tilt of the steering axis. Castor is positive when the steering axis is inclined rearward at the top.

Catalytic converter A silencer-like device in the exhaust system which converts certain pollutants in the exhaust gases into less harmful substances.

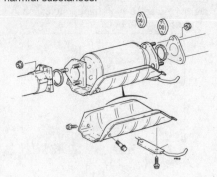

Catalytic converter

Circlip A ring-shaped clip used to prevent endwise movement of cylindrical parts and shafts. An internal circlip is installed in a groove in a housing; an external circlip fits into a groove on the outside of a cylindrical piece such as a shaft.

Clearance The amount of space between two parts. For example, between a piston and a cylinder, between a bearing and a journal, etc.

Coil spring A spiral of elastic steel found in various sizes throughout a vehicle, for example as a springing medium in the suspension and in the valve train.

Compression Reduction in volume, and increase in pressure and temperature, of a gas, caused by squeezing it into a smaller space.

Compression ratio The relationship between cylinder volume when the piston is at top dead centre and cylinder volume when the piston is at bottom dead centre.

Constant velocity (CV) joint A type of universal joint that cancels out vibrations caused by driving power being transmitted through an angle.

Core plug A disc or cup-shaped metal device inserted in a hole in a casting through which core was removed when the casting was formed. Also known as a freeze plug or expansion plug.

Crankcase The lower part of the engine block in which the crankshaft rotates.

Crankshaft The main rotating member, or shaft, running the length of the crankcase, with offset "throws" to which the connecting rods are attached.

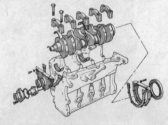

Crankshaft assembly

Crocodile clip See Alligator clip

D

Diagnostic code Code numbers obtained by accessing the diagnostic mode of an engine management computer. This code can be used to determine the area in the system where a malfunction may be located.

Disc brake A brake design incorporating a rotating disc onto which brake pads are squeezed. The resulting friction converts the energy of a moving vehicle into heat.

Double-overhead cam (DOHC) An engine that uses two overhead camshafts, usually one for the intake valves and one for the exhaust valves.

Drivebelt(s) The belt(s) used to drive accessories such as the alternator, water pump, power steering pump, air conditioning compressor, etc. off the crankshaft pulley.

Accessory drivebelts

Driveshaft Any shaft used to transmit motion. Commonly used when referring to the axleshafts on a front wheel drive vehicle.

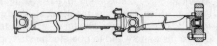

Driveshaft

Drum brake A type of brake using a drum-shaped metal cylinder attached to the inner surface of the wheel. When the brake pedal is pressed, curved brake shoes with friction linings press against the inside of the drum to slow or stop the vehicle.

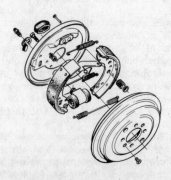

Drum brake assembly

E

EGR valve A valve used to introduce exhaust gases into the intake air stream.

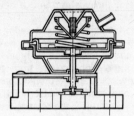

EGR valve

Electronic control unit (ECU) A computer which controls (for instance) ignition and fuel injection systems, or an anti-lock braking system. For more information refer to the *Haynes Automotive Electrical and Electronic Systems Manual.*

Electronic Fuel Injection (EFI) A computer controlled fuel system that distributes fuel through an injector located in each intake port of the engine.

Emergency brake A braking system, independent of the main hydraulic system, that can be used to slow or stop the vehicle if the primary brakes fail, or to hold the vehicle stationary even though the brake pedal isn't depressed. It usually consists of a hand lever that actuates either front or rear brakes mechanically through a series of cables and linkages. Also known as a handbrake or parking brake.

Endfloat The amount of lengthwise movement between two parts. As applied to a crankshaft, the distance that the crankshaft can move forward and back in the cylinder block.

Engine management system (EMS) A computer controlled system which manages the fuel injection and the ignition systems in an integrated fashion.

Exhaust manifold A part with several passages through which exhaust gases leave the engine combustion chambers and enter the exhaust pipe.

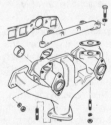

Exhaust manifold

F

Fan clutch A viscous (fluid) drive coupling device which permits variable engine fan speeds in relation to engine speeds.

Feeler blade A thin strip or blade of hardened steel, ground to an exact thickness, used to check or measure clearances between parts.

Feeler blade

Firing order The order in which the engine cylinders fire, or deliver their power strokes, beginning with the number one cylinder.

Flywheel A heavy spinning wheel in which energy is absorbed and stored by means of momentum. On cars, the flywheel is attached to the crankshaft to smooth out firing impulses.

Free play The amount of travel before any action takes place. The "looseness" in a linkage, or an assembly of parts, between the initial application of force and actual movement. For example, the distance the brake pedal moves before the pistons in the master cylinder are actuated.

Fuse An electrical device which protects a circuit against accidental overload. The typical fuse contains a soft piece of metal which is calibrated to melt at a predetermined current flow (expressed as amps) and break the circuit.

Fusible link A circuit protection device consisting of a conductor surrounded by heat-resistant insulation. The conductor is smaller than the wire it protects, so it acts as the weakest link in the circuit. Unlike a blown fuse, a failed fusible link must frequently be cut from the wire for replacement.

G

Gap The distance the spark must travel in jumping from the centre electrode to the side

Adjusting spark plug gap

electrode in a spark plug. Also refers to the spacing between the points in a contact breaker assembly in a conventional points-type ignition, or to the distance between the reluctor or rotor and the pickup coil in an electronic ignition.

Gasket Any thin, soft material - usually cork, cardboard, asbestos or soft metal - installed between two metal surfaces to ensure a good seal. For instance, the cylinder head gasket seals the joint between the block and the cylinder head.

Gasket

Gauge An instrument panel display used to monitor engine conditions. A gauge with a movable pointer on a dial or a fixed scale is an analogue gauge. A gauge with a numerical readout is called a digital gauge.

H

Halfshaft A rotating shaft that transmits power from the final drive unit to a drive wheel, usually when referring to a live rear axle.

Harmonic balancer A device designed to reduce torsion or twisting vibration in the crankshaft. May be incorporated in the crankshaft pulley. Also known as a vibration damper.

Hone An abrasive tool for correcting small irregularities or differences in diameter in an engine cylinder, brake cylinder, etc.

Hydraulic tappet A tappet that utilises hydraulic pressure from the engine's lubrication system to maintain zero clearance (constant contact with both camshaft and valve stem). Automatically adjusts to variation in valve stem length. Hydraulic tappets also reduce valve noise.

I

Ignition timing The moment at which the spark plug fires, usually expressed in the number of crankshaft degrees before the piston reaches the top of its stroke.

Inlet manifold A tube or housing with passages through which flows the air-fuel mixture (carburettor vehicles and vehicles with throttle body injection) or air only (port fuel-injected vehicles) to the port openings in the cylinder head.

J

Jump start Starting the engine of a vehicle with a discharged or weak battery by attaching jump leads from the weak battery to a charged or helper battery.

L

Load Sensing Proportioning Valve (LSPV) A brake hydraulic system control valve that works like a proportioning valve, but also takes into consideration the amount of weight carried by the rear axle.

Locknut A nut used to lock an adjustment nut, or other threaded component, in place. For example, a locknut is employed to keep the adjusting nut on the rocker arm in position.

Lockwasher A form of washer designed to prevent an attaching nut from working loose.

M

MacPherson strut A type of front suspension system devised by Earle MacPherson at Ford of England. In its original form, a simple lateral link with the anti-roll bar creates the lower control arm. A long strut - an integral coil spring and shock absorber - is mounted between the body and the steering knuckle. Many modern so-called MacPherson strut systems use a conventional lower A-arm and don't rely on the anti-roll bar for location.

Multimeter An electrical test instrument with the capability to measure voltage, current and resistance.

N

NOx Oxides of Nitrogen. A common toxic pollutant emitted by petrol and diesel engines at higher temperatures.

O

Ohm The unit of electrical resistance. One volt applied to a resistance of one ohm will produce a current of one amp.

Ohmmeter An instrument for measuring electrical resistance.

O-ring A type of sealing ring made of a special rubber-like material; in use, the O-ring is compressed into a groove to provide the sealing action.

O-ring

Overhead cam (ohc) engine An engine with the camshaft(s) located on top of the cylinder head(s).

Overhead valve (ohv) engine An engine with the valves located in the cylinder head, but with the camshaft located in the engine block.

Oxygen sensor A device installed in the engine exhaust manifold, which senses the oxygen content in the exhaust and converts this information into an electric current. Also called a Lambda sensor.

P

Phillips screw A type of screw head having a cross instead of a slot for a corresponding type of screwdriver.

Plastigage A thin strip of plastic thread, available in different sizes, used for measuring clearances. For example, a strip of Plastigage is laid across a bearing journal. The parts are assembled and dismantled; the width of the crushed strip indicates the clearance between journal and bearing.

Plastigage

Propeller shaft The long hollow tube with universal joints at both ends that carries power from the transmission to the differential on front-engined rear wheel drive vehicles.

Proportioning valve A hydraulic control valve which limits the amount of pressure to the rear brakes during panic stops to prevent wheel lock-up.

R

Rack-and-pinion steering A steering system with a pinion gear on the end of the steering shaft that mates with a rack (think of a geared wheel opened up and laid flat). When the steering wheel is turned, the pinion turns, moving the rack to the left or right. This movement is transmitted through the track rods to the steering arms at the wheels.

Radiator A liquid-to-air heat transfer device designed to reduce the temperature of the coolant in an internal combustion engine cooling system.

Refrigerant Any substance used as a heat transfer agent in an air-conditioning system. R-12 has been the principle refrigerant for many years; recently, however, manufacturers have begun using R-134a, a non-CFC substance that is considered less harmful to the ozone in the upper atmosphere.

Rocker arm A lever arm that rocks on a shaft or pivots on a stud. In an overhead valve engine, the rocker arm converts the upward movement of the pushrod into a downward movement to open a valve.

Rotor In a distributor, the rotating device inside the cap that connects the centre electrode and the outer terminals as it turns, distributing the high voltage from the coil secondary winding to the proper spark plug. Also, that part of an alternator which rotates inside the stator. Also, the rotating assembly of a turbocharger, including the compressor wheel, shaft and turbine wheel.

Runout The amount of wobble (in-and-out movement) of a gear or wheel as it's rotated. The amount a shaft rotates "out-of-true." The out-of-round condition of a rotating part.

S

Sealant A liquid or paste used to prevent leakage at a joint. Sometimes used in conjunction with a gasket.

Sealed beam lamp An older headlight design which integrates the reflector, lens and filaments into a hermetically-sealed one-piece unit. When a filament burns out or the lens cracks, the entire unit is simply replaced.

Serpentine drivebelt A single, long, wide accessory drivebelt that's used on some newer vehicles to drive all the accessories, instead of a series of smaller, shorter belts. Serpentine drivebelts are usually tensioned by an automatic tensioner.

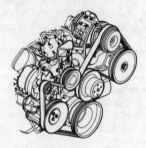
Serpentine drivebelt

Shim Thin spacer, commonly used to adjust the clearance or relative positions between two parts. For example, shims inserted into or under bucket tappets control valve clearances. Clearance is adjusted by changing the thickness of the shim.

Slide hammer A special puller that screws into or hooks onto a component such as a shaft or bearing; a heavy sliding handle on the shaft bottoms against the end of the shaft to knock the component free.

Sprocket A tooth or projection on the periphery of a wheel, shaped to engage with a chain or drivebelt. Commonly used to refer to the sprocket wheel itself.

Starter inhibitor switch On vehicles with an

automatic transmission, a switch that prevents starting if the vehicle is not in Neutral or Park.

Strut See MacPherson strut.

T

Tappet A cylindrical component which transmits motion from the cam to the valve stem, either directly or via a pushrod and rocker arm. Also called a cam follower.

Thermostat A heat-controlled valve that regulates the flow of coolant between the cylinder block and the radiator, so maintaining optimum engine operating temperature. A thermostat is also used in some air cleaners in which the temperature is regulated.

Thrust bearing The bearing in the clutch assembly that is moved in to the release levers by clutch pedal action to disengage the clutch. Also referred to as a release bearing.

Timing belt A toothed belt which drives the camshaft. Serious engine damage may result if it breaks in service.

Timing chain A chain which drives the camshaft.

Toe-in The amount the front wheels are closer together at the front than at the rear. On rear wheel drive vehicles, a slight amount of toe-in is usually specified to keep the front wheels running parallel on the road by offsetting other forces that tend to spread the wheels apart.

Toe-out The amount the front wheels are closer together at the rear than at the front. On front wheel drive vehicles, a slight amount of toe-out is usually specified.

Tools For full information on choosing and using tools, refer to the *Haynes Automotive Tools Manual.*

Tracer A stripe of a second colour applied to a wire insulator to distinguish that wire from another one with the same colour insulator.

Tune-up A process of accurate and careful adjustments and parts replacement to obtain the best possible engine performance.

Turbocharger A centrifugal device, driven by exhaust gases, that pressurises the intake air. Normally used to increase the power output from a given engine displacement, but can also be used primarily to reduce exhaust emissions (as on VW's "Umwelt" Diesel engine).

U

Universal joint or U-joint A double-pivoted connection for transmitting power from a driving to a driven shaft through an angle. A U-joint consists of two Y-shaped yokes and a cross-shaped member called the spider.

V

Valve A device through which the flow of liquid, gas, vacuum, or loose material in bulk may be started, stopped, or regulated by a movable part that opens, shuts, or partially obstructs one or more ports or passageways. A valve is also the movable part of such a device.

Valve clearance The clearance between the valve tip (the end of the valve stem) and the rocker arm or tappet. The valve clearance is measured when the valve is closed.

Vernier caliper A precision measuring instrument that measures inside and outside dimensions. Not quite as accurate as a micrometer, but more convenient.

Viscosity The thickness of a liquid or its resistance to flow.

Volt A unit for expressing electrical "pressure" in a circuit. One volt that will produce a current of one ampere through a resistance of one ohm.

W

Welding Various processes used to join metal items by heating the areas to be joined to a molten state and fusing them together. For more information refer to the *Haynes Automotive Welding Manual.*

Wiring diagram A drawing portraying the components and wires in a vehicle's electrical system, using standardised symbols. For more information refer to the *Haynes Automotive Electrical and Electronic Systems Manual.*

Notes

Notes

Notes

Haynes Manuals – The Complete List

Title	Book No.
ALFA ROMEO	
Alfa Romeo Alfasud/Sprint (74 - 88)	0292
Alfa Romeo Alfetta (73 - 87)	0531
AUDI	
Audi 80 (72 - Feb 79)	0207
Audi 80, 90 (79 - Oct 86) & Coupe (81 - Nov 88)	0605
Audi 80, 90 (Oct 86 - 90) & Coupe (Nov 88 - 90)	1491
Audi 100 (Oct 76 - Oct 82)	0428
Audi 100 (Oct 82 - 90) & 200 (Feb 84 - Oct 89)	0907
AUSTIN	
Austin Ambassador (82 - 84)	0871
Austin/MG Maestro 1.3 & 1.6 (83 - 95)	0922
Austin Maxi (69 - 81)	0052
Austin/MG Metro (80 - May 90)	0718
Austin Montego 1.3 & 1.6 (84 - 94)	1066
Austin/MG Montego 2.0 (84 - 95)	1067
Mini (59 - 69)	0527
Mini (69 - Oct 96)	0646
Austin/Rover 2.0 litre Diesel Engine (86 - 93)	1857
BEDFORD	
Bedford CF (69 - 87)	0163
Bedford Rascal (86 - 93)	3015
BL	
BL Princess & BLMC 18-22 (75 - 82)	0286
BMW	
BMW 316, 320 & 320i (4-cyl) (75 - Feb 83)	0276
BMW 320, 320i, 323i & 325i (6-cyl) (Oct 77 - Sept 87)	0815
BMW 3-Series (Apr 91 - 96)	3210
BMW 3-Series (sohc) (83 - 91)	1948
BMW 520i & 525e (Oct 81 - June 88)	1560
BMW 525, 528 & 528i (73 - Sept 81)	0632
BMW 5-Series (sohc) (81 - 93)	1948
BMW 1500, 1502, 1600, 1602, 2000 & 2002 (59 - 77)	0240
CITROEN	
Citroen 2CV, Ami & Dyane (67 - 90)	0196
Citroen AX Petrol & Diesel (87 - 94)	3014
Citroen BX (83 - 94)	0908
Citroen CX (75 - 88)	0528
Citroen Visa (79 - 88)	0620
Citroen Xantia Petrol & Diesel (93 - Oct 95)	3082
Citroen ZX Diesel (91 - 93)	1922
Citroen ZX Petrol (91 - 94)	1881
Citroen 1.7 & 1.9 litre Diesel Engine (84 - 96)	1379
COLT	
Colt 1200, 1250 & 1400 (79 - May 84)	0600
DAIMLER	
Daimler Sovereign (68 - Oct 86)	0242
Daimler Double Six (72 - 88)	0478
DATSUN *(see also Nissan)*	
Datsun 120Y (73 - Aug 78)	0228
Datsun 1300, 1400 & 1600 (69 - Aug 72)	0123
Datsun Cherry (71 - 76)	0195
Datsun Pick-up (75 - 78)	0277
Datsun Sunny (Aug 78 - May 82)	0525
Datsun Violet (78 - 82)	0430

Title	Book No.
FIAT	
Fiat 126 (73 - 87)	0305
Fiat 127 (71 - 83)	0193
Fiat 500 (57 - 73)	0090
Fiat 850 (64 - 81)	0038
Fiat Panda (81 - 95)	0793
Fiat Punto (94 - 96)	3251
Fiat Regata (84 - 88)	1167
Fiat Strada (79 - 88)	0479
Fiat Tipo (88 - 91)	1625
Fiat Uno (83 - 95)	0923
Fiat X1/9 (74 - 89)	0273
FORD	
Ford Capri II (& III) 1.6 & 2.0 (74 - 87)	0283
Ford Capri II (& III) 2.8 & 3.0 (74 - 87)	1309
Ford Cortina Mk IV (& V) 1.6 & 2.0 (76 - 83)	0343
Ford Cortina Mk IV (& V) 2.3 V6 (77 - 83)	0426
Ford Escort (75 - Aug 80)	0280
Ford Escort (Sept 80 - Sept 90)	0686
Ford Escort (Sept 90 - 97)	1737
Ford Escort Mk II Mexico, RS 1600 & RS 2000 (75 - 80)	0735
Ford Fiesta (inc. XR2) (76 - Aug 83)	0334
Ford Fiesta (inc. XR2) (Aug 83 - Feb 89)	1030
Ford Fiesta (Feb 89 - Oct 95)	1595
Ford Granada (Sept 77 - Feb 85)	0481
Ford Granada (Mar 85 - 94)	1245
Ford Mondeo 4-cyl (93 - 96)	1923
Ford Orion (83 - Sept 90)	1009
Ford Orion (Sept 90 - 93)	1737
Ford Sierra 1.3, 1.6, 1.8 & 2.0 (82 - 93)	0903
Ford Sierra 2.3, 2.8 & 2.9 (82 - 91)	0904
Ford Scorpio (Mar 85 - 94)	1245
Ford Transit Petrol (Mk 1) (65 - Feb 78)	0377
Ford Transit Petrol (Mk 2) (78 - Jan 86)	0719
Ford Transit Petrol (Mk 3) (Feb 86 - 89)	1468
Ford Transit Diesel (Feb 86 - 95)	3019
Ford 1.6 & 1.8 litre Diesel Engine (84 - 96)	1172
Ford 2.1, 2.3 & 2.5 litre Diesel Engine (77 - 90)	1606
FREIGHT ROVER	
Freight Rover Sherpa (74 - 87)	0463
HILLMAN	
Hillman Avenger (70 - 82)	0037
Hillman Minx & Husky (56 - 66)	0009
HONDA	
Honda Accord (76 - Feb 84)	0351
Honda Accord (Feb 84 - Oct 85)	1177
Honda Civic 1300 (80 - 81)	0633
Honda Civic (Feb 84 - Oct 87)	1226
Honda Civic (Nov 91 - 96)	3199
HYUNDAI	
Hyundai Pony (85 - 94)	3398
JAGUAR	
Jaguar E Type (61 - 72)	0140
Jaguar MkI & II, 240 & 340 (55 - 69)	0098
Jaguar XJ6, XJ & Sovereign (68 - Oct 86)	0242
Jaguar XJ6 & Sovereign (Oct 86 - Sept 94)	3261
Jaguar XJ12, XJS & Sovereign (72 - 88)	0478

Title	Book No.
JEEP	
Jeep Cherokee Petrol (93 - 96)	1943
LADA	
Lada 1200, 1300, 1500 & 1600 (74 - 91)	0413
Lada Samara (87 - 91)	1610
LAND ROVER	
Land Rover 90, 110 & Defender Diesel (83 - 95)	3017
Land Rover Discovery Diesel (89 - 95)	3016
Land Rover Series IIA & III Diesel (58 - 85)	0529
Land Rover Series II, IIA & III Petrol (58 - 85)	0314
MAZDA	
Mazda 323 fwd (Mar 81 - Oct 89)	1608
Mazda 626 fwd (May 83 - Sept 87)	0929
Mazda B-1600, B-1800 & B-2000 Pick-up (72 - 88)	0267
MERCEDES-BENZ	
Mercedes-Benz 190 & 190E (83 - 87)	0928
Mercedes-Benz 200, 240, 300 Diesel (Oct 76 - 85)	1114
Mercedes-Benz 250 & 280 (68 - 72)	0346
Mercedes-Benz 250 & 280 (123 Series) (Oct 76 - 84)	0677
Mercedes-Benz 124 Series (85 - Aug 93)	3253
MG	
MGB (62 - 80)	0111
MG Maestro 1.3 & 1.6 (83 - 95)	0922
MG Metro (80 - May 90)	0718
MG Midget & AH Sprite (58 - 80)	0265
MG Montego 2.0 (84 - 95)	1067
MITSUBISHI	
Mitsubishi 1200, 1250 & 1400 (79 - May 84)	0600
Mitsubishi Shogun & L200 Pick-Ups (83 - 94)	1944
MORRIS	
Morris Ital 1.3 (80 - 84)	0705
Morris Marina 1700 (78 - 80)	0526
Morris Marina 1.8 (71 - 78)	0074
Morris Minor 1000 (56 - 71)	0024
NISSAN *(See also Datsun)*	
Nissan Bluebird 160B & 180B rwd (May 80 - May 84)	0957
Nissan Bluebird fwd (May 84 - Mar 86)	1223
Nissan Bluebird (T12 & T72) (Mar 86 - 90)	1473
Nissan Cherry (N12) (Sept 82 - 86)	1031
Nissan Micra (K10) (83 - Jan 93)	0931
Nissan Micra (93 - 96)	3254
Nissan Primera (90 - Oct 96)	1851
Nissan Stanza (82 - 86)	0824
Nissan Sunny (B11) (May 82 - Oct 86)	0895
Nissan Sunny (Oct 86 - Mar 91)	1378
Nissan Sunny (Apr 91 - 95)	3219
OPEL	
Opel Ascona & Manta (B Series) (Sept 75 - 88)	0316
Opel Ascona (81 - 88)	3215
Opel Astra (Oct 91 - 96)	3156
Opel Corsa (83 - Mar 93)	3160
Opel Corsa (Mar 93 - 94)	3159
Opel Kadett (Nov 79 - Oct 84)	0634
Opel Kadett (Oct 84 - Oct 91)	3196
Opel Omega & Senator (86 - 94)	3157

Title	Book No.
Opel Rekord (Feb 78 - Oct 86)	0543
Opel Vectra (88 - Oct 95)	3158
PEUGEOT	
Peugeot 106 Petrol & Diesel (91 - June 96)	1882
Peugeot 205 (83 - 95)	0932
Peugeot 305 (78 - 89)	0538
Peugeot 306 Petrol & Diesel (93 - 95)	3073
Peugeot 309 (86 - 93)	1266
Peugeot 405 Petrol (88 - 96)	1559
Peugeot 405 Diesel (88 - 96)	3198
Peugeot 406 Petrol & Diesel (96 - 97)	3394
Peugeot 505 (79 - 89)	0762
Peugeot 1.7 & 1.9 litre Diesel Engines (82 - 96)	0950
Peugeot 2.0, 2.1, 2.3 & 2.5 litre Diesel Engines (74 - 90)	1607
PORSCHE	
Porsche 911 (65 - 85)	0264
Porsche 924 & 924 Turbo (76 - 85)	0397
PROTON	
Proton (89 - 97)	3255
RANGE ROVER	
Range Rover V8 (70 - Oct 92)	0606
RELIANT	
Reliant Robin & Kitten (73 - 83)	0436
RENAULT	
Renault 5 (72 - Feb 85)	0141
Renault 5 (Feb 85 - 96)	1219
Renault 9 & 11 (82 - 89)	0822
Renault 12 (70 - 80)	0097
Renault 15 & 17 (72 - 79)	0763
Renault 18 (79 - 86)	0598
Renault 19 Petrol (89 - 94)	1646
Renault 19 Diesel (89 - 95)	1946
Renault 21 (86 - 94)	1397
Renault 25 (84 - 86)	1228
Renault Clio Petrol (91 - 93)	1853
Renault Clio Diesel (91 - June 96)	3031
Renault Espace (85 - 96)	3197
Renault Fuego (80 - 86)	0764
Renault Laguna (94 - 96)	3252
ROVER	
Rover 111 & 114 (95 - 96)	1711
Rover 213 & 216 (84 - 89)	1116
Rover 214 & 414 (Oct 89 - 92)	1689
Rover 216 & 416 (Oct 89 - 92)	1830
Rover 618, 620 & 623 (93 - 97)	3257
Rover 820, 825 & 827 (86 - 95)	1380
Rover 2000, 2300 & 2600 (77 - 87)	0468
Rover 3500 (76 - 87)	0365
Rover Metro (May 90 - 94)	1711
SAAB	
Saab 90, 99 & 900 (79 - Oct 93)	0765
Saab 9000 (4-cyl) (85 - 95)	1686
SEAT	
Seat Ibiza & Malaga (85 - 92)	1609
SIMCA	
Simca 1100 & 1204 (67 - 79)	0088
Simca 1301 & 1501 (63 - 76)	0199

Title	Book No.
SKODA	
Skoda Estelle 105, 120, 130 & 136 (77 - 89)	0604
Skoda Favorit (89 - 92)	1801
SUBARU	
Subaru 1600 (77 - Oct 79)	0237
Subaru 1600 & 1800 (Nov 79 - 90)	0995
SUZUKI	
Suzuki SJ Series, Samurai & Vitara (82 - 97)	1942
Suzuki Supercarry (86 - Oct 94)	3015
TALBOT	
Talbot Alpine, Solara, Minx & Rapier (75 - 86)	0337
Talbot Horizon (78 - 86)	0473
Talbot Samba (82 - 86)	0823
TOYOTA	
Toyota Carina E (May 92 - 97)	3256
Toyota Celica (Feb 82 - Sept 85)	1135
Toyota Corolla (fwd) (Sept 83 - Sept 87)	1024
Toyota Corolla (rwd) (80 - 85)	0683
Toyota Corolla (Sept 87 - 92)	1683
Toyota Corolla (Aug 92 - 97)	3259
Toyota Hi-Ace & Hi-Lux (69 - Oct 83)	0304
Toyota Starlet (78 - Jan 85)	0462
TRIUMPH	
Triumph Acclaim (81 - 84)	0792
Triumph Herald (59 - 71)	0010
Triumph Spitfire (62 - 81)	0113
Triumph Stag (70 - 78)	0441
Triumph TR7 (75 - 82)	0322
VAUXHALL	
Vauxhall Astra (80 - Oct 84)	0635
Vauxhall Astra & Belmont (Oct 84 - Oct 91)	1136
Vauxhall Astra (Oct 91 - 96)	1832
Vauxhall Carlton (Oct 78 - Oct 86)	0480
Vauxhall Carlton (Nov 86 - 94)	1469
Vauxhall Cavalier 1300 (77 - July 81)	0461
Vauxhall Cavalier 1600, 1900 & 2000 (75 - July 81)	0315
Vauxhall Cavalier (81 - Oct 88)	0812
Vauxhall Cavalier (Oct 88 - Oct 95)	1570
Vauxhall Chevette (75 - 84)	0285
Vauxhall Corsa (Mar 93 - 94)	1985
Vauxhall Nova (83 - 93)	0909
Vauxhall Rascal (86 - 93)	3015
Vauxhall Senator (Sept 87 - 94)	1469
Vauxhall Viva HB Series (ohv) (66 - 70)	0026
Vauxhall Viva & Firenza (ohc) (68 - 73)	0093
Vauxhall/Opel 1.5, 1.6 & 1.7 litre Diesel Engines (82 - 96)	1222
VOLKSWAGEN	
VW Beetle 1200 (54 - 77)	0036
VW Beetle 1300 & 1500 (65 - 75)	0039
VW Beetle 1302 & 1302S (70 - 72)	0110
VW Beetle 1303, 1303S & GT (72 - 75)	0159
VW Golf Mk 1 1.1 & 1.3 (74 - Feb 84)	0716
VW Golf Mk 1 1.5, 1.6 & 1.8 (74 - 85)	0726
VW Golf Mk 1 Diesel (78 - Feb 84)	0451
VW Golf Mk 2 (Mar 84 - Feb 92)	1081
VW Golf Mk 3 Petrol & Diesel (Feb 92 - 96)	3097

Title	Book No.
VW Jetta Mk 1 1.1 & 1.3 (80 - June 84)	0716
VW Jetta Mk 1 1.5, 1.6 & 1.8 (80 - June 84)	0726
VW Jetta Mk 1 Diesel (81 - June 84)	0451
VW Jetta Mk 2 (July 84 - 92)	1081
VW LT vans & light trucks (76 - 87)	0637
VW Passat (Sept 81 - May 88)	0814
VW Passat (May 88 - 91)	1647
VW Polo & Derby (76 - Jan 82)	0335
VW Polo (82 - Oct 90)	0813
VW Polo (Nov 90 - Aug 94)	3245
VW Santana (Sept 82 - 85)	0814
VW Scirocco Mk 1 1.5, 1.6 & 1.8 (74 - 82)	0726
VW Scirocco (82 - 90)	1224
VW Transporter 1600 (68 - 79)	0082
VW Transporter 1700, 1800 & 2000 (72 - 79)	0226
VW Transporter with air-cooled engine (79 - 82)	0638
VW Type 3 (63 - 73)	0084
VW Vento Petrol & Diesel (Feb 92 - 96)	3097
VOLVO	
Volvo 66 & 343, Daf 55 & 66 (68 - 79)	0293
Volvo 142, 144 & 145 (66 - 74)	0129
Volvo 240 Series (74 - 93)	0270
Volvo 262, 264 & 260/265 (75 - 85)	0400
Volvo 340, 343, 345 & 360 (76 - 91)	0715
Volvo 440, 460 & 480 (87 - 92)	1691
Volvo 740 & 760 (82 - 91)	1258
Volvo 850 (92 - 96)	3260
Volvo 940 (90 - 96)	3249
YUGO/ZASTAVA	
Yugo/Zastava (81 - 90)	1453

TECH BOOKS	
Automotive Brake Manual	3050
Carburettor Manual	3288
Diesel Engine Service Guide	3286
Automotive Electrical & Electronic Systems	3049
Automotive Engine Management and Fuel Injection Manual	3344
In-Car Entertainment Manual	3363
Automotive Tools Manual	3052
Automotive Welding Manual	3053

CAR BOOKS	
Automotive Fuel Injection Systems	9755
Car Bodywork Repair Manual	9864
Caravan Manual (2nd Edition)	9894
Haynes Technical Data Book (88 - 97)	1997
How to Keep Your Car Alive	9868
Japanese Vehicle Carburettors	1786
Small Engine Repair Manual	1755
SU Carburettors	0299
Weber Carburettors (to 79)	0393

C6684.CL04.04/97

Preserving Our Motoring Heritage

< The Model J Duesenberg Derham Tourster. Only eight of these magnificent cars were ever built – this is the only example to be found outside the United States of America

Almost every car you've ever loved, loathed or desired is gathered under one roof at the Haynes Motor Museum. Over 300 immaculately presented cars and motorbikes represent every aspect of our motoring heritage, from elegant reminders of bygone days, such as the superb Model J Duesenberg to curiosities like the bug-eyed BMW Isetta. There are also many old friends and flames. Perhaps you remember the 1959 Ford Popular that you did your courting in? The magnificent 'Red Collection' is a spectacle of classic sports cars including AC, Alfa Romeo, Austin Healey, Ferrari, Lamborghini, Maserati, MG, Riley, Porsche and Triumph.

A Perfect Day Out

Each and every vehicle at the Haynes Motor Museum has played its part in the history and culture of Motoring. Today, they make a wonderful spectacle and a great day out for all the family. Bring the kids, bring Mum and Dad, but above all bring your camera to capture those golden memories for ever. You will also find an impressive array of motoring memorabilia, a comfortable 70 seat video cinema and one of the most extensive transport book shops in Britain. The Pit Stop Cafe serves everything from a cup of tea to wholesome, home-made meals or, if you prefer, you can enjoy the large picnic area nestled in the beautiful rural surroundings of Somerset.

> John Haynes O.B.E., Founder and Chairman of the museum at the wheel of a Haynes Light 12.

< Graham Hill's Lola Cosworth Formula 1 car next to a 1934 Riley Sports.

The Museum is situated on the A359 Yeovil to Frome road at Sparkford, just off the A303 in Somerset. It is about 40 miles south of Bristol, and 25 minutes drive from the M5 intersection at Taunton.
Open 9.30am - 5.30pm (10.00am - 4.00pm Winter) 7 days a week, *except Christmas Day, Boxing Day and New Years Day*
Special rates available for schools, coach parties and outings Charitable Trust No. 292048